Praise for *Love Is Fierce* by Kerri

C000132942

The greatest gift you can give your
relationship with your mother. Kerri Hummingbird's breakthrough
book will stretch you to embrace your mother for all that she is and
all that she isn't, allowing your future female ancestry to unfold with
trust, compassion, power and intimacy. I highly recommend.
— Dr. Shawne Duperon, Project Forgive Founder, Nobel Peace Prize
Nominee

Kerri Hummingbird's latest book is quite simply a masterpiece in
understanding our relationship to ourselves and our bond to our
physical mother and by extension, our earth mother and community
of brothers and sisters. Think the fierceness of Marianne Williamson
and the wisdom of Maya Angelou wrapped into one gem of a book.
Kerri delves deep into the nature of the bond with our mothers, and
more so, has direct, healing steps to support us in creating lasting
peace within and on our planet.

—Karen McGregor, Wall Street Journal Bestselling author of *The Tao
of Influence: Ancient Wisdom for Modern Leaders and Entrepreneurs*

This is an extraordinary and profound book, groundbreaking in what
it brings to light and the possibilities that are manifested. If I were not
reading this book online, by now my yellow marker would have run
dry. It demands to be read and reread, deeply transforming with each
pass. What could be more important in the world right now, than to
shake up what we think we know about mothering, and to make a
quantum shift in the core of our individual and collective being?
Thank you Kerri, for your commitment to yourself...and through
that, to all of us, mothers and children alike.

— Laurie Seymour, Founder/CEO The Baca Institute

Our individual relationship to the Mother is at the core of our being, and it has the power to shape our lives, whether it's the birth mother, Mother Earth or the Divine Mother energy. For centuries the Divine Feminine has been in the shadows of the Masculine. Only through balance and alignment will we be able to bring Peace... within ourselves and in the world.

Kerri Hummingbird-Sami guides us through a journey of awakening to, and stepping into, this incredibly powerful energy, healing and bringing balance within, and therefor also in our lived life experience. This is a raw, honest and deeply personal story, that gives the reader permission to experience his or her own mother wound and find the courage and power to heal. I cannot think of a more timely message in this time.

— Eva Charlotte, Founder of R.I.S.E. In Love

Kerri Hummingbird's new book, Love is Fierce: Healing the Mother Wound, continues to stretch us further into the beauty way of walking upon this earth while held in the loving embrace of the infinite mother love available to us all. Journey into the depths of you with this book and emerge ready to unleash yourself in power and splendor into the world. The time is now. The way is here in this extraordinary literary and energetic contribution to humanity.

— Christine Powers, Founder/CEO of The Philosophers Camp

Kerri Hummingbird's ability to tell her story with full openness and authenticity is the core power of Love is Fierce. I was drawn to this book from a similar 'Mother Wound" and, through Kerri's powerful presence on these pages, I found a partner with whom to navigate my healing with love, gratitude, and acceptance. I thank her for her leadership and guidance in this area...and you will too.

— Daniel Olexa, CIHt, PCC, author of *A Pessimist's Guide To Manifesting*

The healing message of Love is Fierce: Healing the Mother Wound is urgently needed today. For sure, we are the walking wounded. Without transforming the Mother Wound into Mother Wisdom, humanity will sink deeper into despair and possibly extinction. Hummingbird-Sami is direct and powerful. She walks us through the narrative of her healing and awakening. Spanning the spectrum from traditional psychology, spiritual psychology to shamanic transformation, she enables us to understand the path to greater consciousness, connection, and sustainable love.

Having outgrown shame, she weaves us through her childhood abuse, teenage sexual acting out, young adult grasping and greediness, birthing two sons, divorce, and the traumatic separation from her mother to the liberation of her soul into spiritual adulthood. Her life story is relatable. We can all identify with the struggles of growing up in a materialistic culture devoid of true universal love. We all yearn for the perfect mother that makes us feel safe and whole. The vacancy created by the lack of feminine wisdom sets the stage for her soul's journey. Without immersion in the Great Mother, how can any physical mother be a true and trusted guide or any child emerge as the divine's full, unique expression?

Hummingbird-Sami shares the wisdom of her psychological and spiritual teachers with us so we can benefit too. This is a very generous book. Her energy, spirit, and fierce heart radiate through each carefully chosen word.

Her main message is this: Wake up to your relationship to the Great Goddess, Mother Earth, and the infinite feminine wisdom. The Great Mother Wound results from thousands of years of taking the masculine to a toxic extreme. Our path to healing is through the feminine, which will bring our lives and our hearts into balance. Hummingbird-Sami expresses the message of our time. The feminine wisdom is rising powerfully now. We need to heal the Mother Wound to align with our higher consciousness and the consciousness of the beautiful Mother that holds us so wisely and dearly.

— Sarah Weiss, MA, Spiritual Teacher, Keeper of the Light, and Medical Intuitive

This page left intentionally blank.

From the #1 Int'l Bestselling Author Of "The Second Wave"

LOVE IS FIERCE
Healing the Mother Wound

Kerri Hummingbird Sami
guided through embodiment by
White Buffalo Calf Woman

First published in the United States of America by Siwarkinte Publishing

Love Is Fierce: Healing The Mother Wound
Kerri Hummingbird Sami guided through embodiment by White Buffalo Calf Woman

Cover design by © Kerri Hummingbird Sami
Illustration by © Kerri Hummingbird Sami
Photograph of Kerri Hummingbird Sami by The Perfect Headshot
Photograph in cover artwork by © Evgenyatamanenko

This book may be ordered directly from Amazon.com.

ISBN-13: 978-0-578-77454-1

For more information about Kerri Hummingbird, visit:
Web: www.kerrihummingbird.com
Twitter: @KerriHummingbrd
Facebook: Kerri.Hummingbird
Instagram: kerri.hummingbird
Pinterest: kerrihummingbrd
YouTube: Kerri Hummingbird

Fight for the things you care about, but do it in a way that will lead others to join you.

—Ruth Bader Ginsburg

♥

To describe my mother would be to write about a hurricane in its perfect power. Or the climbing, falling colors of a rainbow.

—Maya Angelou

♥

I alone cannot change the world, but I can cast a stone across the waters to create many ripples.

—Mother Teresa

♥

Integrity is choosing courage over comfort; choosing what is right over what is fun, fast, or easy; and choosing to practice our values rather than simply professing them.

—Brené Brown

Acknowledgements

My heart pours out gratitude to my husband Akeem Sami who from the first moment I met him encouraged me to shine my brightest. He held my hand through the darkness of these last four years to claim my wisdom, always having faith that I would. Mesumobo Akeem.

To my sons Garrett and Tanner: you forever open a flood of agape love in my heart, and I promise to honor you as grown men even as I hold dear the memory of cradling you for the first time as tiny beings of light in flesh. My heart sings for you, and always will.

To my newest teachers, Yamina and Chi: thank you for giving me another chance to be a mother as your bonus mom.

I am eternally grateful to my ancestors for guiding me to the Red Road and walking every step with me.

Thank you to the Q'ero, Huichol, and Shipibo shamans for sharing your medicine and wisdom and waking me up to Walk the Beauty Way.

Thank you to the PowerPath School of Shamanism community, Red Foxes, Jose and Lena Stevens, and Anna and Aaron Harrington for community.

Thank you to Tracey Trottenberg and George Kansas and our messenger tribe for helping me own, honor, and unleash my message into the world.

Thank you to my Four Winds Light Body School teachers and mentors for powerful energy medicine and a fresh start in my life.

Thank you to HeatherAsh Amara, Diana Adkins, Gerry Starnes, and Chrispy Bhagat Singh for helping me lift out of darkness into my purpose.

Thank you Teresa de Grosbois and the Evolutionary Business Council for always lifting me up to shine even brighter.

Eternal thanks to my Dad for watching over me and demonstrating unconditional love throughout my life.

And thank you White Buffalo Calf Woman for helping me remember the love of the Divine Mother.

Contents

LOVE IS FIERCE: HEALING THE MOTHER WOUND

Dedication

This book is dedicated to my mother, who as a young woman grew up in a conservative religious suburban world where women were polite, wore little white gloves with their tea dresses, and demurely took care of the home while the men climbed the corporate ladder. Leading up to my surprise entrance into her world, she was confronting the social norms of her own upbringing by moving to Dallas, Texas and marrying my natural father who was seduced by the Summer of Love and introducing her to hippies, drugs, and free-love. Into the clash of these worlds, I was born in June 1969.

What I most admire about my mother is her tenacious pursuit of an authentic life for herself. She landed the most genuine, caring, and supportive partner with her third husband: the man I call my Dad. For 45 years they enjoyed what many people observed was a rare soulmate connection; the kind of love relationship people dream about receiving.

Most people don't realize that a love like that has a price to pay upfront. Or at least, it did in our world. And those early bumps in my mother's journey to love cost her, and me, dearly. From my birth until 5 years old when we met my Dad, it was not safe for me because it was not safe for my mother. My natural father, wounded himself from early childhood trauma, was beginning to sexually abuse me as a one year old toddler.

My mother did not look the other way. She fought for me. When the courts would not protect me, my mother married a professional man with a good income who agreed to move us far away from my natural father. She did not let her daughter become another statistic.

And still, another series of lessons befell us as my first step father physically abused my mother, and terrified me that he might take her life. As a toddler, I was biting my arms and leaving red welting marks. My eyes had dark circles from sleepless nights.

Determined to not stay in an abusive relationship, my mother secretly stowed away small amounts of money for our escape. And then, grace arrived with a humble funny man who was willing to be a Dad to another man's child.

Fierce love is what I received as a child from my mother. Yet the trauma planted in my brain from those early years formed a foundation that has woven itself into the very fabric of my life, up until now. My brain was hardwired for a perception of life that created suffering in my relationship with myself, my mother, friends, and every partner. That perceptual hardwiring has created content to fill thousands of hours of psychotherapy sessions, and exhausted my life savings to heal myself through retreats, plant medicine, coaches, alternative healing certifications, and so on.

I love my mother deeply for her sacrifices every step along the way. I know she persevered where many women have looked the other way and drowned in guilt and shame. My mother is a powerful force to be reckoned with, a role model of a woman going after what she wants for herself. Beyond her dedication to finding the right partner, she persisted until she received her Masters degree in Early Childhood Education in mid-life and never passed up an opportunity to email her government representatives her perspective on issues of the day. Because she loved her daughter and wanted me to have the best opportunities, she sent me to the home of strong educated women: Smith College.

As it turns out my deep love and loyalty for my mother is what, finally, stood in the way of my own healing until I was willing to value my own life and voice as the top priority.

And so I courageously faced the hardest thing a person can do in life: I faced my mother. Or rather, the mother I created in my mind that caused me to shut down my voice, suppress my light, and self-sabotage.

Becoming a mother myself woke me up to this part of the spiritual journey in 1999, and yet the calling lay dormant until after my Dad passed away in 2017.

The last three years have been some of the most painful in my life in terms of loss, and the most rewarding in my life in terms of inner happiness and success in the world.

With fierce love I offer what I've learned in the pages of this book. I have come to realize the absolute power of a mother to set into motion the life experience of her children. I have also come to realize the absolute power of humans to love and care for the planet or to destroy everything in sight. The key is the consciousness with which humans are birthed into the world, raised into adults, and dedicate themselves to self-mastery.

I love and honor my mother.
I love and honor myself.
I love and honor Mother Earth.

And, I have to speak the truth with fierce love.

♥

this is the recipe of life

said my mother

as she held me in her arms as i wept

think of those flowers you plant

in the garden each year

they will teach you

that people too

must wilt

fall

root

rise

in order to bloom

—rupi kaur

it was when i stopped searching for home within others

and lifted the foundations of home within myself

i found there were no roots more intimate

than those between a mind and body

that have decided to be whole

—rupi kaur

Foreword

It takes a special kind of woman to write, rather birth, a book about Healing the Mother Wound. It takes a special kind of woman to say yes to such a large—monumentous, even—calling. It takes a courageous woman to take step after step from gestation through birth, and beyond.

It takes a special kind of woman to render herself open and available to be used as a conduit of universal wisdom. To share her heart and expose the vulnerabilities that—while not always looking good—are packed with gold. Kerri Hummingbird is such a woman, and the gold offered here in this book is priceless.

The Dalai Lama is often quoted as having said *"The world will be saved by the Western Woman,"* and with deep respect and reverence, we offer an additional twist to this important wisdom.

As I, Tracey, wrote in my book "Faces of the New Feminine Leadership," I believe it's a woman who is willing to do the deep inner work to face her own shadows and shame, fears and darkness within, and bring love and light to these places that will make a true and lasting difference. A woman who is willing to go within and love all parts of herself in a way that she's not been loved, and by doing so—and continuing to do so because it's a life-long practice—this woman emerges with a capacity to love, heal and hold space for others. This woman is willing to be supported and held, and do for herself what is required to navigate the deep healing that comes up in the inner work and in the process of healing the mother wound. It is this kind of woman who can share her journey as she invites us all to heal alongside her.

Kerri is such a woman. She is a magnificent messenger, divinely designed and guided to bring forward this profound work as she continues to master her own path and lead this fundamental conversation in the world when it's needed most, right now.

It takes a big person to hold a big space. And a courageous person to be held while holding others.

Having the honor of witnessing, holding and exploring these edges and dark places with Kerri over the course of more than 3 years, as well as fanning the flames of her brilliance and great wisdom, we know the moments of deep pain, great love and unshakable commitment she has lived authentically. Her light is undeniable, and her love immense. Her courage and knowing to dig deeper, lift higher, love more and surrender over and over to the healing that is shared in this book is inspiring and heroic. We've held Kerri in breakdown, build up and integration. We've witnessed firsthand, Kerri making herself an instrument for the song of divine truth and healing to play through her. Not trying to be some version of perfect, Kerri has walked this path and still does her evolutionary work for herself, and others.

We honor and adore Kerri's devotion to be the messenger and feminine leader she's here to be. This book goes to the places that we need to explore to heal the 'nooks and crannies' of human consciousness and create a world that is safer, more kind and caring for all living beings. We continue to walk this path with Kerri, and together, we do this for the children and their children, and theirs, and so on for generations to come.

We hold reverence for Kerri's children and her mother, and for all children and all mothers, as we all wake up to the truth of the love that we are. We're all here to help each other on this path of awakening as we each fulfill the principle we practice in our Amazing Community, called our "soul's curriculum." This is why we believe that though the details may often be challenging and sometimes even terrible, the blessings are there to be found. As these wounds get healed and the gifts are discovered through the lens of love, compassion, patience, discipline and devotion, we learn to love our inner child as we learn to mother ourselves lovingly. This is the work we've been immersed in together, on the path of learning and embodying how to love all parts of ourselves.

We're grateful as we honor our own mothers, and the mother in all of us. We invite you to honor the mother in you as well. We invite you to work through the gold in this book and find yourself in it, and know you're not alone.

It's a blessing, honor and pure joy to walk this journey with Kerri and share with you what we know—the countless hours of tears, willingness, courage, kicking and screaming, laughing and loving, that this Amazing Woman, this divine messenger, this powerful feminine shaman, this human mom, wife and daughter has been navigating to heal her own wounds and allow herself to be a vessel to birth this important work.

Tracey Trottenberg-Kansas and George P. Kansas

Spiritual Ignitors, Conscious Leadership and Communication Alchemists, and Co-Founders of Amazing International, Inc and Voices For Love

Love isn't the work of the tender and the gentle;

Love is the work of wrestlers.

The one who becomes a servant of lovers

is really a fortunate sovereign.

Don't ask anyone about Love; ask Love about Love.

Love is a cloud that scatters pearls.

—Rumi

Why Read This Book

Do you see yourself as a strong wise human able to make decisions that positively impact your family, community and the world? Or do you struggle with self-doubt, lack of worth, and self-sabotage? Do your relationships lift you to your fullest potential, or wear away at your energy and resolve?

When I began writing this book, I was estranged from my mother and part of my family, recovering from the loss of my Dad, and doing my best to support my eldest son in launching into the world. For years before beginning to write this book I had already been learning the lessons and taking the steps to heal the Mother Wound. I just was not aware of the process I was in until I was Spirit-tapped by White Buffalo Calf Woman to channel this book. I said yes and committed, without really knowing what I was signing up for.

As I began this book, I hoped that through the healing process I would be able to be connected with my mother while maintaining my personal power and respecting both of us, and that I would be a better mother for my sons. Upon finishing this book, my reason for doing it, and sharing it, is first a matter of **self-respect**. Because I respected myself to do the work in this book, I am able to show up with greater compassion, wisdom, love and kindness.

What I have come to realize through writing and embodying the teachings of this book, is that it is vital that you **know** yourself as strong, wise, and capable. This is especially important for women and mothers as we enter the Age of Aquarius where the Divine Feminine rises, and we embrace the Divine Mother as a teacher.

Strong wise women are the weavers of the web of family and community. When in their rightful place of honor, our families, communities and planet thrive from the benefit of the intuition, deep listening, divine connection, and fierce love of wise women. Our wise women support and teach our new mothers how to hold compassionate loving presence for our children and the words they speak come from wisdom earned through direct experience...not from outside authority but from **inner authority**.

A woman in her true power gives everyone a space to flourish because she is the constant gardener, she is the Mother Earth. She is not afraid to let the forest burn down or weeds to grow rampant because she knows life is a process, a cycle, and has innate wisdom. She is tapped into a greater consciousness through her feelings and intuition and surrenders to this all knowing presence to guide her way. She knows she is the voice of her ancestors, and her children are their greatest hope. She listens to the Mother Earth and feels the early tremors of the quakes and storms so she can lead the tribe to course correct and come back into harmony before a natural consequence is needed. She knows that every member of the tribe is dreaming a unique dream of their Soul, and she helps teach the **respect and tolerance** that allows all of these dreams to coexist.

For the last thousands of years, the web of our wise women has been torn apart, and in its departure humanity has brought itself to the brink of destruction. What we can witness is how when things are not in right relationship, the world topples over and over on itself.

Without the temperance afforded by ancestral wisdom, unbridled masculine energy penetrates and claims until everything that can be consumed, is consumed, from singular focus on self-interest. Our corporations convince us to be dependent on them for our comfort (and their profit), and we forget how to grow our own food. Our nations fight over limited resources (bypassing omnipresent ones), we build our societies as a power-ladder of haves and have nots, and our families divide from the dark pole of the toppled matriarchy which infects our mothers with programs that fester manipulation, jealousy, competition, objectification, and abuse (mental, emotional, physical, sexual, spiritual) out of the powerless nightmare of the downtrodden feminine.

Where is the mother with confidence enough to stare straight into the tormented eyes of a pedophile father and declare an end to the abuse through whatever means necessary? **How can mothers stand for the children if they can't stand for themselves?**

Can you hear the tremors and quakes of impending doom when you are consumed with talking about yourself and your suffering (from a far greater comfort than your ancestors ever had)? When you are so busy trying to escape the pain of your opulent yet unfulfilling life that you lose precious moments of presence with your children? **The volume of the mental chatter drowns out the quiet voice of our Divine Mother.**

As above, so below: your personal life is a micro version of what's happening in the macro Earth experience. Contemplate how the content of this book relates to your relationship with your own mother, your feminine energy and your masculine energy. Consider the larger ramifications of the messages in this book for the human collective and for Mother Earth.

If you are a mother, where do you need to deepen your relationship with Mother Earth and claim your power to speak truth into your family, community and world?

If you are a daughter or son, what aspects of this book help you to heal that inner Mother Wound so you can show up with your gifts in service to help restore and revitalize our planet?

How can you dream bigger and more powerfully than the drama that you were born into?

Realize that if you've experienced the patterns described in this book, your mother has passed the Mother Wound to you despite her best efforts, since she has also been infected with it.

Women began truly waking up to these patterns in the 1960s and doing their best to break them by following teachers like Dr. Benjamin Spock whose revolutionary message was that women should show their babies love and affection, and not just strict discipline, and that they should trust their common sense (or intuition). After centuries of being taught to be afraid of their intuition from a religious context, mothers were now being encouraged to see their innate knowing as a valuable asset.

This message being widely adopted was possible because women were finally feeling respected (in the United States) with the passage of the 19th Amendment in the 1920s which gave women the same rights and responsibilities of citizenship as men. Women began respecting themselves as a generation, and then a generation later, their daughters were able to begin loving and caring for their children in a new way. A generation later, their daughters began refining and lifting love and respect and care to new heights; thus, this book you are reading here today.

This effort to elevate love is generational because healing the patterns caused by the Mother Wound takes time, persistence, and dedication from women who are Warriors of Love. My mother is one of these women. I am one of these women. You need to see the greater context to appreciate that your mother's generation did their part to lift you to the place where you can now have greater expectations of love for yourself and your children. You are able to experience nuance and refinement in the conversation of Love to the degree to which your ancestors dug into the work to heal the layers of the Mother Wound they were addressing.

In the larger conversation, you are healing the Mother Wound of your relationship to Mother Earth. No matter what body you're in during this incarnation, you are fully a part of the consciousness of Mother Earth. You are born of her earth, fire, water and air. You are a product of the human collective programming that we are transitioning now for the survival of the species into the Age of Aquarius.

The path to ascension is through honoring our Mother Earth. Her steady heart beat calls you home to your Source, to Love. At all levels micro to macro you must honor the Divine Mother beginning with Gratitude to unlock the Love that leads to Awe. The Divine Father, God, helps to steer you with presence, structure, clarity, and penetration to deepen into the Divine Mother where you surrender to the unique self-expression that you are as a multidimensional being and you embrace all that you are in her steady agape love that honors your journey of self-discovery as a loved child of the Oneness.

It begins with the literal, tangible expressions of Mother: your mother, yourself as a mother, the Earth as our mother.

As you awaken to the Age of Aquarius, you are called forth to fully embody the Divine Feminine and Mother energies and express them as you deepen your roots. You must use your voice, serve as a nurturing guide to Let Others Voluntarily Evolve, and become a conduit of the Divine Mother to help awaken yourself and all of humanity. You must dream a new powerful dream for the planet that lifts you into greater self-mastery of Love. You must learn to listen inside and trust your inner guidance, even as you may receive pushback from the wounded masculine within, or in your life, who feel threatened by this feminine power that shines light into all the vulnerable nooks and crannies of the ego.

There is a natural contraction as you expand the Divine Feminine consciousness because the patriarchal consciousness strives to reassert its influence; this temporary recoil creates the space for a deeper expansion of the Divine Feminine as you move steadily into the new age. Trust the process because as you learn to be a vessel of Divine Mother energy, everything falls into right relationship and the masculine aspects of consciousness will naturally be guided to their rightful thrones and purpose.

The lesson begins with Gratitude and a suggested daily practice: place your hands on the Mother Earth and express gratitude from your heart through your hands in prayer.

Thank you for my life.
Thank you for this Earth school.
Thank you for all the support you've given me for my lessons.
Thank you for guiding me every step of the way.
Thank you, thank you, thank you Divine Mother.

As you shift your consciousness with *Gratitude*, you will see that a doorway opens to *Love*, and as you enter that doorway you experience *Awe*. This is the state of consciousness we must embody to re-envision human society to uplift and serve all of life on Earth. Practicing *Gratitude* demonstrates your dedication to dream from integrity and *Love*, and your commitment to the path unlocks more blessings with each step. By demonstrating you are committed to acting and speaking from integrity, you will be honored by the Divine Mother with new revelations and opportunities.

With this book, I humbly offer you revelations I have received from the Divine Mother and White Buffalo Calf Woman. *I ask you to read with an open mind and heart, and to let the messages of this book transform you.*

Our children's children are depending on us to turn our upside-down world right-side up.

You may not have personally created the conditions that are hurting humanity and all of life on Mother Earth, but you are response-able for it. You are response-able for the decisions, choices and actions that build the foundation of a New Earth. You must help to rebuild the foundation of our society and culture for sustainable living that honors our home and humanity.

It starts with you rewiring your individual consciousness to align your thoughts, choices and behaviors for your highest good, so you become a healthy cell in the body of Mother Earth.

In ceremony with a prayer for help to heal the Mother Wound, I heard thousands of ancestors say "We've tried, and we were not able to heal the Mother Wound. We do not think it can be done." My heart tells me otherwise. I know that is what we are here to do, and I know we can do it. There are sisters who have led the way, who have healed the Mother Wound within their own hearts. They shine as examples for us that it is possible to heal it for yourself, and then to ripple that healing backwards to your ancestors, and forwards to your children's children.

For our brothers and sisters who yearn to explore the galaxy, realize that the gateway to that freedom lies on the other side of loving, respecting, and honoring Mother Earth with every thought, word, and deed. Until you can take care of your planet and yourself, you remain in Earth School.

You are a piece of the puzzle of Heaven on Earth, as my friend Jennifer Hough says. Once you know that, and embody yourself as the unique Divine Spark that you are, your life becomes an act of service to the collective that lifts others to become the piece of the puzzle of Heaven on Earth that they are.

Together, we can set into motion a conscious humanity that honors all of life on Earth, and accepts response-ability to be Earth Keepers. Mother Earth has so much to teach you once you are willing to quiet yourself to listen and learn. Aren't you interested in expanding your consciousness with wisdom from the greatest teacher in all of Creation? *I Am.*

As I was writing this book and sharing thoughts on social media, I had a woman comment on a post "Is the Mother Wound even real?" Just the fact that she wrote that comment is an example of the Mother Wound. We are each perceiving life through a unique lens, here to understand life with our Soul's curriculum. When a person of color says he has experienced systemic racism, and a white person says "But is systemic racism even real?" it is the same issue. Just because you do not think you 'see' something, does not mean that your brothers and sisters do not see it. Showing respect to others is to say "Tell me more about that, because I'm not sure I have experienced it, and I am curious."

In this way, you are invited to adopt an attitude of curiosity and to empty your cup of all that you 'think' you know so that you will be able to receive what is humbly offered here. Suspend any disbelief, and let your mind open to the possibilities that this Mother Wound is very real…and it can be healed when you are willing to see it and do your personal shadow work to heal it.

There are no guarantees that doing the work in this book will change your relationship with your mother, children, or loved ones. **Focus on the love of your life, YOU, and do the work for yourself.** Self-respect is a huge gift I received from being motivated by circumstances with my mother and my children to commit to this work. And respect is the gift I am able to give to my mother and children from having dug into the shadows revealed within the pages of this book. I hope the teachings serve you as well as they have served me, or even better.

Why bother to do the work of healing the Mother Wound as described in this text? Do it because life is so much more enjoyable when you're not lugging a dumpster of resentments and misunderstandings around with you. Do it to experience what it feels like to be gentle, loving and kind to yourself. Do it to discover the magic inside you that is just waiting for you to remember it's there underneath all that crust that built up around your heart. Do it because Love is All That Is, and it wants to express fully as the unique design you are. Do it so the sparkle returns to your eyes, and the world returns to the technicolor fullness you knew as a child.

Do it because you deserve to know what it's like to feel the simple joy of being yourself.

♥

White Buffalo Calf Woman Returns

White Buffalo Calf Woman is a sacred woman of supernatural origin, a prophet of feminine power, who brought sacred wisdom and gifts to the Sioux people.

In the traditional story, it is said that there was a time of famine where all the Sioux tribes gathered together. The chief of the Lakota sent out two scouts to hunt for food. These men came across what appeared to be a white cloud in the distance, and as it came closer they saw a beautiful woman in white buck skin.

One of the men was filled with lust for her and reached out to touch her.

"This woman was 'lila wakan', very sacred, and could not be treated with disrespect. Lightening instantly struck the brash young man and burned him up, so that only a small heap of blackened bones was left. Or some say that he was suddenly covered by a cloud, and within it he was eaten up by snakes that left only his skeleton, just as a man can be eaten up by lust."
– Lame Deer, told in 1967 at Rosebud Indian Reservation in South Dakota

The remaining man was frightened until the holy woman beckoned him forth, telling him that no harm would come to him as he did not have the same lustful motives as the other scout. She explained she was a wakáŋ, having supernatural powers, and that if he did as instructed, the Lakota would rise again. He returned to his encampment as instructed, called the Council, and prepared a feast for her arrival.

When the holy woman arrived she had a gift for the people.

"Halting before the chief, she now opened the bundle. The holy thing it contained was *chununpa*, the sacred pipe. She held it out to the people and let them look at it."

"She told them that the smoke rising from the bowl was Tunkashila's breath, the living breath of the great Grandfather Mystery."
– Lame Deer, told in 1967 at Rosebud Indian Reservation in South Dakota

She taught the Lakota seven sacred ceremonies to protect the Mother Earth and gave them the chununpa, the sacred ceremonial pipe.

"With this holy pipe," she said, "you will walk like a living prayer. With your feet resting upon the earth and the pipe stem reaching into the sky, your body forms a living bridge between the Sacred Beneath and the Sacred Above.

Wakan Tanka smiles upon us, because now we are as one: earth, sky, all living things, the two-legged, the four-legged, the winged ones, the trees, the grasses. Together with the people, they are all related, one family. The pipe holds them all together."

– Lame Deer, told in 1967 at Rosebud Indian Reservation in South Dakota[1]

As she left the people, she stopped and rolled four times. The first time she rolled she turned into a black buffalo. The second time she turned into a brown buffalo. The third time she turned into a red buffalo. And the last time she turned into a white buffalo calf. She told the people that when the white buffalo started being birthed again into the world, it would signal her return.

Starting with Miracle the White Buffalo in 1994, white buffalos have been birthed, and many believe this is the fulfillment of the prophesy of the return of White Buffalo Calf Woman and the rise of women into leadership of our tribes and nations. It is time to mend the Sacred Hoop of life with matriarchal wisdom.

♥

---

[1] Read the full story from Lame Deer at https://www.firstpeople.us/FP-Html-Legends/White-Buffalo-Calf-Woman-Sioux.html

My Name

This section is channeled from White Buffalo Calf Woman.

Many of you know of me through the legend passed down through the Oceti Sakowin (The People of the Seven Council Fires, also known as the Lakota, Dakota and Nakota, or the 'Sioux'). Two thousand years it has been since my visit to the people with whom I shared many sacred ceremonies, songs and dances because these people demonstrated being prayerful and grateful. I shared seven sacred rituals that every prayerful person can perform to live harmoniously and abundantly on the Earth. And I told the people that the women and children were sacred vessels. I told the people to honor women because they are made in the image and likeness of Mother Earth: vessels of creation.

When I appeared to the people, it was to two brave scouts who had been sent by the Chief to find food during a famine. I turned myself into a beautiful young woman to teach the first lesson. One of the scouts instantly felt lust upon seeing me, and tried to take my sacred vessel into his hands to satisfy it. I turned him into dust. This was the first lesson. The other scout upon seeing this felt fear at my power. But there was no need for fear. The lesson was to honor the feminine vessel.

And now Kerri is having trouble with the channeling because she feels unworthy to be delivering this message. And this is perfect timing for this to arise because it is the point of why I have returned. The women walking the Earth today have not been honored as sacred vessels of the Mother Earth. The women walking the Earth today have been subjugated, denigrated, abused, shamed, controlled, and stripped of self-worth; for many, the abuse begins while they are still children.

And because the women have been stripped of self-worth, humanity has been stripped of self-worth.

The chanunpa, or sacred pipe, is one of the gifts I bestowed upon the Lakota people. It is an external representation of what happens by alchemy inside every woman. The bowl of the pipe is the woman's womb. Tobacco goes into the bowl of the pipe externally because protection and strong medicine go into the woman's womb for effective prayers. Prayers and blessings go into the tobacco that enters the pipe in the outer world because prayers and blessings are what is needed to birth beautiful creations from a woman's womb.

The smoke from the bowl of the pipe must travel through the will center, heart, and throat with the intention of the mind/third eye and an open connection to the Great Spirit before it is released out into the world. Just so, a woman – who is a walking chanunpa – must bring her creations up from her womb, through her will center, her heart, and her throat to be expressed by her words into the world.

What happens to a creation that is being birthed inside a toxic soup of shame, blame, judgement, grief, unworthiness, and victimhood? The well of Love is empty in such a vessel because it has been stripped of self-worth.

Now let us talk about creations because certainly humans have demonstrated an ability to proliferate creations from their mind upon the Earth. The skyscrapers, highways, shopping malls and technology gadgets to entertain restless unsatisfied minds prove that humans are able to create things. However, creating material things for egoic gratification is very different than creating something sacred.

Sacred creations are inspired by Divine connection, serve a greater purpose, bring beauty, and serve as a fountain of Love that restores the Garden of Earth even as it is derived from the Mother Earth's materials. A baby is a sacred creation. This book is a sacred creation. A chanunpa is a sacred creation. A ceremonial cloth is a sacred creation.

To birth a sacred creation you must prepare the vessel. You must honor the vessel through which the creation is birthed. You must open the vessel and flood it with the Divine through sacred ritual and prayer. And then you must surrender to the Great Spirit that is the only force that can birth a sacred creation…through you as the prepared vessel.

You are not doing it. The Great Spirit is the one that answers the prayers from the chanunpa. And if you have prepared your vessel for the sacred, the Great Spirit can birth the sacred creation through you.

Being in a female body automatically requires sacred work to prepare the vessel so that the Great Spirit can birth a sacred creation through you. Being a living chanunpa means that your prayers have power. Women's prayers have been influencing the world without them realizing it. Psychologically women have been trained over thousands of years to think they are not being heard; that the content of their hearts does not matter. Women have been violated by lustful men and made to think that being a receptacle of semen is their purpose.

Nothing could be further from the truth. Remember what happened to the lustful scout who attempted to take my sacred vessel to fulfill his physical desires?

For centuries women have been falsely conditioned to think that they are lower than men, and that the way to please 'God' is to subjugate yourself to men's control. That the way to survive in the world is to 'get a man and keep him.' Kerri is now remembering when her grandmother, who was trained in the Southern Baptist beliefs, told her that 'the Bible says woman serves man.' Kerri felt repulsed by this statement and hurt, and that was the correct response.

Now let us turn our attention to Christianity that has worshiped Jesus. Indeed, Jesus is an incredible teacher of love, forgiveness and compassion. And, Jesus was born of Mary. Mary prepared her vessel to receive the sacred gift of the Divine. Without this preparation, it is possible that a baby would have been born….but not a great spiritual teacher. Because Mary had prepared her vessel to be a living chanunpa, she lived in walking prayer. Because Mary lived in walking prayer, she reared her child in walking prayer.

Because Mary mothered Jesus in walking prayer, the world received the great spiritual teacher Jesus. It all began with the Mother and her decision to honor her sacred vessel...even if the prevailing culture did not honor her as a chanunpa, she found it within herself to do so.

Everything is connected. The fires rage across the planet, the heat rises, and the polar caps melt because the Earth reflects to humanity the state of its consciousness... or rather, the state of the consciousness of billions of chanunpas who have been desecrated. The rage and shame inside women's wombs is boiling, and so the planet is boiling.

The Divine Mother says through all sacred chanunpas: honor me or be destroyed.

There is a corollary teaching in Christianity about not honoring 'false prophets' above 'God'. Money is a false prophet. Oil is a false prophet. Thinking you own anything on the Earth is a false prophet. Nothing here belongs to you. It belongs to Mother Earth. She has only graciously allowed you to borrow her materials, including your own body, to have an experience in her garden. How have you treated her body? How have you treated her garden?

And now I speak to the souls that inhabit those bodies. It is time to respect the Mother Earth who is the Mother of your human incarnation. ASK before you take. If you have a desire, PRAY with Divine Mother to manifest it in a way that honors all of life on Earth for the highest good. Let her guide you to the solution that creates harmony. You have been taking from your sisters and brothers long enough. You have disregarded the animals, the plants, the stones, the birds, the dolphins...you have mistakenly elevated yourself above all of life on the planet.

Being on Earth is a privilege, and privileges can be revoked.

Things are out of balance on Earth from too many centuries of taking without asking, entitlement without gratitude, false superiority complexes, and enslaving the feminine to satisfy base desires.

And even as Kerri is channeling my message, there are distractions. There is a call from the bank that not enough money is available. There is a man across the street disturbing the peace with his electric blower…and isn't that a perfect demonstration of the loud masculine thinking mind disrupting the peace of the feminine connection to the sacred? Kerri feels aggravated by the lack of financial support and the intrusion of this noise into an otherwise peaceful and perfect environment for channeling. But this also was orchestrated as a demonstration of the human condition which interferes with the delivery of sacred messages into the third dimension in every way it can.

You thought the white buffalo calf was the sacred gift. It was a gift from the sacred. Notice how I rolled four times, changing colors, and then vanished leaving the gift in my place? This was to demonstrate many messages including the mutability of the feminine, the cycles of the seasons, the diversity of Creation, and the ephemeral nature of the Divine.

It is harder for Kerri to hear me when I go into softness. Her heart is so conditioned by the masculine for being pounded over the head with it that the gentler messages slide under the surface of awareness. And it is the same for most humans on the planet today. The Great Spirit offers a constant stream of subtle impressions that you can quiet yourself to hear and follow. Many ascended masters are here at this time to help you move out of the mind and back into your heart so you can hear these gentle messages. In the stillness is an understanding that liberates you from the conditioning of your mind from thousands of years of masculine energy domination.

As the women soften their hearts, the grief in their wombs can be released. With this clearing, there will be space for Love to grow again. It takes courage to soften your heart, to set down the armor, and to listen to your inner landscape with compassion, rather than judgment. It takes courage to claim responsibility to prepare your vessel for the sacred because it means facing the inner destruction caused through human conditioning and forgiving it to reclaim your chanunpa.

Women: no one can honor you until you first honor yourself and restore the sacred to your vessel. No one will give you honor because of the fear of a woman standing in her power. Remember back to the second scout who treated me with respect because of his fear for how I turned his fellow into dust? The reason why men have subjugated women on Earth for centuries is from this same fear...the fear of your power.

When a woman has prepared her vessel for the sacred, and learned to pray through herself every day, she is a conduit of the power of the Great Spirit. Certainly, depending on the level of toxicity within her womb, a woman can misuse this power for manipulation, control, and self-aggrandizing prayers. And in this phase of healing and transition into the Age of Aquarius, women will falter until they learn the self-awareness needed to avoid these misuses of power. Healing a woman's chanunpa and liberating it from passed-down patterns of suffering is necessary at this time, and that is what this book is about. It's about healing the Mother Wound.

The Mother Wound is created when a woman births a baby from an unprepared womb...from a womb that has not been prepared to receive the sacred. A woman who has not prepared her chanunpa for the sacred has not activated the inner wellspring of Divine Love that supports her to become a giver of life. Birthing a life is actually assisting a Soul to incarnate into a physical body. You can only fulfill the function of assisting a Soul to incarnate into a physical body when you have prepared your sacred chanunpa. This is why so many humans are born without knowing they have souls. They are born with Earth 'amnesia' not remembering who they are.

A woman who has prepared her chanunpa can channel into her womb the incarnating Soul and assist it with integrating into its physical form. This is a form of Soul midwifery.

As a result of so many women being deterred from accessing their spiritual power, we have had thousands of years of mothers birthing babies into the world that struggle with a sense of lack and emptiness because their souls are not fully integrated. The more that women have been punished and abused over generations, this unprocessed karma becomes the burden of the new babies who are birthed into the world without the guidance of their souls to heal it.

So you see you have learned a big lesson. People of Earth did not heed the message to honor your women, to lift them, to elevate them. As a result, you have learned what happens when you devalue, desecrate, demoralize, and demonize women. You create a world where there is hate, lack, greed, suffering, perpetrators, victims, helplessness, confusion, doubt, blame, shame, judgment, competition, and war. Sons who watched their fathers disrespect their mothers grow up to disrespect their wives and daughters. The cycle repeats and repeats; it is a spiral into darkness and destruction. The yearning for more is insatiable inside the loveless heart of the soulless human, and it will consume everything like a hungry ghost until there is nothing left, desperately trying to fill the void.

What reverses this cycle is women reclaiming their sacred chanunpas and honoring themselves. As women honor themselves, they restore the connection to the Divine that creates the inner wellspring of Love. This inner wellspring of Love satiates all desires with daily prayerful activity, and allows the woman to be gracious towards other women—ending the competition between women and rebuilding community. As the women rebuild the community, cooperation and understanding expand, elevating the group consciousness of the planet. And as the women teach their sons and daughters a new way of being, then a new generation of children can rise to embody healed masculine and feminine energies, and to lift women as sacred conduits of Divine creation.

When a healed masculine lifts a woman who honors her sacred chanunpa, her Love overflows with a bounty that replenishes his efforts to provide.

The turning of the tide begins with the women reclaiming their honor and healing the Mother Wound to become conduits of Divine Mother wisdom and Love.

You have called me White Buffalo Calf Woman because of the gift I gave to you. This book has messages from the White Buffalo Woman who birthed the calf, and is a call for each woman on Earth to become a White Buffalo Woman.

What the world needs now is the fierce love of a mother, our Divine Mother, and women who know their inner power and stand as White Buffalo Women for the mending of the Sacred Hoop of life on Earth. This book will point the way through the shadows and into the fierce love that you are invited to birth into the world. All humans are welcome to read this book regardless of physical body or sexual orientation; there is healing here for all.

I will share the teachings through the lens of Kerri Hummingbird.

Let us begin.

Suggestions

Connect with White Buffalo Calf Woman To fully receive the teachings and activations of this book, set the intention to connect with White Buffalo Calf Woman and allow her to be an etheric guide for you as you read. Simply choosing to welcome this connection is enough. If you want to go deeper, you can get an image of White Buffalo Calf Woman to see her and feel her presence. The artist Katherine Skaggs has a wonderful image on her website (www.katherineskaggs.com). You can also do the activation for White Buffalo Calf Woman in the book "The Sofia Code: A Living Transmission from the Sofia Dragon Tribe" channeled through Kaia Ra by Sofia, The One Divine Mother Creatrix of All Life.

Remembering Yourself Repeat this mantra daily from Paul Selig's channeled works, and begin listening to the Audible versions of his books starting from "I Am The Word." What do you feel as you say the mantras? What do you notice about your knowing after a week or a month?

I know who I am in truth and love
I know what I am in truth and love
I know how I serve in truth and love
I am here, I am here, I am here
I am free, I am free, I am free
Word I Am Word with this intention
Word I Am Word

Choose Kindness and Compassion Some of the content of this book can be challenging. Be kind to yourself as you explore it and have compassion for your life journey.

Quotes

"Above all, be the heroine of your life. Not the victim."
— Nora Ephron

"She overcame everything that was meant to destroy her."
— Rumi

"Family is supposed to be our safe haven. Very often, it's the place where we find the deepest heartache."
— Iyanla Vanzant

"What you do makes a difference. And you have to decide what kind of difference you want to make."
— Jane Goodall

"It took me quite a long time to develop a voice, and now that I have it, I am not going to be silent."
— Madeleine Albright

"My idea of feminism is self-determination, and it's very open-ended: every woman has the right to become herself, and do whatever she needs to do."
— Ani DiFranco

"The women whom I love and admire for their strength and grace did not get that way because shit worked out. They got that way because shit went wrong, and they handled it. They handled it in a thousand different ways on a thousand different days, but they handled it. Those women are my superheroes."
— Elizabeth Gilbert

The Power Of A Mother

I remember my mother's prayers and they have always followed me.
They have clung to me all my life.
—Abraham Lincoln

You may believe you have no power, but every mother has tremendous power with her children. That power can be used to uplift your children or to subjugate them to a lifetime of low self-esteem. It is vital that you heal her own Mother Wound so a generous nurtured heart guided by the Divine leads the way to raise your children.

This passage is from the book *Daughter Detox: Recovering from an Unloving Mother* by Peg Streep in which she offers scientific studies into the power of a mother with her children.

James Sorce and his colleagues took the cliff experiment one step further, exploring what a one-year-old does when her eyes are telling her one thing —Yikes! There's a drop ahead!—while her palms and knees, solid against the plastic, are telling her another. When her sensory perceptions contradict each other, how does she resolve the ambiguity?

She looks to her mother for guidance. The researchers had the babies' mothers stand on the deep end and assume various facial expressions. It's in this experiment, among others, that the extent of maternal power becomes crystalline.

When the researchers had the mothers look happy and smiling, they discovered that an astonishing 74 percent of the babies began crawling and kept going, even over the deep end. The signals conveyed by their cheery mothers' faces—All is well! You're safe!—caused the babies to ignore the danger of a drop ahead that their own senses registered.

In contrast, an angry face from their mothers on the other side was enough to stop every baby in his or her tracks. Some babies actually retreated, crawling backward, at the sight of their mothers' disapproving expressions.

Every nuance of a mother is registered by her child: facial expressions, emotional energy, tone of voice, smell, energy. You are finely tuned to your mother for guidance on all of life's challenges from the moment you are in her womb until you manage to parent yourself through inner healing of the Mother Wound. The relationship with your mother is a huge factor in whether you can identify your feelings and communicate, have the confidence to take risks, be resilient in the face of setbacks, and feel strong self-worth and self-love.

I never realized how important I was as a mother until my children were nearly grown. I spent most of their young lives swimming in self-doubt, feelings of inadequacy, and fear of mothering them wrong from my own unhealed Mother Wound. Together, we must break the cycle and help our young mothers begin parenting from a healed place.

The Mother's Womb Weaves Children's Consciousness

As a baby grows inside his mother, her thoughts, emotions, beliefs, patterns, stories she tells about herself and world—all of this weaves the web of consciousness with which he is born into the world. It is an ingenious system created to ensure that each child is born onto Earth equipped to live in the times into which the child is born.

In times and cultures of human history where mothers were revered as sacred vessels of creation, where people understood that humans were born into a web of life created by the consciousness of the mothers who birthed them, attention was paid to ensure that mothers understood their own worth. Mothers were honored and cherished and uplifted and taught to honor, cherish, and uplift themselves. Special attention was paid to girls to ensure that they were wise, discerning, of high integrity and good listeners of Mother Earth, knowing the inherent magic of creation their bodies possessed that could birth a human into a life of joy or a life of suffering.

Girls were prepared to be warriors of love and community, taught to keep the fabric of family together through cooperation and diplomacy. Intuition and empathy were honed skills for detecting unrest in the family before gossip turned into manipulation and division. Every voice heard and respected was the understood pathway for peaceful tribal living. Patience for each individual to learn at his or her own pace without shame or ridicule was facilitated by the wise female elders who were tapped into all the nuances. Many matriarchal traditions wisely encouraged girls to choose their own mates, listening deep within themselves for the truth of their bodies and spirits for the best alchemical combination to produce a new life into the tribe.

Curanderas, or medicine women, were known to be extremely powerful healers due to their access to Spirit and Mother Earth, and the innate gifts of their bodies so finely tuned and sensitive. The courage of a mother bear, the lightness of a butterfly, the swift conviction of the jaguar, the suppleness of a flower, the seduction of the serpent, the sensuous allure of the papaya...women were trained to shapeshift through all the faces of the feminine, knowing the moment demands its perfect medicine.

The range of expression of the feminine was not feared, it was revered as it spoke emotionally and sensationally to the human experience. She gave us permission to feel, to cry, to laugh, to moan, to be still with no answers in the mystery of Spirit. The medicine women were as tough as centuries-old oak trees, and as gentle as a spring breeze lightly touching you.

Imagine for a moment being birthed inside a woman in her power, in her knowing, in her truth. Marvel at the web of life created by a boundless woman in touch with all of life on Earth. A woman knowing herself in this way births her baby into the Garden of Eden.

And perhaps it was this inexplicably uncontrollable feminine power that led patriarchal leaders to disassemble all matriarchal cultures, and condemn, disempower, disrespect, torture, rape and kill women...especially medicine women. The truth was flipped upside down and women learned through the Bible that they were actually the shameful ones who must repent for their sinful natures, and succumb to the exulted power of God in a masculine form.

The masculine ideology has made women into property and trophy wives, more concerned with being beautiful and catching a rich powerful man than making sure life on Earth is sustainable for the children. How small, petty, and competitive women have become believing the lie of powerlessness.

Our culture reveals what we are conditioned to value from women. In the unconscious matrix, the 'valuable' woman is the young pretty one willing to reveal her sexy body in an alluring way for the pleasure of men, and then surprise him with her intellect (as long as she remembers who is boss). She feels so powerful in her sexiness until she is replaced by a younger woman, and then she goes after plastic surgery and botox and endless hours at the gym to keep her looks (and thereby, her value). She demeans herself adhering to the 'standards' that were never created to help her honor herself—only to create a system for producing trophies that men want to acquire.

All the shapeshifting gifts that women have access to are modeled as ways to attract a man, and to compete with other women for 'desirable' men or for other forms of power. These gifts are now tools of manipulation because that is what happens when women are raised in systems where they don't have access to their inner power: they use their innate gifts to stealthily manipulate the outcomes they want, and they tear down other women in the process (including their own daughters who become 'competition' as well).

Imagine for a moment the mother web that births a child from this consciousness. Does the child feel secure in his mother's wisdom? Protected by his mother's fierce love? Or does he feel uncertain and afraid in the world because his mother hasn't found her own power and is unpredictable in her reactions to circumstances? How does a girl child feel? Uplifted and celebrated by her mother?

In this living Barbie production system, women who shirk the system and express their unique individual selves are called weird, and so dye their hair all wild colors to mark themselves as renegades. Women who think for themselves and challenge the status quo are called bitches, and so often find their place of power as entrepreneurs outside the systems of masculine power. Or women straight up battle men using their own masculine power matrix, leaving unexplored their inherent divine feminine and ending up burned out in midlife.

Is it any wonder that humanity is at a point of crisis where Mother Earth hurls at us fires, tornadoes, melting icecaps, earthquakes, and viruses? Collectively, we are disrespecting our mothers, we are birthing humans fixated on consuming, penetrating, conquering, and claiming—and very few humans are listening as our skies fill with smog and our plant medicines burn in the jungle.

We have reached the end of the patriarchal drive to conquer the feminine and control Mother Earth. Humanity will never dominate the Earth. She will flick humanity off her back like so many fleas if we do not start listening to her.

She's been listening to us, and she knows our every anticipated move. Take a moment and consider how ridiculous it is to be concerned with a manicure when in just a few generations from now we may be extinct if we don't take action now to course correct. Please, we need to get our priorities straight for the benefit of future generations.

To survive, we need humans tuned into Mother Earth. We need our medicine women to rebuild the fabric of human society with wisdom, compassion, patience, and diplomacy. We need our men to put down their tools of destruction, stop building stuff we don't need, stop trying to 'outwit' Mother Nature with new biohazards and drugs, and stop playing Monopoly to control and subjugate life on Earth.

We must humble ourselves to learn from the sacred power of Mother Earth that is beyond our comprehension.

Those of us on the frontier of the return of the divine feminine are doing the tough spiritual work to dismantle distrust of other women, to speak our truth from love (it often starts with anger, frustration and grief), to be straight up and direct with each other by learning how manipulation has seared itself into our cultural consciousness, to be present with ourselves so we can actually hear one another, to witness each other without fixing each other, and to heal the Mother Wound passed down to us ancestrally.

The qualities that best serve every human now are humility, presence, integrity, and willingness to take personal response-ability to clean up this mess we have collectively created.

You've got to stop listening to that hungry ghost you picked up in the womb of your mother who was trained to believe she was not worthy, not good enough, not loved, not wanted, not respected, not appreciated; and so birthed you into a web of consciousness where you never felt worthy, good enough, loved, wanted, respected and appreciated.

When you heal the Mother Wound within you, you awaken to the powerful connection you can have with Mother Earth, and she leads you through breadcrumb steps to claim the Garden of Eden that is right here, right now.

The indigenous cultures around the world have guarded these secrets for this Great Awakening, waiting for you to be ready to heal yourself and reconnect with Mother Earth.

Admit that you are not smarter than the Earth that birthed you. You are a student in Earth School: so start listening and learning.

❤

How The Mother Wound Is Formed

Gestating in your mother's womb, you marinate in her state of consciousness. If she doubts herself, you marinate in the energy of doubt which can manifest itself later in distrust of the feminine. If she feels unworthy, you marinate in unworthiness. If she lacks confidence, then you marinate in lack of confidence and also fear that you will not be supported. If she has fears or worries about her circumstances, fear and worry become a mental pattern in your tiny forming brain, becoming more deeply grooved the more she obsesses.

If she thinks or talks about not wanting to be a mother, and considers terminating the pregnancy, you begin life knowing you were not wanted nor loved.

The patterns you absorb in utero, and experience from birth to 5 years old, set the dream of your life (or nightmare), and your life's experiences begin to unfold in ever widening arcs to present you with circumstances that are opportunities to witness and heal these patterns as you evolve.

Teaching safe sex is the minimum we need to be doing to prepare women to become mothers. Mindfulness, self-empowerment, clear boundaries, empathy, and self-honoring are a starting point for the spiritual work women need to birth strong confident humans. **Preparing a woman to be a mother is training her to be a warrior of love—fierce love.** Yet what often happens is that a woman finds herself pregnant before she has learned how to be a warrior of love.

When I got pregnant with my first child, I thought I was ready. I was 30 years old and had over a decade of weekly psychotherapy under my belt which began at 15. What I did not predict was that birthing the baby would unleash a flood of unhealed childhood trauma and Mother Wound from my body in tidal waves of post-partem depression.

I remember one day just a couple of weeks after the birth I was standing in the shower and seeing – with eyes open – a dark hole leading to an abyss of despair in the tiles of the shower floor. At other times while driving I was getting a near uncontrollable urge to jerk the wheel into the cement highway barrier as my baby wailed from the backseat.

He was born inconsolable. Of course he was. He was born in the web of my Mother Wound. There was a black aching cloud around my heart of shame that I inherited from my mother at one year old when she found my natural father molesting me. In the years to follow as my mother left my natural father to protect me, and found her way to a safe place for us, we went through more trauma and violence from my first step-father who appeared to be a 'good man' and then proved to be a violent alcoholic.

These early life experiences birth to 5 years old placed in my brain the patterns for feeling a deep insecurity, a need for achievement to cover up feeling unworthy, clinginess and desire for security contrasted with inability to form secure attachment from abandonment, lack of confidence in myself, doubt in my intuition, extreme need for external validation, shamefulness about my body and sexuality, and a profound sense of being to blame for just about everything.

Even having the best father from age 5 onwards could not undo the early programming. It influenced my thoughts and behaviors my whole life, and splashed up to the surface for healing when I birthed my son at 30.

Holding my little precious son, I felt like I was doing motherhood wrong, and he knew it. I didn't honor or trust myself, and that scared him. *How can you relax when your caretaker doesn't think she can take care of you?*

Within a few weeks, I had hired a nanny and I returned to work. Then I repeated the pattern of abandonment every time my son escaped the nanny to reach out to me in my open office and could not get past the child gate. There, but not there. In sight yet inaccessible.

My relationship with my mother felt tenuous to me, and I was never certain if I was truly wanted or loved; now the Mother Wound of not feeling wanted or loved was getting passed to my son through my choice to focus on what I was good at (work) rather than step into this new frightening territory of being a mother. I needed my own space and identity separate from being his mother; otherwise, I felt I might drown in motherhood and lose myself entirely.

I thought I was doing a better job with my children since I worked at home throughout their lives. I was a latch key child, I was all alone every day after school. Yet the main complaint both my sons have made is that they always saw me at my desk working, and did not feel that I cared about them to take time out. They spent a lot of time in their rooms after the divorce from their father, thereby repeating my exact experience of feeling alone and entertaining myself as a child. **The Mother Wound was transferred through me to them despite my thinking I had done it differently.**

Only now, as my younger son is in his last year in high school, do I have enough self-awareness to see what's been happening, and the supportive relationship to help me attempt to create a different family environment and unravel this persistent pattern. The Mother Wound is the deepest of wounds, and has taken me a lifetime of psychotherapy, and nearly a decade of intense spiritual work to unpack, process, and transmute. It took me until I was 49 to realize that the source of my deepest wounding was from the unloving patterns I experienced through the words and behavior of my mother, who herself had been conditioned with unloving patterns from her mother that were even more painful to endure.

Remember, it takes generations to break the cycles, and Warriors of Love to stay committed to taking personal response-ability to do the inner work that changes the patterns. Despite my mother's dedication to breaking the patterns, her commitment to earning a Master's degree in Early Childhood Education, and her continued engagement in psychotherapy for personal growth: she could not eradicate the patterns in me because I had already been born into her Mother's Web before she dove into all that training and healing work.

In fact, it was my birth and her love of me that brought her to do the deep hard work of healing the Mother Wound; time and again my mother reinvested herself to work on her relationship with me as her daughter, and despite her conflicted feelings about her mother, she dedicated herself to understanding and loving my grandmother until she passed in her early 90s.

My love for my sons brought me to begin healing the Mother Wound within me just like my mother's love of me brought her to work on healing her Mother Wound. When all my shadows and pain surfaced at the birth of my first son, and I witnessed how out of control I was being with my fits of anger and suppressive depression, I dug into healing myself so I could be there for him as his mother.

We will often heal for our children because we love them more than ourselves; they are the reason we will finally face and heal the Mother Wound within.

I am now the kind of mother who can do for my kids what I always wanted to receive from my mother: listen and unconditionally love. They've said some pretty rough things to me, things that I never would have been brave enough to say to my mother. I have listened and guided as best I could. I have humbled myself rather than forced my will, controlled or manipulated them.

I have done all this deep spiritual work on myself and with my children in the midst of my family 'taking sides' and shunning me; the elders that my sons look up to have told them that their mother is not parenting them with love, which has introduced doubt and distrust in their hearts that they have had to contend with. It's made them question my motives, my love, my parenting, my integrity, and whether they want to be in relationship with me when 'everyone says' [fill in the blank].

This is the Mother Wound that medicine women today bear the brunt to heal on behalf of humanity. The family is still operating from the painful conditioning even as we are healing the Mother Wound within ourselves. We pass on the Mother Wound before we are aware we are doing it, and then we work through the patterns and the shadows in ourselves and our children and families at the same time. Projection runs rampant, blame divides us into 'sides', and the pain is unbearable so we leave each other. Mothers are drug through the mud one last time, often without our family realizing they're doing it or that there's another potential for how to perceive and resolve these familiar and painful cycles.

When you have the capacity to see the bigger picture of the evolution of our species, you can have grace and compassion for those souls mired in the mud of the Mother Wound.

Those of us who can see the bigger picture have a response-ability to heal ourselves of the patterns and cultivate the emotional capacity to stay in the conversation during the healing process with our children and families. In so doing, we offer new seeds of potential to our children and children's children.

The healing vibrations of all this deep work to heal the Mother Wound will penetrate the consciousness of our sons and daughters, and a new way of being will unfold before them as we collectively step into the Age of Aquarius.

In the meantime, as a participant in this process, I hold myself as the mother I always wanted for myself, my children, and even my mother.

♥

A Mother's Heart Is A Powerful Influence

The potential of agape love lives within every mother's heart. Agape love is defined as "the highest form of love, charity" and it is universal and unconditional love that transcends and persists regardless of circumstances.

On the high road, a mother allows this seed of agape love to grow within her heart, and to reveal all her self-interest, judgments, fears, attachments, and self-delusions as her children grow and go through their lessons. To fully reap this potential and embody agape love, a mother must be willing to open her heart fully to her children, and keep her love open even as she takes the inspired actions that her child needs to grow. She must learn the hardest lessons about loving unconditionally, without expectations, and without taking it personally. She must hold her love of herself in balance to her love of her children, and sometimes act with fierce love to help her children course correct back onto the golden line. **The golden line is the beauty way through life, a path of honesty and gratitude, compassion, forgiveness, understanding, listening and loving unconditionally.**

Embodying agape love requires great wisdom to see the coyotes at work, the mischief-makers that will wreak havoc in your home and bring drama and suffering. As a mother, you cannot be afraid to confront these coyotes and call them out in yourself and your children. Expose them, feel the discomfort and shame and blame and all the tricks that keep you from fully embodying agape love. Fearlessly walk through the shadows and demonstrate your strength in Love and your faith that all is well, even if it looks like a huge mess.

A mother who embodies unconditional love gives her children the permission to be imperfect as they learn their lessons in Earth School. She resists the temptation to judge herself for her children's choices, or to shame them because she feels ashamed.

She refutes the coyote that whispers in her ear that her child is broken, damaged, and lost, and she maintains her faith that her child is in the necessary process for growth that the Divine is orchestrating on his/her behalf.

A mother who is on the path to embodying agape love admits her mistakes to her children, demonstrates forgiveness and compassion, and calls them forth to their highest expression – even if that means taking away all safety nets and letting them forge their own way without material support.

A mother who embodies agape love resists the urge to buy her children's love with material things, holds steady in dismantling entitlement and manipulation tactics, and leans into uncomfortable conversations to reveal the coyote within her child to himself/herself—while holding unconditional love.

A mother who embodies agape love respects her child as sovereign, and works to dismantle her own judgments and projections about the dream of life her child is creating for himself/herself. She knows that her child has his/her own unique path to healing, and she is a beacon of love as that pathway is discovered and walked.

A mother who embodies agape love knows that her children will blame her and get angry and fight because they are just beginning the journey to tame that coyote within. She holds steady in her faith that she has passed along all her wisdom and fully demonstrated what to do, and what not to do, to her children and that they are strong, smart and capable. She knows that when things look messy, it is a really good sign that her child is grappling with that coyote and in the process of claiming his power from it.

A mother who is listening to the Divine Mother will take actions that go against her desire to coddle and protect her children. There comes a moment where a human mother can learn a great lesson by watching a mother bird who pitches the babies out of the nest; it's the only way they learn how to fly.

One day leading up to pitching my eldest son out of the nest (for the first time), I was out praying by my fairy garden when something caught my eye in the grass. Just a few feet away from where I was standing was a plump baby bird sitting in the lawn, partially hidden by blades of grass.

The mother bird kept swooping down to the plump baby, feeding it more food from her beak. She was agitated because every time the plump baby fluffed its wings, it was clear those little wings were not strong enough to move its body off the ground. I could very much relate to the mother's predicament. This plump baby has been so well cared for, its every need met, that it literally was not strong enough to lift itself using its own wings.

The mother sensed urgency in this lesson around self-motivation, knowing that the neighborhood had a natural predator for that plump baby: *cats*. In fact, there was a stray orange tabby around at that time who claimed the entire block as his domain, allowing several neighbors to feed and care for him. Just a couple of years before, that orange tabby had lunged all the way up my front door to knock loose the bird nest in the wreath hanging there; he had a meal from all those baby birds that had just hatched.

Watching the mother swooping down to counsel the plump baby, to encourage it to use its wings and legs to propel itself out of danger, made me start to feel concern for that baby bird as well. Knowing that human scent can make a mother bird abandon her baby, I stayed out of it and watched from a distance, using this opportunity to explore how this synchronous scene related to my own mothering challenge with my eldest son.

What I felt in my heart was the question I often felt: am I doing the right thing? Is my decision to pitch my son out of the nest going to help him use his own wings? Or is this decision going to lead to a negative spiral where he feels he has lost the one place he felt safe? Is my role to give constant nurturing and support, or is my role to sometimes be the conduit for Spirit's two-by-four lesson?

For much of my time as a mother, I gave into my own fears and overly protected my children, not giving them a chance to sort things out for themselves. I was concerned about others' opinions and placed the burden of upholding my public image as a 'good mother' on them, expecting them to be visibly successful in socially accepted ways to affirm their love for me. When their lives conformed to my expectations, I felt safe in my role as mother. I felt threatened by other females in my children's lives, afraid I didn't measure up to the competition.

Part of the Mother Wound passed down through my mother's lineage (her generation and ones before) was the pattern of bullying children into compliance through control or manipulation. This pattern creates a sense of powerlessness that a child carries forth into adulthood, creating a dynamic where the mother can feel victimized by her own child when the child expresses his/her own power.

This is what happens when the mother does not know she has inner power, and in fact that she is extremely powerful in her role as a mother, and is afraid her power can be taken away. I was aware of this pattern at work in our family, and I saw it in myself when my sons began claiming their power; I wanted to do whatever I could to stop perpetrating this pattern and support my sons to express their own voices.

What I have learned through my life's experiences is that a mother who feels fearful and insecure sets the tone in the family of competition, manipulation, posturing, expectations, entitlement, family gossip, conformity, and disempowered children who are afraid to claim their own truth because they know that if they do so, and their truth challenges their mother's sense of safety, they will be shunned and shut out.

I experienced being excluded from the family when I began using my voice to express my truth in the public forum, and I felt myself wanting to block family members who were using their voices to tear down my fragile sense of inner power. On the other side of this challenge, I know that a woman in her true power of Love can speak gently in a way that respects others' journeys while still honoring her own.

Getting to this place of understanding was pretty rocky for me and my family as I ventured onto the public stage as a messenger of Spirit. In the words of my first female mentor, HeatherAsh Amara: "When a woman starts learning to speak her truth, it's not very elegant at first." Indeed. There were many times I thought that I was being rational and diplomatic as I spoke publicly of family situations; however, I was actually moving through layers of crust around my heart and speaking from pain.

As I have healed through the years, I see more clearly because in some ways the spiritual journey is like climbing a mountain: the higher you climb, the more clearly you can see as you elevate your understanding above the clutter of your mind that obstructs the view of the bigger picture.

Unraveling the fear patterns set into place from a mother who feels fearful and insecure can take generations. It takes courage to break from the family and set out on your own to discover other families or communities or teachers with healthy patterns. It takes dedication to face all the uncomfortable coyotes that have built cities inside your brain, and dismantle them without resorting to the manipulation tactics that put those coyotes in your brain in the first place.

And if you're the mother in the middle, with a living matriarch still healing the fear patterns within her, you need deep spiritual roots to weather the storm and build your own safe haven of unconditional love for yourself and your children. You've got to be strong enough to unconditionally love your mother as she heals her Mother Wound, and to hold space for your wayward children who are tousling with the coyotes that you passed along to them before you knew better.

As soon as you wake up to this truth, you must claim your throne as the matriarch of your family, and declare your 'house' to be a house of Love.

I Declare This Is A House Of Love
- *This is a house of unconditional love.*
- *This is a house where every member of the family is honored for their journey.*
- *This is a house where you are invited to bring yourself as you are, including hurt feelings and mistakes.*
- *This is a house where you can express yourself, and where you'll be invited to rise up to a higher expression that truly honors you.*
- *This is a house that receives the wisdom of our ancestors to help us through the tough moments.*
- *This is a house of fierce love which allows the Divine to guide our hearts into the most supportive actions to help you face your coyotes and claim your power.*

Making this claim may leave you trembling as the fear shakes you from deep inside. The coyotes start to taunt you and provoke fear that your children will be consumed by darkness and never find their way home to you. You may feel tempted to agree with that fear and build walls and try to barricade those coyotes out of your home—all of which simply lets those coyotes know that what they're doing is working. You believe they can win.

Your mother's heart knows better. Your mother's heart knows that LOVE WINS EVERY TIME.

You feel the proof of that when your heart aches for your children even as they're misbehaving in terrible ways. You love them no matter what, don't you? It doesn't matter what they do, you'll try to find a way to help them through it. That's the power of love that flows through your mother's heart. It's stronger than those pesky coyotes.

You've just got to trust yourself. Trust your heart. Trust your womb. And know that your ancestors are holding you and helping you to rise to this challenge. Your ancestors have your back until you can stand up straight and embody that agape mother love you came here to experience. You are their hope, and the hope of your children's children. It starts with you.

It's the mothers that are going to really turn the tide of the planet because of our capacity to feel powerful love for our children.

Be courageous enough to let your child sit in the stench of his coyotes as you shower him with love. Let your child witness his stubbornness to receive, to act, to speak. Let him witness his self-destruction in the face of your clear boundaries and your undying love. Don't rescue him from his pain, and be there to hold his hand.

Trust yourself and the lessons you imparted as you were fire-hosing him with love. Now that he knows the vibration he's aiming for, he has to create it for himself on the inside, and he knows he has a long way to go until he can love himself as much as you love him from your mother's heart.

Don't follow him into his drama and fear by agreeing with him that he is lost. Know with total faith that his current mess is temporary, and that it's actually the way laid out for him to walk to discover his own love. It's not a problem that he's having problems. Those problems hold the gold nuggets of wisdom he must claim for himself on his path to love.

Don't make your children dependent on your love. If you do, they'll never get the joy of discovering love for themselves. Beware of the urge to create this codependency because that is just your ego wanting to feel important. There is a far greater love that your mother's love points the door to, and that's the discovery of inner love. You want your children to shine on the inside? Let them walk the way to claim their own love.

One more thing: resist the urge to judge other mothers for how they're raising their children and gossip about it. That's actually a sign that you're avoiding the deep work you're here to face within yourself. Tend to your own mother's heart and to your unique Soul agreements with your children. Trust me, that's plenty to keep you busy when you're actually doing the work.

Our children have their own Soul agreements and lessons and timing; they'll get there when they're ready and in their own way. As mothers we must let go and trust our children to live their own lives and follow their own paths to Love. Hold the knowing of your child's brilliance; be in your knowing that he'll get that coyote by the tail and toss it out.

Realize that mothers have egos, and that ego thinks she knows better than the Divine how her children need to learn their lessons; the Divine lays the path for each Soul to learn, and while we may glimpse the curriculum, it's not for us mothers to say what lessons our children are here to learn or how they should learn them.

The mother's sacred commitment is to be a constant source of agape love for our children that they can tap into as they need on their journey. Let the Divine move through you on behalf of your children; if you're listening, you'll know what to do in right timing.

♥

Be Careful The Stories You Weave

As a mother, you have a powerful ability to tell the stories that weave the narrative that create the perceptions through which you see your children, and through which they form their identities. It is a huge responsibility and easy to abuse that power unconsciously by simply doing what you have seen others do your whole life: *gossip.*

Perception creates reality. Perception shared where two or more are gathered creates big reality, and it can be a prison of identity that is hard to escape when you start waking up to new perspectives about yourself.

You have been programmed from the day you were birthed through other people's perceptions and 'realities'.

- You were programmed by the stories your parents and siblings told about you; those stories that became part of family lore and get chuckles or a rolling of eyes at family gatherings.

- You were programmed by the educational system to think a certain way about life, society and history. If you are in America right now, you may be aware of a huge wakeup call that history books inaccurately portray our forefathers as champions of liberty, when the truth is that people of color have struggled against systemic racism long after formal slavery ended with laws passed by elected officials that unfairly target and suppress them.[2]

- You were programmed by what you were taught when young and impressionable with a mind like a sponge, soaking up every detail as 'truth'. Movies, television, children's programs, news, subliminal advertising: these are all ways you have been culturally programmed into accepting things as true, and then encouraged to act in a way as to conform with this programming as part of your individual identity.

---

[2] 13th Full Feature on Netflix offers a starting point for understanding systemic racism against black people

Whatever you give your attention to and agree with becomes an influencing force for the reticular activating system of your brain. The reticular activating system is like a window through which you perceive the world. It brings to your attention things that match your subconscious beliefs, and you unconsciously ignore everything else that doesn't match your beliefs. Unconscious bias is a product of the function of the reticular activating system.

Unfortunately, there are certain professions that understand these principles and use them to program you to push their own agendas, many of which lack moral integrity or concern for the bigger picture of community and planet. They know what demographic of person you will 'trust' and therefore agree with to take action; the action they want you to take so they can profit from your choices.

No one is immune to this programming. You will be influenced by it until you choose to become aware and uncomfortable, and push across your edges to consider other perspectives. You must choose new experiences, fresh ideas, and venturing into the unknown if you want to be free of your programming. For example, visiting another country is an experience that can help you push through the discomfort of something foreign to you; it challenges you by revealing your underlying subconscious programming.

Once you have that uncomfortable feeling of the 'foreign', lean into the discomfort and listen. Let it percolate and expand in your body. Notice any inner resistance. Be with the resistance. What words bubble up from the discomfort? What judgments or objections or impulses?

This kind of inner exploration reaps gold because **you can discover a program that was previously part of the invisible matrix of your mind and make it awkwardly and uncomfortably visible**. Because you are aware of it, you have the ability to explore its truth for you. You may keep it or you may change it. But you'll consciously decide, and that's the whole point.

Waking up is doing exactly this: pushing yourself past your comfort zone to become aware of your programming and then reprogram yourself with conscious choice.

Until you wake up to the power of subconscious programming and the ways your stories program your identity and experience of life, you can be weaving quite the web around yourself. It's a prison of your own making: you are the spider weaving the web with your stories and trapping the fly (yourself) in the web.

Collectively, we have created an entire industry around telling stories for healing, and it's called talk therapy, a form of psychotherapy. After decades on a therapists couch for weekly sessions, I realized that the stories I told about myself and my life, coupled with the powerful emotions I was feeling, were creating more of the life experiences I said I did not want. If I focused on things being a problem, more problems sprung up. If I kept saying "I don't know", I kept having the experience of not knowing (and denying my intuition). If I believed I was crazy, I would act in ways that caused others to agree with that assessment through self-sabotaging behavior.

I had to lean into the discomfort of alternative healing methods, foreign to me at the time, to finally realize that I had powerful spider medicine that I had been using against myself—and I could use it FOR myself.

I learned that I could spin different stories to get more desirable results for myself. I could perceive situations through a new lens with beneficial outcomes for life challenges. I could feel better about myself and elevate to a higher vibration where more positive experiences happened for me.

I learned how to use my spider medicine to consciously create the outcomes I wanted for myself. I reinvented myself and my life with my spider medicine and rediscovered aspects of my personality that I previously thought were 'bad' were actually huge gifts when put into right relationship within myself.

Through trial and error, I learned that what you place your attention on expands. What hooks your attention leads your mind to focus on it, and where you focus your mind, you focus your energy, and where you focus your energy that thing expands. **Every event that happens is neutral until your mind creates a story about it, and that story leads to an expansion of energy.** Then you can identify with the story as if it is who you are, and become attached to that story as part of your identity.

Which leads back to the stories you tell about yourself, and that your mother and your family tells about you. Beneficial stories create beneficial outcomes. Better yet, allowing stories to just be stories and not part of personal identity gives you greater access to the vast inner potential available in each moment.

You are not your history. You are what you make of yourself as a result of the history you experienced. You can choose in any moment to change a belief, thought or behavioral pattern; but if your family identifies you as your history, it's hard for them to perceive you as the person you are choosing to be now, in this moment.

In the words of Tracey Trottenberg and George Kansas, the greatest freedom is when you can 'paint with a new brush' the people in your life. Let go of the past perceptions you had of them, and open up to the unknown of the blank canvas. When you can let go of your perceptions of yourself and your loved ones, you leave them space to evolve and grow, and you give yourself space to witness that evolution and growth.

Give yourself the grace to evolve as well. Listen to the stories you tell about yourself without believing them, and then realign to the truth that your body is holding for you as a vessel made of Earth, of our Mother Earth. The truth will be revealed to you as you hold presence. Then you'll know what you want to expand with your attention, for the highest good.

If you're a mother, catch yourself in the act of deciding who your child is based on your historical perceptions of him/her. **Let your child be an artwork in motion, ever changing and morphing into**

the unexpected. Of course you have your favorite moments, and you can hug those close to your heart when feeling wistful reverie; just realize that is your meaningful moment, not your child's. Your child will decide what moments define him/her.

As a child, realize that the stories that your mother tells about you have been made real in her perception by telling them over and over for years, collecting more evidence to support her version of you that lives in her mind. **You can't change that perception of you that lives in your mother's mind.** Only she can choose to change it. But that perception of you that lives in your mother's mind is not you and has no power over your authentic self that lives and breathes in your body. You are free to express your authentic self as you grow through experiences that shift your perspectives, and that evolve you to new understandings of yourself, without limitation from others' perceptions of you.

It's a beautiful gift to be seen by your parent as the evolution you are. I longed for this gift from my mother. This desire is what inspired me to erase the construct I had built in my own mind about who my sons were, to give them the freedom to evolve without the limitation of my perception of them.

What if you woke up every day wondering who your loved one really was, and set out to discover it? How would you feel to be truly seen in this moment, without the family stories chaining you to past versions of 'you'? Would you feel loved unconditionally? Would you feel free to explore who you truly are at the core? Would it be easier to trust your own heart, and believe in yourself? You're invited to this very worthy experiment: paint yourself and your beloveds with a new brush every day, and see what happens.

The Deepest Wound

The deepest wound a person can experience is a mother who is incapable of loving her, a mother whose love and wisdom he cannot trust. This wound lives in the heart as a profound sadness, an insecurity of being abandoned, a fear of being unworthy of the life received. This wound affects every area of a person's life: her wealth, her expression, her relationships, and her own capacity as a mother.

You were born with a strong bond to your mother to help you navigate life on Earth as a 'separate' being, and when that bond also breaks, it can feel devastating to your sense of belonging and having a lifeline. When your mother cannot acknowledge your recollection of a shared experience, when her perspective is opposite of yours, it can feel so invalidating by the one person from whom you desperately wanted acknowledgement. I imagine this is the pain that children of a mother with Alzheimer's feel.

The Mother Wound has been passed down through generations from mother to children, and our societies are a reflection of this wound. The subjugation of women around the world is a reflection of this wound. The objectification of women is a reflection of this wound. The masculinization of women is a reflection of this wound. And the deadening of hearts, the lack of empathy, the cold indifference to others' plights or to the suffering of the animals and the condition of the planet—this is all a reflection of this wound. Suicide, genocide, pornography, rape, insane asylums, over-industrialization, mass pollution, school shootings, violence of all kinds—this is all a reflection of the Mother Wound.

How can you demoralize, disempower, shun, shame, ridicule, and dishonor a woman, and then expect your progeny to thrive in such a vessel? The fetus forms its consciousness within its mother's belly for 10 months before ever seeing the light of day. The mother is the primary programmer of her children's consciousness.

Whatever exists in a mother's consciousness is what becomes the child's invisible operating system as he or she enters the world. Invisible because a child is completely unaware that his or her mind has been programmed to view the world in a certain way, through the lens of his/her mother, and that this world view is only one option in a limitless sea of options.

Inside the mother's womb, the child not only tunes his/her consciousness to the mother's current experience, but to the experiences of the ancestors for generations before. Ancestral experience is stored within each person's consciousness as records in the DNA. Ancestral DNA reinforces a world view within a child's mind before he/she is even born, and this world view is compounded once the child exits the womb and rearing begins.

Even if you silently criticized the mother of your children, thinking they don't know how you really feel—the mother of your children knows, and because she's connected inextricably to your children, they know too. They feel it as an undercurrent to every interaction in the family. This undercurrent destroys trust which invites doubt, confusion and fear.

A mother who is afraid can likewise never instill a sense of security in her children. They can feel that she is afraid deep inside and just covering it up with a show of 'having it all together'. A fearful mother creates a home that feels superficial in its attempt to create a safe environment. Her fear and insecurity prevents her children from stepping out of 'line' which actually means they don't learn how to deal with the depths of their human experience which is extremely messy and uncomfortable at times.

If you're not allowed to express anger because it makes your mother uncomfortable, where else can you express it? If your own mother doesn't have the emotional capacity to hear your pain, who can? And so you learn to stuff and hide your pain even from yourself so you can please your mother who really just wants you to look the part of the perfect child so she can feel good about herself that she did a 'good job'; all the while ignoring that she already knows the truth that you've been infected by the very fear she's too afraid to explore within herself.

So perhaps it is clear why our world has youth lost in technology and shooting up classrooms. A human's heart that has not been awoken by Mother Love is empty, aching, and desperate. Not being able to feel, the boy cuts himself to stir sensation. Not understanding how to honor herself, the girl flaunts her breasts because she's learned that's how women get attention which is 'power.'

There is a cycle of evolution that humanity has been experiencing. This part is the 'hard road' that parents often mention when informing youth that they have a choice in how to go about life. The hard road has been allowing the egoic self to lead the way.

Mother Earth obliged her wayward children to learn their lessons of what happens when you disrespect your Mother, and those made in her image and likeness. Every drop of water on the planet has been consumed by every human being alive today and that ever was alive throughout history. What you do to one being, you do to yourself. How you mistreat a forest or a dog or a child is how you mistreat yourself. So what better way to learn than to reincarnate again and again, experiencing all the ways that disrespecting your Mother hurts you in the end.

Have we had enough of the 'hard road'?

Our Mother is demonstrating that she's done teaching us that lesson. Time to listen up. Divine Mother's got things to say to our children through us who agreed to be conduits of Mother Love.

Your Children's Lessons Belong To Them

The mother's job is to teach her children everything she knows, everything she learned on her way to healing, and to be a witness to their own growth and development. A mother guides and steers her children to the best of her ability onto the golden line, the pathway of Love through life. And I have learned through significant effort and frustration that you can lead a horse to water, but you cannot make it drink. All you can do is plant seeds—a lot of seeds—and patiently shower them with Love.

When you find yourself feeling resonant with the adage that you can lead a horse to water but you can't make it drink, consider that the water you are leading the horse to is the water in which you found your salvation. This is your water. Your salvation. And it serves as a guidepost for your children to know what salvation feels like. But they have their own water to drink. If they drink of your water, and it's not their pathway to salvation, it potentially causes disruption to their true path.

I learned this lesson in a powerful way with regards to my eldest son as he was nearing his 21st birthday. He had participated in a year-long spirituality program at my encouragement, a path that I walk for my own edification, and I had done a personal ceremony on the night before his graduation day. During the ceremony I felt his presence strongly, and heard very clear wisdom from White Buffalo Calf Woman when she said to me: "Your children's lessons are not your lessons. Your lessons are not your children's lessons. Your job is to hold the love steady now that you found it, with patience and kindness, as he finds his own way to it."

The next day I found out why I had received this message when I discovered that my son had chosen not to culminate his year of training with his fellow tribe members, and did not graduate.

I drove 10 hours to New Mexico for the graduation holding hope that my son would choose to consummate the path to which I had guided him. He had not been answering communications from me for two months, and yet I felt sure he would finish as planned. Reflecting back on the ceremony the night before graduation, I remembered that I heard his spirit tell me that he would choose the path on his own terms…not mine. I realize now that was his way of telling me that he was not going to walk the path that I had shown him.

In my direct family lineage are some patterns of stubbornness and self-destruction. I experienced these patterns in my own life, and spent two decades on a psychotherapy couch trying to extricate myself from them using the tools provided to me by my parents. It was only after I found my own pathway to healing that my life began improving for the better, and I stepped into my power. My parents brought me partway with their tools, but to go all the way, I had to find my own path to healing.

With my son, I made the mistake of thinking that my discovery would also serve his growth. I tried everything I could think of to keep him from fulfilling my fear that he would dive down to rock bottom. In the end, I realized he was going to go wherever he needed to go for his spiritual journey.

The part that I needed to reconcile was a question: what is love? How does a mother express love to her children? Is the mother's job to prevent her children from suffering? I had always gotten the message that was a mother's role, and if she didn't do it well, then her suffering children would expose her to the world for the failure she was at mothering. This fear created a sort of narcissistic urge to pretend that everything was going well, even when the evidence was clear that there was a lot of suffering happening.

From my vantage point as mother, my son seemed uncomfortable in the world. I saw the signs and behavior of a struggling child, and defended him and championed him against other forces in the family calling for stronger measures. It's like he wanted to be punished, so stubbornly refusing to conform to norms or behaviors expected of him. I wondered if there was something that needed healing within him. Why does he struggle and resist being loved? Why does he not speak up for himself, always allowing others to speak for him? Why doesn't he engage and participate and advocate for himself?

For much of his life, I was his lifeline—the one person he would actually speak to. And then, I wasn't his lifeline anymore. He ignored my messages and calls. And he refused to show up to conclude his training on the path that I had invited him to walk.

Before my years of healing, if this had happened, I would have assumed this outcome was terrible and blamed myself for my son's choice. I would have become self-destructive, reviewing every perceived mistake I ever made that could have led to my perception of brokenness inside him that refused love and community. I would have taken his choices personally, and made his experience all about me.

Now I see, through years of stepping off the Triangle of Disempowerment, and through years of channeled messages about sovereignty: his choice had very little to do with me, and a whole lot to do with him. He has his own path to discover and walk, and he wants to do it on his terms. His rejection of my path does not mean that he's broken or there's something wrong with him. It means that the water I've led him to is not the water he is meant to drink. So he very smartly did not drink it.

I've imagined so many wonderful outcomes for my son and me. I've wished and dreamed that we walk the spiritual path together and be healers and host community together. It's a dream I have had to let go of because it's my dream, not my son's. And if I hold onto my dream, and he doesn't come along with it, then he is in the uncomfortable position of disappointing me simply because he is being true to himself.

So I let my imagined dream die so my son can live, as he is, and I can be a witness to it as he lets me.

A witness to his life does not mean offering him a safety net. It means listening to Spirit and the ancestors, and taking the actions that will best serve my son. Every child walks a unique path, which is why there is not one set of guidelines that creates the best strategic parental plan. In my case, my Dad provided a safety net for me, which I rarely used because I have always been self-motivated. But having that perception of a safety net helped me take bigger risks in my life, knowing that my Dad would help me if I got stuck.

My son is not me. In my perception as his mother, I came to the conclusion that a safety net kept him from hitting the hard brick wall that he needed for his pathway to truly unfold for him. After a year and a half of having my son back home after his first exodus, I witnessed that being in his mother's house when he needed to be out exploring life as an independent young man was crumbling his self-esteem. I knew he needed to leave my protective cocoon to discover his own truth. I worried about him winding up under a bridge in a tent with the surging homeless population of Austin. If that is the lesson he needs to find the door to his Soul, then who I am to judge it and try to prevent it?

My role as his mother is to keep the love and faith burning in the home hearth, and stay out of the way of destruction as he tears things up to find himself.

The second birth is the one where the child tears apart his cocoon, biting and scratching the lining to set himself free. His cocoon is the mother's womb, her web of protection, her constant remembrance of who he has been up until the moment he is ready to birth himself. To birth himself, he has to bring himself to reject his mother so he can propel himself out of the cocoon, out of the story of him she told, and into his own truth. He tears her down so he can break from his addiction to her love and find himself on the other side of his mother's dream.

It hurts like hell if you take it personally. You've got to be strong inside to endure it.

Love is patient and kind and unconditional, and all of this is possible with good boundaries. As White Buffalo Calf Woman said, "Your children's lessons are not your lessons. Your lessons are not your children's lessons. Your job is to hold the love steady now that you found it, with patience and kindness, as he finds his own way to it."

♥

Teaching Each Other

Your children are born into this life with their own Soul's curriculum, perfectly matched to yours in the opposite. Oh, did you think the Mother Wound was just yours as the child? Well, it is also the wound in the mother's heart and womb from being a mother and the messy terrible wonderful that comes from that experience.

Perhaps you hold grievances against your mother for how you were mistreated. You may feel your life was torn apart from your mother's abuse of you. Are you comfortable on the victim corner of your life because of a mother that was mean in some painful way?

You're invited to reframe the relationship with your mother as a Soul agreement where you agreed to be born into her mother web, and navigate your own way through a life experience with that as your starting point. Something about your mother's web, and her ancestral patterns, made being her child the perfect beginning for the journey your Soul designed you to embody. I realize that if you were abused by your mother, this statement can feel affronting and like 'victim shaming'.

Did I 'ask for it' when my natural father began molesting me at a year old? Was my adorable little baby body to blame for his illness being attracted to it? Absolutely not. And yet, the abuse became part of my inner matrix that formed many of my life's experiences around sexuality; by moving through the discomfort of this abuse pattern in my own consciousness, I have reclaimed my power.

I am only a victim if I allow what happened to me when I was defenseless to imprison me on the inside.

Curiosity opens the doorway out of victimhood and into self-empowerment, and an initial very helpful question is: What inner strength or wisdom did I gain from the experience of being abused?

Similarly, if you are a mother, your child selected your mother's web as the perfect starting point for the Soul journey they chose for this incarnation. Rather than protecting your child from all discomfort, or ruminating over how your flaws disrupted the perfect childhood you imagined for your child, perhaps your role is to open your heart and guide your child from love as he or she moves through life lessons. Maybe your flaws and mistakes were exactly 'the way' your child needed to live in order to fulfill his or her Soul journey and its incarnation goals.

"We do the best we can with the tools we have at the time" is what my Dad always said, and anything that happens is what was necessary for growth for the mother and the child. In my healing work, I have realized that some ancestral patterns take generations to heal; meaning, each generation does its part to rewire unhealthy dynamics as they travel down the family line.

A powerful life lesson was given to me in this incarnation around making other people happy. I was born into my mother's web which has a life incarnation plan to be critical and to point out the perceived flaws in integrity; to see the shadows and the negative aspects, rather than the possibilities. Then here I come, unplanned and unexpected, with my life plan to see the rainbow in the storm, to have faith and trust that something better is around the corner.

I tried for the first part of my life to please my mother, thinking that if I pleased her she could be happy at last. Then I married a man very similar to her, with a critical untrusting mindset, and spent the next two decades trying to please him and make him happy. The result was I was twisted up like a pretzel on the inside and angry because none of my pleasing behavior fixed these people I loved. They still chose to be exactly as they were. In my perspective at the time, they were addicted to pain.

'The Mastery of Love' by Don Miguel Ruiz offered me reflections that helped me understand I was operating from conditional love in my relationships. Was it my job to 'fix' my mother or former partner?

Nope. From my experience I learned that you are not here to fix your mother or your partner or anyone else in your life. You may perceive that some people in your life are addicted to pain, and it is your perception because that feeling you feel from them feels painful to you. I spent a period of my life entangled in this dynamic, and as an empath, embodying the pain of others without clear boundaries and a sense of self, and without realizing what I was doing. Because I did not have a clear sense of myself, I was not able to discern other people's feelings from my feelings, and so I took all of it on for processing as if it all belonged to me to 'fix' and lighten up.

Through my training in energy medicine, I learned how to discern what is 'me' and what is 'others' and to create strong energetic boundaries around my own auric field with new agreements that I am only responsible for processing my 'stuff'. If someone I love is in pain and that makes me feel pain, then it's my responsibility to sort out my own pain to make myself feel better; it's not the other person's job to stop feeling pain so I don't have to feel it. In that way, I can truly show up for the people I love and serve and allow them to be just as they are.

I had come to some peace around this premise, until I realized I was still heartily engaged in trying to fix my eldest son. The hardest thing to do was to reconcile the mama bear within me, and the truth that nothing you do to try to take away the pain for someone else does anything to alleviate the pain. Some people choose to be defined by their pain in order to work through a Soul lesson; and that lesson is not your lesson. You can't solve the puzzle for them even if you can see the finish line and exactly all the steps to take to get there.

To try to take away their pain is, in a way, trying to thwart their Soul lesson; it can feel like you're judging them and getting in the way. And a part of the twisted dynamic is that they feel enabled to hold on tighter to their pain when they see it causes you pain to see them in pain. **This is a trauma bond.** And when the relationship is forged by trauma, the fear is that in letting go of the trauma and pain, they actually lose the 'love' when in fact it was never love to begin with. It was attachment formed in pain.

Love is what helps you heal from pain. And as the healed person in a trauma bond, love is what helps you witness the attachment to the pain of the person you love….breaking your heart over and over and over. Sometimes you wonder why you stay. Why not just close the door and walk away? Let that person live in pain. Then your heart calls you forth again to be a witness.

You must break the loyalty to the trauma bond while staying loyal to the love for this person.

Realize you are blessed to be a witness to the journey of your beloved. Put things in right relationship by realizing you made an agreement to teach each other lessons of love. You are only responsible for learning your own lessons, and holding compassionate space for your beloved to learn their lessons. You are the teacher and the student, and the more you allow the Divine Mother to flow through you and guide your interactions with your beloved, the more smoothly the process will go. Trust the process.

A song that really helped me to feel gratitude for my own realignment to witnessing is Ben Harper's song, Blessed to be a Witness. This song helped me grieve and renew my gratitude after the second time my eldest son moved out, and was choosing to not communicate with me. It helped me explore and realize everything I have shared in this section.

Some have flown away
And can't be with us here today
Like the hills of my home
Some have crumbled and now are gone
Gather around for today won't come again
Won't come again

I am blessed
I am blessed
I am blessed to be a witness

So much sorrow and pain
Still I will not live in vain
Like good questions never asked
Is wisdom wasted on the past

Only by the grace of God go I
Go I

I am blessed
I am blessed
I am blessed to be a witness

I am blessed to be a witness. To me, it is a reminder that I am blessed to be incarnated on Earth at this time. I am blessed to have birthed two beautiful sons, and to have watched them grow over the years. I am blessed to have felt their pain, and seen their spirits shine through their radiant smiles. I am blessed to have felt the most expansive unconditional agape love burst forth from my heart at the thought of my sons. I am blessed for every truthful conversation, every heartfelt hug, and every "I love you momma."

I admit I deeply desire more of these moments with my sons, and that's why I remind myself that I am blessed to be a witness. To keep it all in right relationship.

❤

Quotes

"Being a mother has been a master class in letting go. Try as we might, there's only so much we can control. And, boy, have I tried - especially at first. As mothers, we just don't want anything or anyone to hurt our babies. But life has other plans. Bruised knees, bumpy roads and broken hearts are part of the deal. What's both humbled and heartened me is seeing the resiliency of my daughters."
— Michelle Obama

"A 'healthy' woman had children; a 'happy' and 'fulfilled' woman was a mother."
— Peg Streep, author of "Daughter Detox"

"A wise mother knows: It is her state of consciousness that matters. Her gentleness and clarity command respect. Her love creates security."
— Vimala McClure, The Tao of Motherhood

"She was imperfect. She made mistakes. But she was her best self more often than it's reasonable for any human to be."
— Cheryl Strayed ("Sugar")

"Mother love is the fuel that enables a normal human being to do the impossible."
— Marion C. Garretty

"As you enter positions of trust and power, dream a little before you think."
— Toni Morrison

I Don't Want To Be Like My Mother

As long as you have unexplored and unhealed resentments towards your mother, you will not fully receive the benefits of a healed mother within yourself. This is because you form a mother and a father figure inside your mind created from your perceptions of your parents as you are growing from a child to an adult. The slightest incident can create a negative core belief that festers until it is the only 'truth' you can see, and it colors all interactions with your parent. Your actual parent might be completely unaware of the impact of the small incident in activating the Mother Wound within you.

The version of your mother that lives in your brain is a collection of stories you started telling yourself in childhood, and often were unable to speak aloud for fear of punishment. Were you able to speak it aloud at the time, it might have been addressed and dissolved before it became a pattern of perception in your mind. In fact, even the pattern of not speaking aloud your resentments is part of the Mother Wound and can lead to a grown adult woman not being able to speak her feelings to her aging mother. In every other relationship, this woman is able to speak her truth; but when it comes to her mother, she is locked up inside herself as her mother freely vents her frustrations. This was me before I healed the mother within.

Who doesn't want to be like my mother? The child within me whose caregiver alternated between playful laughing mommy and irritated angry mother, that's who. To heal my inner mother I had to give my inner child a safe space to speak her fears, frustrations, and resentments towards my biological mother; or the idea of my biological mother that my inner child created through my childhood and young adulthood.

To help my inner child find her voice, I gave her prompts and information about things mothers do that are unloving. These prompts helped her to point to the things that were true for her and say yes, that happened to me and it made me sad, angry, or afraid. For this work, I used the book *Daughter Detox: Recovering From An Unloving Mother* by Peg Streep.

Reading this book brings awareness of the patterns that have been passed down for generations and that keep you from experiencing Love. It's not as if mothers consciously chose to be unloving; this is the underlying matrix that has resulted from dishonoring women in all the ways mentioned in this book. Your ancestors have been working to heal these patterns and elevate you to Love for generations. Bringing awareness to the patterns gives you the choice to heal and transform them. Healing the patterns is a daily decision to be mindful, and a moment-by-moment noticing of the pattern and redirection to desired thoughts that welcome Love.

The first obstacle that must be addressed is the fear and shame of 'telling' on your mother. This text is not encouraging you to publicly talk 'bad' about your mother; it is encouraging you to explore on a personal basis the patterns of un-love you have experienced so you can heal. You must face the uncomfortable truths you feel deep inside to heal the Mother Wound. "She did her best." Of course she did. In no way does this text suggest that your mother intentionally set out to be unloving. She was part of a larger framework of mental conditioning that normalized unloving patterns. Also, the Divine Mother is a powerful teacher, and can use every person in your life as the means for you to learn your lessons: including your mother.

If you were to bring your perception of your mother's unloving patterns to her, she may be completely taken aback and hurt. Her perception of the world as your mother is very different than your perception of the world as her child. I have had a heightened experience of this dynamic in my life, most likely because of the purpose I came here to serve in healing the Mother Wound. My mother and I very rarely agree to even the smallest of details from a shared experience; it is almost as if we are experiencing two entirely different realities. I believe this is because I had to learn in the strongest way possible the lesson that each Soul is living their own perceived reality based on the Soul's curriculum they are here to learn.

You can be holding onto resentments about your mother, and she can be feeling helpless, clueless and sad about why you're so upset. So, in fact, the point of doing the inquiry of this section is not to convince your biological mother that she did X, Y, and Z; the point of the inquiry of this section is to reprogram the avatar of mother that you created in your own consciousness so that you can heal yourself, dump a lot of not useful baggage, and have the opportunity to 'see' your actual biological mother a bit more clearly as her own person independent of your projections.

To honor your mothers desire to raise the best possible human, you must start by bringing awareness to the unloving patterns that she unconsciously passed onto you so that you can be free to fulfill the promise of being the best possible human.

Explore the following statements and listen to your body to hear your inner child. What happens as you read the statements? Do you feel tight, uncomfortable, anxious, sad, or angry? Breathe deeply in your belly through any feelings that arise while holding one hand over your heart, the other over your belly.

- I feel guilty, terrified, and like a traitor for even contemplating the ways I feel abused by my mother.

- I did not often feel validated nor accepted by my mother for things important to me.

- I feel that my mother did not want me as a baby, and I feel that I have been a burden to her.

- I often felt that I had to perform well in school or other ways to win my mother's love.

- Not being able to win my mother's love made me feel like I must be unlovable.

- My mother often withdrew love if I broke a rule, made a mistake, or disappointed her. She would look at me coldly, refuse to speak to or look at me, or banish me from her presence.

- My mother often shifted the blame to me or made me feel like I was bad. "You are impossible and difficult." "You're a bad little girl." "You're a pain in the neck."

- My mother often ignored me and it was hard to get her attention, even when I was doing what she wanted me to do.

- When I questioned my mother, I was ridiculed, batted down, denied, punished or called crazy.

- I have grown up having trouble regulating emotions, either flooded with feelings or disconnected from them.

- My mother often used harsh words or behavior to 'discipline' me into compliance.

- My mother treated me differently than my siblings, and I often wondered if it was my fault or if I was flawed; my siblings did not see that she was treating me poorly and thought I was making it up.

- My mother dismissed my concerns by ignoring me while I was trying to tell her about it, or say things like "It's not a big deal. You'll get over it."

- I don't really feel like I belong to my family.

- My mother controlled every aspect of my life, and said things like "Without me, you would fail at every step."

- My mother taught me that love comes with strings attached, and if you fail or disappoint, no one will love you.

- My mother was not emotionally available to me; she was distant and withdrawn emotionally and physically.

- My mother vacillated wildly between being unbearably present—intrusive, invasive, utterly without respect for my boundaries—and being absent and withdrawn.

- My mother favored me when I reflected well on her to her friends, and ostracized me by belittling me when I did things that embarrassed her with her friends.

- My mother seemed to like being angry at me and yelling for any slight infringement of her rules.

- My mother was always intruding into my life and I felt choked by her needs of me.

- My mother confided things in me that were adult matters, and overburdened me as a child.

- I lost my childhood because I had to grow up too quickly and help my mother run the house.

Exploring all of these difficult realizations is important to your healing process. You must elevate to the level of consciousness what your inner child experienced: how she/he felt and the ideas she/he created about herself/himself because of those feelings and events.

Notice whether you can connect emotionally to the statements, or whether you feel denial and numbness. If you feel numb and in denial, it may be your ego feeling unsafe and deflecting you away from exploring these statements out of fear of feeling the painful submerged feelings from childhood. There can be a lot of protection between your conscious mind and the suppressed memories of childhood; be patient and make it safe to open up the locked compartments for healing.

Comfort your inner child as you allow feelings to rise up for healing that were stuffed all those years ago. There is beneficial work here in acknowledging the ways your inner child feels he or she was treated by your mother. As you listen to your inner child and do this inquiry, your inner child begins to trust you as an advocate for him or her.

This trust is essential to the healing process. As your inner child feels heard by you and trusts you, you can begin to calm the storms that previously got kicked up when triggers happened. You can learn to detect the voice of your inner child in the anxious feelings within your stomach, for example. This is a process of listening, exploring, and contemplating the nuances of the voices in your head and the emotions and sensations in your body as triggers happen in your life.

To get started in this type of exploration it is helpful to have a mentor guide you with an inner child healing. When I guide clients through this process, I open sacred space and invite my client to discuss a trigger that happened in their life. I ask the client questions about the trigger, to kick up the inner dust so to speak, and then I ask questions to help the client identify where his or her body holds the reactivity to the trigger. It's helpful that my gifts allow me to be an overlay for a person's body so that I can detect where energy is stuck and needs exploration.

Once the client is fully aware of the body sensations, thoughts and emotions related to the trigger, I shift the client into an etheric healing space I call the Sanctuary where the client invites his or her inner child who first felt this way to come forward. This child always comes forth, and now the client can work directly with the inner child to remove false agreements and heavy emotions, and fill up with light. This child healing process is like a reclamation of a frozen-in-time aspect of self that can now speak and be heard, receive love and come home to the larger Self.

Sometimes in these healing sessions there is an ancestor who, in her lifetime, was a healed mother; meaning, she was in touch with motherly love and able to express it in healthy ways. Your ancestors are often quite willing to offer support you in healing, or to activate healed patterns into your own ancestral DNA. You can open to receive this kind of ancestral support from your matriarchal lineage. Somewhere back a few generations is a mother who had a generous capacity for agape love that is willing to be a guide for you on your way to healing your inner mother figure.

And that is truly what is needed to heal the Mother Wound within you. You must reprogram the mother figure created by your inner child into a mother figure who is fully capable of expressing agape love for YOU, inside of you. This healed mother figure helps you to reclaim possibility in your life in all areas because it helps you have self-worth, confidence, resiliency, strength of conviction, and self-soothing.

Before you can be powerful in the world, you must be powerful within yourself. To be powerful within yourself, you must heal your inner child and the Mother Wound. Every healing layer reveals greater inner power that results in outer power. As you heal more deeply within yourself, your possibilities expand in the outer world.

❤

Suggestions

Understand the Context What was your mother's state of consciousness as you were gestating in her womb? What were her fears, desires, beliefs, and conditions? If possible, interview her to illuminate what she may have been feeling and thinking as you were growing inside her.

Review Your State of Mind During Pregnancy What were you thinking and feeling as you were growing your baby in your womb? What doubts, fears, and worries did you have? Were you feeling peaceful or burdened or excited? All of the above? Do you see any of these patterns playing themselves out in your children?

Rant About Your Mother In a private journal, give your inner child free reign to say all the things about your mother that she was repressed from expressing in your youth. Let your inner teenager tell it like it is—no holding back! Air your inner daughter's grievances from all ages. If you feel anger, express it by stomping your feet and growling. If you feel sad and disappointed, let yourself cry.

Celebrate Your Mother We all have flaws and gifts, including your mother. Make a list of all the things you admire about your mother and aspire to be like yourself.

Compare Notes In what ways do you carry forth the behaviors and patterns from your mother that you ranted about? In what ways do you emulate the aspects of your mother that you celebrated?

Self Care Do something to deeply nurture yourself.

Quotes

"I know the answer now, and that knowledge absolutely coexists with a terrible longing for the mother love I never had and never will have."
— Peg Streep, author of "Daughter Detox

"Just give yourself permission to tell the truth to yourself."
— Iyanla Vanzant

"Women are still in emotional bondage as long as we need to worry that we might have to make a choice between being heard and being loved."
— Marianne Williamson

"That place of true healing is a fierce place. It's a giant place. It's a place of monstrous beauty and endless dark and glimmering light. And you have to work really, really, really hard to get there, but you can do it."
— Cheryl Strayed ("Sugar")

"Embrace the glorious mess that you are."
— Elizabeth Gilbert

"We forget that we were put on Earth to learn something. If everything were perfect in this life, we would never learn anything new. We would not be able to elevate our spirits through the events that happen to us."
— Lynn Andrews

Quotes

"I am proud of the woman I am today because I went through one hell of a time to become her."
— Unknown

"You wanna fly, you got to give up the shit that weighs you down."
— Toni Morrison

"Emotional pain cannot kill you, but running from it can. Allow. Embrace. Let yourself feel. Let yourself heal."
— Vironika Tugaleva

"Every woman's path is difficult, and many mothers were as equipped to raise children as wire monkey mothers. I say that without judgment: It is, sadly, true. An unhealthy mother's love is withering."
— Anne Lamont

"Trauma creates change you don't choose. Healing creates change you do choose."
— Michele Rosenthal

"Wisdom is nothing more than healed pain."
— Brené Brown

"Being a mother is the hardest job on earth. Women everywhere must declare it so."
— Oprah Winfrey

The Pathway Forward

Now that we've gotten ourselves in quite a mess by disrespecting our Mother Earth, and all Mothers on the planet for thousands of years....how do we untangle ourselves? How do we rectify this situation?

Have you noticed how many people feel a call to return to the Earth and ancient spiritual practices? That is because Mother Earth is speaking to all of our hearts. It's time to quiet your mind and listen to the Earth for wisdom that will help you to heal the Mother Wound within so that together we can take the inspired actions that will bring humanity into a new era of enlightenment.

This book tackles the paradigms of suffering caused by the Mother Wound, and shares spiritual practices for untangling yourself from the egoic matrix so you can awaken love within your heart. The teachings are applicable to all humans. Some of the messages may resonate more strongly with women who are in their 40s and 50s, and more potently for mothers, because this has been my life experience.

The way forward is to go within and rewire your consciousness with the loving guidance of our Mother Earth.

♥

Aligning To The Divine Mother

The Earth is our mother just turning around, with her trees in the forest and roots underground. Our father above us whose sigh is the wind, paint us a rainbow without any end.
—John Denver

A vital aspect of healing the Mother Wound is to give yourself connection to a healed mother. The Mother Earth is the most obvious healed mother energy we have access to, and you can align yourself to our home planet as you heal your inner mother figure.

This was a first big step I made in my own healing. I chose to invite Pachamama, Mother Earth, to be my mother. I have learned through daily prayer and meditation how to connect with her and rest back into her. She supports me to walk with confidence and a clear heart. She gives me endless support with her stones, plants, trees, animals, birds, mountains and oceans. She lets me know how much she loves me and that I am wanted. Letting Mother Earth love me has allowed me to create enough space with my biological mother to allow forgiveness and compassion. We human mothers are only doing the best we can to emulate the master...the Divine Mother.

Invite a relationship with the Divine Mother by making space each day to open sacred space and express thanks and praise as you acknowledge and welcome all the Earth allies into your day for guidance and healing. Even if you have never consumed plant medicines, you can invite the wisdom of these sacred teachers to support your path through life. You can begin with pinching a bit of tobacco in your fingers, blowing prayers into the tobacco and offering it to the ground with gratitude for the support in releasing toxic energy from your body and mind, and protecting you.

Another way to support your healing process is to create an altar, or intention space, where you spend a few moments each day connecting with the Divine Mother and speaking from your heart. On this altar you can place candles for the Four Directions (South, West, North, East), stones and crystals, tobacco, feathers, and any other allies you welcome by placing little figurines (such as jaguar or eagle).

A personal altar is a space to invite support from Divine Mother teachers like Guadalupe, Mother Mary, or Quan Yin; you can put little artworks or figures of them on the altar, or say specific prayers to them. Let the altar evolve as the Divine Mother brings you gifts (like feathers), or you find items and feel in your heart their significance to your healing process.

A special ritual that the Divine Mother offered to me at the beginning of this work is especially healing for the Mother Wound. This ritual is the creation of a mandala on the Earth to support the healing of your heart and your Mother Wound by the Mother Earth. Find a private safe space outside on the Earth to create this mandala where it will be protected as you perform the work of healing over weeks and months.

When I created mine, I acquired a rose quartz crystal in the shape of a heart; this was to represent my own heart. I gathered together white beans (lima preferred), pinenuts, tobacco, and tiny flowers to my liking. Collect what your heart calls forth for your mandala.

Open sacred space over the ground where your mandala will be created. Then use the white beans to create a circle on the ground by intentionally placing each bean as you contemplate healing your Mother Wound with Divine Mother love.

Once the circle is complete, begin in the south point of the circle and place pinenuts with intention as a line leading to the center of the circle to call the energy and healing power of the South to your mandala.

Then create a line of pinenuts from the west point of the circle to the center of the circle to call the energy and healing power of the West to your mandala.

Repeat to call the energy and healing powers of the North and East into the center of the mandala.

Create an inner circle out of pinenuts to designate the Center of the Wheel of Life.

Now place the rose quartz crystal heart in the center of the mandala where the pinenut lines intersect, inside the Center.

Sprinkle tobacco all around the mandala, welcoming healing energies and protection from Spirit of Tobacco.

Lastly, decorate from your heart and gratitude the mandala with the tiny flowers in a way that feels beautiful to you.

Now that the mandala is complete, say a little prayer to the Divine Mother: "Thank you Divine Mother for healing the Mother Wound within me, and helping me to love myself unconditionally."

Every day, visit your mandala and say prayers, remove 'full' tobacco and replace with fresh, add new tiny flowers and any other items you're called to add. You may sprinkle flower water over your crystal heart, for example. Notice the healing that happens in your life.

To open yourself to receive more connection, love and support from the Divine Mother, you can also play the crystal singing bowl that is tuned to the root chakra, and is typically a ruby garnet red.

During a special ceremony to support the empowerment of a female client, I played the crystal bowl for the root chakra. In a deep meditative state my perception was altered so that I became aware of my root chakra opening, unfolding, and expanding as I played the bowl with intention to connect with the Divine Mother. I felt a profound healing of the Mother Wound, and knew that the Divine Mother was encouraging me to step fully into my power and channel her wisdom through me and into the world.

Healing the root chakra with the love of the Divine Mother is an ongoing process that will fortify your courage to weather the storms of the collective consciousness transformation as you speak the truth that is bursting forth from the very womb of your knowing.

And for more third-dimensional support in this physical reality, it is beneficial to keep exposing yourself to greater expressions of Divine Mother love by being led to communities and mentors who can model this higher vibration for you. As you witness and receive this heightened love, you can emulate it within yourself and make it part of the rewiring of the mother figure within you. Together, we rise.

♥

Prayer To Welcome Earth Support

To welcome support from Mother Earth and all the allies she has gifted you for this journey as a human being, you can practice Opening Sacred Space. This prayer is a starting point for your own invocations that will unfold over time as you learn to connect with the energies and speak from your heart to them.

I welcome the Winds of the South to surround me in love and protection so I know I am fully capable of healing, I am unconditionally loved, and I am supported in every way through my connection to Mother Earth. Help me drop into deep presence so I can tangibly feel this love, support, and protection.

I welcome the Winds of the West for your wisdom and discernment to help me see deeper into my shadows to reveal the beliefs, patterns, and blocks that no longer serve me. Help me to release what no longer serves with ease and grace, and to choose new ways of being that expand my love, joy and prosperity.

I welcome the Winds of the North for the support of my ancestors and guides for myself and my children. Help me receive your gifts of wisdom and strength through my ancestral DNA, and help me to clear away inherited ancestral patterns and energies that no longer serve my highest good. I welcome my guides and the ascended masters that support my growth. Help me Winds of the North to align to my true self, my true vibration, and to guide my life from this higher alignment.

I welcome the Winds of the East for a new sunrise in my life where the old slips away into the darkness of night as the light expands bringing joy, love and laughter. Help me to fly like Eagle high in the sky to see the bigger picture. Help me to step into the void of not knowing so that something awe inspiring beyond my wildest dreams can come into being for me.

I welcome Mother Earth, Divine Mother, to guide my heart to right action along the heartbeat of love pulsing through her body ... feeling her through my bare feet. I welcome all the allies you've gifted me for this journey Mother Earth: the mountain spirits, the tree nations, the rocks stones and crystals, the plant kingdom, the animal guides, the bird spirits, the four elements...all of life on Earth.

I welcome Father Sky, the Sun, Grandmother Moon, and the Star Nations. Fill me with upper frequencies and wisdom from the stars to ascend my consciousness, learn new perspectives, and help me forgive.

And I welcome the Great Spirit, *you who is known by a thousand names. Help me dance on the Earth once again in innocence.*

♥

The Path To Reclaiming Your Power

Your power, your sovereignty, deepens and expands through every initiation you encounter as you Walk the Beauty Way. As it has been introduced to me by indigenous teachings, Walking the Beauty Way is seeing the beauty and harmony in all of the experiences that life delivers to you for your growth and expansion. It's deepening into trust, softening your hard edges, and breathing gratitude into all of it.

Each challenge is viewed as an initiation or doorway into a greater level of love, compassion, forgiveness, gratitude and awe. Meeting 'unwanted' events with gratitude and trust in the process helps you to more gracefully receive the lessons that are leading you where you say you want to go. **Even the most painful things can be a doorway opening you to greater personal power and sovereignty**; in fact, they often are initiations designed to help you step more deeply into your voice, truth, and capacity to serve with your gifts.

The more you realign to the Divine, the more power you can harness and the more deeply grounded you are within yourself. Every layer of conditioning from the Mother Wound that is peeled away removes attachments, expectations, entitlement, and patterns rooted in suffering so that you can open your Love channel ever wider. **Each initiation can be like a rebirthing—painful to endure the birth canal, yet rewarding in the expansion on the other side.**

The people in our lives are used as unwitting accomplices in our evolutionary path to reclaim our power by healing the Mother Wound. Sometimes their actions will lure you into a sense of 'it's not fair' which pulls you into the blame game until you can remember that you asked for something tremendous—you asked for your power—and this 'not fair' event is a doorway leading to the fulfillment of that request.

Sometimes they will have totally opposite perspectives from you so you can learn to soften, listen, be mindful of any assumptions you're making, and feel into what is actually true for you.

To reclaim your power you must let go of all thoughts, behaviors, patterns, and energetics that entangle you with others as the 'source' of something you need. The only source, ultimately, is the Divine; and every initiation is designed to lead you to that ultimate alignment in your conscious awareness. You must pass through many challenges, and you can discover your primary shadows for this lifetime by reviewing your Gene Keys. A source for information about your Gene Keys is Richard Rudd's work (www.genekeys.com). Let his contemplation audios and books spark your own inquiry into overcoming your shadows so you can receive and embody the gifts of your life plan.

The more refined your alignment to the Divine, the more the flow opens up to reveal even greater blessings and initiations towards higher levels of power and capacity. When you are aligned with the Divine, and you listen and allow yourself to be guided, you can avoid many of the unnecessary pitfalls and traps that up until now were part of your journey. Messages come from the Divine Mother to place you exactly where you need to be for maximum benefit for yourself and others.

Each layer of conditioning that arises for release can be uncomfortable to witness, and fear-provoking to remove as you transform the foundation of your consciousness from egoic programming to Divine design. This book explores some of the conditionings and patterns that we are collectively witnessing and transmuting at this time as we shift into the Age of Aquarius.

As you heal the Mother Wound within your human consciousness, as you realign yourself to the Divine, you learn to be grateful for the gifts of Mother Earth and to make the choices that honor yourself and your home. As you reclaim your personal power and tap into the Divine for guidance, you have the strength to speak what needs to be spoken, to change what needs to be changed, and to hold space for others who have not yet chosen to Walk the Beauty Way.

❤

Suggestions

Practice Opening Sacred Space I invite you to make a daily practice of opening sacred space in the morning to start your day. Notice as you run this experiment how your life unfolds on the days that you open sacred space, and on the days that you do not. Become aware that your commitment to the relationship with the Great Spirit and Divine Mother makes all the difference in the results. You can use the invocation provided in "Prayer To Welcome Earth Support" as a starting place, and then let your prayers evolve as you speak from your heart to each Direction. This practice helps you build personal relationships with Earth forces that will support your continued growth.

Create Your Mandala for Healing the Mother Wound As shared in "Aligning To The Divine Mother", you are invited to initiate deep healing of the Mother Wound by creating your own mandala on the Earth. Use the instructions as a guideline for your mandala, and follow the inspirations of your own heart as you create it. Periodically visit your mandala with offerings and prayers as you move through your healing process. As you drop into stillness, you give the Divine Mother a chance to inspire you with wisdom that contributes to your healing.

Set Up Altars for Healing the Mother Wound The section "Living As A Sacred Ceremony" describes several altars you can create to facilitate healing your Mother Wound.

Quotes

"You carry Mother Earth within you. She is not outside of you. Mother Earth is not just your environment. In that insight of inter-being, it is possible to have real communication with the Earth, which is the highest form of prayer."
— Thich Nhat Hanh

"You are a guest. Leave this earth a little more beautiful, a little more human, a little more lovable, a little more fragrant, for those unknown guests who will be following you."
— Osho

"Love is the Divine Mother's arms; when those arms are spread, every Soul falls into them."
— Hazrat Inayat Khan

"And forget not that the earth delights to feel your bare feet and the winds long to play with your hair."
— Khalil Gibran

"The Earth is alive and contains the knowledge you seek. It is your consciousness that determines what it reveals. The Earth speaks. Love her, honor and respect her, and she will reveal her secrets..."
— Barbara Marciniak

"The most profound thing we can offer our children is our own healing."
— Anne Lamont

The Mud For Your Lotus Blossom

If you have chosen to be alive during this transition to the Age of Aquarius, you may have experienced some of the following patterns which we are now collectively clearing within ourselves and our families:

-   The pattern of a mother figure with a fearful heart who, not knowing her inner power, derives a sense of safety by diminishing your sense of power with patterns of control or manipulation. Manipulation includes criticism that erodes your confidence, being unimpressed or disappointed in you, guilt, shame, judgment, coercion, silent treatment, denying your feelings, gossiping about you to 'help' you, taking 'sides' with others against you, excluding you, yelling or toxic dumping of energy, jealousy, and untrue accusations.
    A mother who is not able to express herself to you transparently and clearly.

-   The pattern of narcissism in people close to you who avoid deeper levels of self-introspection, including: not accepting responsibility for problems in the relationship, deflecting and avoiding blame, projecting fault back to you, refusing to 'see' the problem, disrespecting you, undermining your confidence, challenging your sense of reality through gaslighting, and preventing honest actionable conversation where change happens for the better. At the largest sense, it is the consuming of the planet's resources while denying the impact to life on Earth. Western culture has narcissistic elements, especially our corporations that destroy the planet without conscience.

- The pattern of codependent relationships that are based in a false belief that you must do or say what people want so you can get their love. This creates a very tangled mess of people saying and doing things that are not authentic to get power over others and protect a false supply of love. This pattern holds a system of lies in place and also encourages drama and suffering when you don't get what you need that you think someone else has. This codependency has led to the creation of egoic masks that people wear to pretend to be something they are not to get what they need. In codependent relationships, the false personality shifts as needed to present the image of what you think the other person wants so you can manipulate the other person and get your desired outcomes.

- The pattern of blaming your parents and your circumstances for your Soul curriculum when you chose exactly your parents and your circumstances to have a set of lessons for growth and understanding.

- For women, the patterns of disempowerment: being disrespected, feeling challenged to speak up, feeling uncertain of yourself, feeling sexualized or objectified, feeling ashamed of your sexuality, doubting your intuition, being mocked for your intuition, being called crazy or other names to discredit you, being undervalued at home or work, being expected to sacrifice yourself for others, being shamed for self-care, being judged and bullied for not conforming to expectations, being stonewalled for exerting your independence.

The following sections address these patterns and ways to elevate them to a new paradigm.

♥

From Thinking To Listening

If you want to learn from the Divine Mother, you must make the switch from too many thinking to deep listening. Too many thinking happens at the surface of the mind in the shallows of consciousness. Listening opens you to the depths and expanse of consciousness which is multidimensional and multifaceted and much too large to wrap your arms around in a single soundbite. Soundbites are for the masculine mind as are debates of right versus wrong that volley 'facts' back and forth in rapid succession. I begin with this section because it will help you explore the content of all the other sections.

Churning in the mind is caused by obsessively reviewing historical events and retelling stories of perception over and over; this past-focus creates a 'reality' that is then reinforced by new experiences. An overactive mind is also plagued by endlessly anticipating future-based worst case scenarios and predicting what might happen if this action is taken, or what could happen if something else does not happen. In essence, most thought within a mind burdened by too many thinking has to do with **past regrets and insecurity, or future fears of potential poor outcomes** which becomes the justification for actions or inaction today.

Traditional talk therapy heavily emphasizes analyzing past events to reveal the conditions that led to the current experience. Any discussion of a past event is automatically a story because it is a relation of a perception of events through the lens of one person. The story reveals events on which a person places significance, and how the person connects events of significance to form meaning which then leads to a justification of why they feel the way they feel and act the way they act. **A story repeatedly told gains some measure of substantiality simply in the act of retelling it over and over.**

In this lifetime, I experienced how weekly storytelling combined with powerful emotions can create literal experiential outcomes for you. You get more of the same experience you keep talking about while you're feeling big emotions. I spent over two decades trapped in my own thought tunnels.

The more the mind chatters away, the less you can listen. Listening occurs in the present moment, in the experience of being in your body and feeling its sensations.

Thank the stars for my ancestor who became my teacher of listening and presence. He joined my awakening process a couple of years into the journey when I visited Cherokee in the Smokey Mountains to reconnect with my ancestry. I tell the full story in "The Second Wave" book, and I'll share a brief version here.

Upon asking for a medicine person's help to reconnect beyond the veil to my Cherokee ancestors, I was led to a man called Bruce who agreed to meet me after his work was done. I was walking away from him toward the designated meeting spot when I suddenly felt a ball of energy the size of a softball enter the back of my head where it meets my neck. Subsequently I learned that this area is called the Mouth of God, and is the place that ancestors can enter your being. The impact of this energy ball in my brain was dizziness and a new perception that for several days allowed me to see trees breathing.

As I came to know this ancestor through healing work and inner inquiry over a period of six years, I realized he was a White Eagle Peace Chief at the time of the Trail of Tears. He was a medicine man, and he often appeared to psychics and clairvoyants who were helping me on my journey. He stood with arms crossed, leaning back, shaking his head and saying "Too many thinking" for a good part of our early time together.

My mind was trained to have 'too many thinking' by our culture and by my upbringing. In Western culture, you are expected to think quickly, make deductions quickly, have answers and solutions quickly—or else you lose credibility with others. Just delay your start from a traffic light by a few seconds to prove this point to yourself. **The problem with quick solutions is that you are only capable of considering a surface-level bit of information in that amount of time**—until you are aligned with your Soul where wisdom can effortlessly flow into the presence of your mind because there's no resistance or egoic blocks to receiving it.

Reviewing volumes of data to make a simple decision can equally be a symptom of too many thinking and caused by fear of being wrong. Also called analysis paralysis, this condition combined with stubbornness can keep you trapped in unproductive patterns for a very long time.

Fear of being wrong stems from the system of punishment and reward that you are conditioned with from birth. When you cannot anticipate an outcome of being 'wrong' because the person who is deciding you are 'wrong' and exacting punishment is unpredictable, then you develop a condition called 'walking on eggshells'. Walking on eggshells feels like a constant inner shifting and realigning to your surroundings in an effort to re-harmonize yourself with others in a position of authority over you so that you avoid being out of sync, and thereby being punished for some unanticipated wrong doing.

Aligning and harmonizing yourself to your surroundings, rather than to your Soul's guidance, is what leads to a disempowerment that can make you feel desperate, disillusioned, directionless, and even suicidal.

How you decide what is right and what is wrong is also a conditioning from culture; the 'right' answer is usually considered to be the one held by the more assertive person who has certainty in their position. However, favoring assertiveness does not necessarily lead to a brilliant answer, since true genius comes from the presence that allows your Soul to flow wisdom into your heart and mind.

So far this section has called attention to some reasons you might have a chattering mind with too many thinking which keeps you from being able to listen.

True listening is deep, wide, expansive, and takes stillness, presence and as much time as you need to get there. **Deep listening involves all of your senses – taste, touch, smell, sensation, hearing, visuals, knowings.** It requires that you put aside whatever you've been thinking about, or whatever is coming next, or whatever just happened, so that you can be present and open to the mystery of this exact moment…whatever may come.

True listening requires curiosity and don't know mind. If you already know, then you won't really be listening — you'll be filtering what you receive to accept what matches what you know and reject what doesn't match what you think you know. **It's a mastery practice to 'not know' something so that you can know something more profound and true.**

True listening requires feeling which means you must face your feelings locked away deep inside of you in all your storage lockers so you can clear the clutter and listen better to what's being felt NOW.

True listening requires less inner noise which means you must practice good mental, emotional, and energetic hygiene to clear away what is causing the noise. For example, many people do not realize that their energy bodies have parasites just like their physical bodies, and that the parasites instigate certain thought patterns to get the desired emotional response from you which is their 'food'. Daily cleansing of your chakras and auric field is needed to maintain clarity as well as periodic deep cleansing by a practitioner who can see your 'shadow' which has learned to hide from your conscious awareness.

True listening doesn't require talking to communicate. The day I was listening for wisdom about this section in meditation on my front lawn, my son came roaring home in his Mustang fox body. He seemed to desire some answers and so I sat facing him cross legged on the lawn, gazing left eye to left eye for a while in silence. At some point he shifted his gaze and said he got his answers, but still had a question for me. He asked it, and I invited him to find the answers in my reflection. And so we resumed our left eye to left eye gaze, and I felt him shift as he found his resolution. Information shared through speech was not necessary; it's only needed as you learn to flex the listening muscle so you can convince your mind through validation that what it thinks happened just happened. And then it can relax a bit more control and allow you to go deeper into listening presence.

True listening is to ask the question and drop down deep within yourself, becoming aware, curious and still. True listening requires patience to be still while being attentive. True listening is holding steady through the distractions presented by the ego through thought, bodily discomfort, and other disruptions to stillness. The answer you seek may be presented in such a way that your mind does not register it as having been received. Yet as your subconscious unpacks the response over an hour or a day, you now 'know' something different than you did before, and it was because you chose to be still and listen.

There is a calm wise one within you that knows what is most beneficial for you. The point of meditation is to listen to that one, your Self, your Soul.

Wanting immediate gratification is what keeps many of us from practicing true listening. If you do not get a clear response from the stillness within a few minutes of listening, then you get restless and decide it's not 'working.' In our culture, people also have an addiction to busyness and action, and a fear-based belief that you have to stay busy to be productive and make things happen to pay bills and put food on the table. I have experienced many times where magical connections to new clients are made without my effort just hours after a period of true listening. I have learned from these experiences that a pathway to fulfillment of my desires is to create and maintain the channels through which Spirit can flow connections to me, and then practice true listening to open up access by aligning myself to my Soul and replenishing myself.

Once you've experienced true listening, you know when you're skating in the shallows of the masculine mind rather than the depths of feminine presence. When there is something sensitive about to be revealed to your consciousness, defense mechanisms can keep you from that revelation. These defense mechanisms can make you distracted by details, or wrapped up in stories that lead you in mazes in your mind that never actually land below the protective membrane where the truth is waiting to be revealed that you need to move yourself forward into the next part of your evolution. **The trick**

is to notice when you're deflecting away from depth, and drop yourself into the deep waters for exploration. The deep feminine is beyond time because going into the depths is a process that takes patience to unweave and untangle the defenses that protect and defend against the next unfolding.

The more you practice true listening, the greater ease with which you can communicate with your Soul, 'hear' the collective consciousness, and tap into wisdom in the 'field' of the Earth plane and beyond. At first, you might practice true listening as distinct meditations for windows of time. I began practicing deep listening in this way with a morning meditation where I sat still and listened. When I began facilitating healings for others, I practiced deep listening as they were telling their story of what needed help, and as I tuned into their energy and body during the healing session.

It was healing sessions that taught me most about true listening. I learned that I could empty myself of my own 'stuff' and become totally present with the person in front of me. I could become so present with my client that I could feel stuck energy or density in their body, I could feel their emotions, and I could even see visions related to their presenting issue. At first, I would see elaborate visions of the client's past life that told a story of why they were experiencing their current challenge. Over time, the story has become less and less important as now I tune into a highly complex field of energy that is hard to describe with words, or even to comprehend entirely, and allow myself to be guided in whatever actions are needed for the session. As I have practiced true listening, I have had enough validation from my clients that I have grown to trust my guiding force and let go of control. The more I let go, the more I feel incredible sensations and experience mystical moments of Soul connection where I can viscerally perceive White Eagle stepping into my physical body to perform a healing on a client.

In some way, true listening requires you to let go of your identity and control over your mind and body so that you can be reborn with a new understanding that is guided by your Soul. To listen to messages from the Earth or a guide like White Buffalo Woman, you must refine your listening to pick up on nuances in energy and sensation, and you must be willing to be patient to keep listening until the window opens where you can receive the message in whatever form it is going to take.

I've learned that you cannot demand a message on your timeline from any Divine Feminine guide. She will pop into the spaciousness you create to receive her, and she'll do it when she feels the time is right. The Divine Mother is always with you, patiently observing your state of consciousness, timing her appearance for the moment when you can best receive the message she has to deliver to you.

Of course, if you refuse to stop and listen, at some point the Divine Mother will whack you with a spiritual two-by-four. For your own good. So let's learn our lessons when Divine Mother sends us pebbles; it's much simpler to course-correct at pebbles than it is at rocks, two-by-fours, and brick walls.

For example, let's take a look at the 'gentle' collective lesson from the Divine Mother we all received in 2020 with COVID-19. This illustrates how she works when you are listening to her messages.

- There's no separation. You can't build a wall to keep it out. Everyone has the potential to be affected by the virus no matter what country they live in, or color skin they have, or how much money they have. Be humble and realize what affects one of us, affects all of us.

- You can't control it or predict it. Just because someone's not sneezing doesn't mean they're not carrying it and spreading it. Your Soul is in control of whether or not you experience this virus. Do you need the virus for growth? Is there a lesson it's teaching that you need to learn?

- You can't solve it with a pill. If your solution for dealing with your health up until now has been to pop a pill or get a Z-Pack and then continue doing all the behaviors that stress your body into illness...this is your wake up call. The only thing that keeps you from having a bad time with this virus is a healthy immune system and good self-mastery around taking care of your body.

- The virus affects the lungs and throat primarily. Where are you not speaking your truth? Are you holding onto grudges and grief, reluctant to forgive? This virus will force the issue and make you purge the content from your lungs that you've been clutching. It's here to help you let go and move on.

- There are bigger things to worry about than how much money you're making; like how much you're living (or not living). Do you appreciate your life? Are you grateful for the gifts? Or have you allowed your mind to go into stress and complaint on the daily?

- Are you in so much fear that you stockpile supplies to 'protect' yourself, and then leave your brothers and sisters without any? Are you still in the consciousness that you're in competition to survive?

- Have you been focused on perceived threats to your freedom? If so, you may have viewed the Stay In Place as restricting your freedom to live, work, and travel. You may view masks as a way to strip you of your freedom of expression. You may wonder whether the pandemic has been artificially created as a slow slide into martial law. You may view those who trust the government as ignorant sheeple, blindly giving up their freedom to congregate and protest. You may be terrified about your body choice being violated by a mandatory vaccine that you are quite sure will have long-lasting negative effects.

- Have you been focused on perceived threats to your safety? If so, you may have believed the Stay In Place is necessary to protect lives, and you may feel it necessary to control others through shame or force to ensure safety for all. You may view the mask as a sign of a good person doing their part to protect others. You may view people protesting as endangering the lives of others out of selfishness. You may not have considered that many millions are starving behind closed 'safe' doors right now due to lack of income. You may be waiting for a savior like a vaccine to save you from the virus because you believe that vaccines save lives.

Try to flip your perspective to see what this virus is teaching you, and bring yourself into gratitude for the exposure of shadow within that will lead you to make new choices that open up greater love, gratitude, connection and joy in your life. As yourself: how do I know what I think I know, what meanings have I assigned to ideas, and how am I reacting to ideas and meanings?

To practice listening, create spaciousness for a meditative experience with your body. Turn off all external noise and find a space to sit comfortably, preferably on the Earth herself. Close your eyes to put your external world awareness on pause and tune inside. Take deep breaths into your belly to start, turning your attention to the sensation of the breath entering your airways and traveling down to fill up your lungs and expand your chest and belly, and then the air releasing from your lungs as your chest and belly relax back down and contract. Start to sway your body and notice where your body is tight, and where it is loose. Pause in an expansion of a tight area and breathe into that spot to loosen it up. Reach your hands high over your head to stretch and elongate your spine upwards. Pause and breathe to release any tight spots; you might notice heat emanating from your back. And then stretch and arc one hand at a time, slowly, to stretch your ribcage and sides. Breathe through this stretch. If you notice your hips are tight, experiment with ways to move your body that focus stretching on tight areas. In this way, move into a slow meditative exploration of your body that is designed to identify tight areas, curiously explore ways to stretch to expand those areas, and breathe spaciousness into them. This exercise in listening to your body can last for hours if you give yourself the space to explore. You may notice thoughts, emotions, or memories surface during this meditation; allow them to be witnessed and released with your breath. Allow compassion to stir within your heart for your life journey.

♥

Being Right To Curiosity

The mind that opens to a new idea never returns to its original size.
—Albert Einstein

As it happens, I've met a lot of argumentative people in my life. I learned to identify that moment where a conversation turned into a debate: the moment of entrenchment where it was clear the other person was committed to being 'right' and would fight over it.

Being a sensitive empath, I could feel the onset of the anger in the other person and the fear within myself; I could feel their heels begin to dig into the ground as they leaned into the debate, pulling 'facts' out to prove they were right. In response, I learned how to let go within myself, almost like letting go of a rope during a tug-of-war game, and then shield myself against the attack. The other person invariably took this retreat as a sign of weakness, which would strengthen their inner bully the next time a conversation between us turned into a debate.

I call this the Right Vs Wrong Game. I've witnessed people amassing lots of data in support of their perspective in order to 'win' a conversation by being 'right', which is essentially being more certain than the other people involved in the conversation. Sometimes, a person's need to be 'right' is such a powerful motivator that they will alter facts, consciously or unconsciously, to support their perspective and conclusions. They may 'forget' something they said or did because it does not align with the perspective they have adopted, or the story they are telling, as the person who is 'right'. For these people, it's all about 'winning' and being 'right' and having other people support their point of view by, typically, dividing along party lines and excluding from the conversation anyone who disagrees.

People who need to be 'right' have a hard time seeing grey. They think in very black and white patterns: with me or against me. To stay 'with' such a person is to agree to their world view, even if it causes you to feel disempowered or to accept undue responsibility in a situation.

Admitting fault is difficult for people who need to be 'right' because by being 'right', they remain in control (or they perceive that control is derived from being right). Therefore, it's rare that a person who is dedicated to being 'right' will apologize. To do so would be to admit being 'wrong' and weak and powerless.

Therefore, people who have learned to be highly certain of themselves, or at least project the image of being highly certain of themselves, are actually desperate to get some feeling of control by being 'right' and being proven 'right.' They require validation and consensus from the people closest to them.

I gave up so much ground throughout my life in these Right Vs Wrong battles, that to compensate for the dynamic I would simply escape into my own world where I was the only 'boss'. I believe this is why I chose to become an entrepreneur; the passive aggressive and overt aggressive posturing in work environments made my stomach churn. It took a great deal of effort to maintain my emotional composure when surrounded by people with a strong need to defeat others to feel good about themselves.

Being in a relationship for twenty years where the Right Vs Wrong game was a regular occurrence, I was called to examine the dynamic closely because escaping it was hard. We always went to sleep in the same bed, so I was bound to see him at some point. Often, we each stubbornly did what we wanted to do because our perspectives were so different that it was hard to compromise. Increasingly though, agreeing to disagree was not enough for my former partner; he wanted me to put aside my point of view and agree with him. He wanted to force me to abandon myself; at least, that is what I perceived. It was threatening to me at every level.

Underneath his insatiable desire to be 'right' was an ocean of insecurity. He sought to control me to keep me from being a wildcard that could turn his world upside down any moment. In fact, I did turn his world upside down when I decided I no longer wanted to be controlled, and I left the marriage.

Nearly a decade later, with deep healing and extensive exploration of my subconscious realms, I see there was potentially some missed opportunities for us to have learned how to stop the Right Vs Wrong game. We just did not have the tools at the time that were needed to address the root cause of all that entrenchment, debate, and need for control (and my need to escape it).

The Right Vs Wrong game is fueled by insecurity and fear, and often there is a wounded inner child at the center of that storm. The one who wants to prove the point, and force the other to concede, actually wants to affirm his perspective and world view as the truth so he can have a sense of security that he knows something provable.

Although the impulse to dig heels into a perspective feels like security, it actually instigates a much less safe outcome because it causes conflict. Entrenching in a perspective often leads to 'taking sides' and then name calling and eye rolling to establish the idiocy of the other person who believes the 'wrong' point of view.

Notice that the attack is often on the person, rather than the perspective. The person who believes he is 'right' seeks to establish dominance over the other person by proving that she is 'wrong', and not only that, an idiot. The person who needs to be 'right' fights for it because it's a matter of identity and self-worth to win; if you challenge his perspective, it's almost the same as punching him in the face. His opinion is part of who he is on an identity level. His self-worth depends on his opinion being correct, otherwise if he is wrong he could lose worth in the eyes of others because his worth is based on what other people think about him.

Often, entrenchment leads to finding others who agree with the 'right' perspective, who validate it, and then forming a group identity around the perspective to have more power as a group when battling people of competing perspectives. Secretly inside, the person feels completely insecure about their perspective and that's the true motivator for building consensus.

An underlying influence of needing to be right is the parental system of punishment and reward. You are punished when you are wrong, and rewarded when you are right. Since being punished is not desirable, it's important to not end up wrong. The bigger the consequences for being 'wrong' as a child, the deeper the entrenchment later in life to avoid being wrong.

Another underlying influence is the way that parents who 'won' debates, won them. If the parent who typically 'won' debates did so by being verbally aggressive, then the child learns that being verbally aggressive is how to win debates and avoid being wrong. Later in life, the adult version of that child perpetuates the use of verbal aggression whenever he feels he is losing an argument.

Any time perusing social media during the pandemic revealed the negative effects of the Right Vs Wrong game as people tore each other to shreds over 'the mask' and 'Stay In Place' and any number of other arguments that arose during 2020. The vehemence of the arguments indicates the depth of emotional wounding of the people engaging in entrenchment.

The way to disrupt and open up the Right Vs Wrong game is to become curious. Being curious with an entrenched person keeps you from getting snared by the egoic traps, even if that person is wrapped up in them. Curiosity disrupts confirmation bias which is what happens when your reticular activating system in your brain keeps showing you evidence of what you already believe so you can confirm it more strongly and become entrenched. Curiosity takes courage because anyone playing the Right Vs Wrong game believes that if they win, you lose (power, ground, status, respect).

Therefore, to use the Curiosity tool, you must be centered within yourself and not have your identity or worth wrapped up in the outcome of the debate. You must also be able to stand alone in your perspective, and not need to surround yourself with a group identity as protection or strengthening of your opinion.

What is your identity and self-worth based on? The more your inner world drives your worth, and your Soul leads your life, the more Curiosity you can embody without feeling threatened by others' perspectives. **Why feel threatened by something as small and fleeting as a perspective?** Perspectives are temporary, conditional, and ever changing as new information presents itself; at least, when you're willing to allow evolution to transform your identity.

A perspective is simply an expressed idea. You can defeat a perspective's power over you with a simple word: No. A perspective has no power to make you afraid until you give it that power.

Better yet, because perspectives are so mutable, you have great power when you use the tools of Curiosity and Empathy. Lean into the discomfort you feel when an opposing perspective is shared with Curiosity. Ask questions to dig deeper into the perspective to open it up, and even consider trying it on for size with your Empathy.

What does that perspective feel like? Does it disorient you when you feel into it? After the initial discomfort, do you understand that perspective better? What happens to the person who was oppositional when you become curious and empathetic about their perspective? Are they still entrenched, or do you sense them breathing and opening and relaxing?

You can explore another person's perspective without adopting it or agreeing with it. The part of you who feels fear at considering an opposite perspective has incorrectly attributed part of its identity to this perspective; and so it is a gift to release this attachment and realign the aspect to the Source of your being and worth.

Very likely, the other person who began entrenched will be challenged to hear and consider your perspective with Curiosity and Empathy. If you feel that is unfair, or start to hear the inner retort and resentment from having gifted listening without receiving it, you have a new opportunity for healing and realigning. You do not require anyone's validation to know your perspective is true for you; therefore, it is unnecessary that another person hear your perspective for you to know it is right for you. Surely, it is a gift when you can share your perspective and have it received by another; just release the expectation that it will happen so you can fully enjoy the experience if it does.

In the book "The Second Wave", White Eagle shared that each of us is living a 'thumbprint' life with a perspective as unique as the print on your thumb. It is unreasonable to think that anyone will ever truly understand you because we are all so different. There is some overlap to the experience that we can share with others from time to time, and that always feels reassuring; but it is a trap to rely on that commonality in order to validate yourself or feel secure in your knowing. **Realizing that each person has a unique perspective by design can help you embrace Curiosity even more because you see the differences as part of the overall kaleidoscope of the Divine.**

You can allow others to be who they are, and see life as they see it, because you can embrace the truth that they are not wrong or broken in seeing the world differently than you; and you are not wrong or broken in seeing the world differently than them. It's even possible to experience a sense of awe that the Divine has created so many billions of unique human expressions, and let that fuel your Curiosity even more to understand ever greater pieces to the puzzle of human consciousness.

With the Great Awakening, we are being invited to let go of control, to let go of the world as we knew it, and to open to a larger force to guide us. The unknown surrounding us is an invitation to NOT KNOW. **By *not* knowing we can surrender to the Divine unfolding that shows us something new.**

If the Great Awakening is a river, the ego is the part that grasps for the branches along the shore to get out of the flow; to entrench itself somewhere fixed and immovable so it can control where it goes and how fast.

When you see yourself or another grasping for a branch, or becoming entrenched in a position, realize it is from fear. Inside each of us is an aspect that fears change, that fears flow, and that fears awakening. The greater the fear, the more entrenchment, name calling, eye rolling, shaming, judging and bullying.

Let it fall apart. In the falling apart, and loss of control, people are revealed for their shadows that need healing. It's all exposed. Those playing tug-of-war think they've won. There's no winning a losing game.

Bring love and compassion to that aspect within that is in fear. Bring love and compassion to your brothers and sisters who are in fear.

None of us know anything. We are being awakened from a dream where we thought we knew everything.

♥

Letting Go Of The Blame Game

We are the product of what we are exposed to growing up. However, at some point, you have to move on. You cannot blame your parents forever.
—Iyanla Vanzant

I spent a good deal of my life looking for something or someone to blame for the way I was feeling, reacting, and behaving. My identity was wounded by unfavorable diagnosis labels from psychotherapy and shaming stories from those close to me who knew my flaws. To elevate myself out of the dumps, I used my weekly psychotherapy sessions to complain about my husband, my mother, my boss, or even a stranger who did something rude to ruin my day. I often felt like a victim of circumstances, blaming how I was feeling on mean people who were making life hard for me.

When someone criticized me, I took it personally as an attack on my character and integrity; then I cycled the criticism in my mind and made myself feel even worse. **I tore myself down on the inside with other people's opinions.** Then I would feel so badly I would resort to some form of self-destructive behavior as an act of defiance. Finally, I would blame the person who hurt me for making me hurt myself.

I felt I was the victim, but actually I was perpetrating violence on myself constantly. Others were just catalysts for my self-torture.

To reach this understanding took a great deal of energy healing to unlock my inner Triangle of Disempowerment (victim, rescuer, perpetrator), and release ancestral patterns and childhood trauma. My brain had been conditioned by early childhood trauma to think I was a powerless victim to the anger and aggression of large adults in my life. I was still operating from this powerlessness as a 42 year old mother when I finally met a guide who revealed the paradigm to me.

My life's perception was that I was provoked for over 42 years with passive aggressive and covert aggressive behavior designed to tear down my defenses and make me subject myself to control by others in positions of authority in my family. I perceived that I had been treated in a way that disrespected and minimized my authority as a mother by my family. Now seeing the Triangle of Disempowerment in my brain, I questioned what I thought I knew, layer by layer.

What I realized is that the subconscious conditioning from childhood trauma to self-sabotage was what actually most harmed my sense of self-worth. When I claimed response-ability for this self-sabotage, I liberated myself from disempowerment, and I began to see that blaming others actually kept me suppressed. By believing another person could hurt me, I gave my power away to that person.

Wounded people do wounded things. This realization was a key step that helped me dismantle the Blame Game. It spoke to the truth that the hurtful actions people take towards you are not about you; hurtful actions are a reflection of the inner state of consciousness of the person doing the actions. What you do with those hurtful actions, how you respond to those hurtful actions, is a reflection of your inner state of consciousness. Will you agree that you deserve to be the recipient of those hurtful actions? Will you agree that you deserve to be hurt? And then will you reinforce that belief with self-sabotaging actions that actually end up hurting you?

Or will you make a clear boundary between the person doing the hurtful actions towards you, and your inner sense of self and worth?

When I began exploring my reactions to hurtful actions at a deeper level, I found the places of agreement with self-harm and held those aspects of me with great love and compassion. I found the places within where I thought it was my fault, and realigned to only claim response-ability for what was truly on my side of the fence; I released the rest to Spirit.

There were many painful tests of this lesson in my life: tests that challenged my self-worth as a daughter, a woman, a mentor, and a mother. In fact, my eldest son was the start of my true journey to the self-love that finally liberated me from the Blame Game. My love for him as a tiny defenseless baby, and my desire to protect him, became a deep subconscious desire to love him as I was not loved. To have his back the way I wanted to feel my mother having my back.

During the course of my eldest son shifting into manhood, there were many painful events in my family where I felt him lose the support of key individuals in his life who were judging his character for some poor choices. I felt myself the target of blame for how he 'turned out'. And along with grief for the tearing apart of my family, I felt blame towards those who abandoned him in his deepest shadows. This time of my life was a huge opportunity to extricate myself from the Blame Game and empower myself and my eldest son to reclaim our self-worth, self-love and honor.

Part of the dissolving of the Blame Game was to notice one of its underlying support structures: **What If**. What if the family had guided him rather than derided him? What if the family had respected me rather than diminishing me in front of my sons? What if the family had been secure enough to stick through the hard parts of raising my son, instead of me having to do it alone?

All the What Ifs served to make me feel worse about how things turned out because they highlighted the gap between ideal circumstances that never happened, and the reality of the situation my eldest son and I now faced together. I realized I could get lost in the Blame Game if I let myself. I could wrap my mind in stories of What If and keep feeling worse about what actually was happening; thereby increasing the sense of being a victim of bad circumstances.

To heal myself, I let myself feel the resentments towards my family: from a river of boiling lava until it was just smoking embers. I blew light through the smoke, liberating myself and my eldest son.

Releasing the resentment revealed underlying self-judgments where I agreed with the wounded words of my family. I held so many judgments about my mistakes as a mother, and the mistakes I perceived that others made in my family. Becoming curious about these judgments and mistakes, I explored them and found places of wounding that needed my love and compassion. Greater perspectives opened up that helped me expand self-love and empathy for all the players in this drama.

No one's hurtful words and actions can diminish your self-worth and confidence to create your dreams—unless YOU allow it.

Gratitude offered another layer of healing as I realized that my eldest son showed me how I was allowing myself to be abused. He gave me the courage to stand up and walk out. I did it for him, and then I started doing it for me. The bigger perspective of personal response-ability and letting go of the Blame Game gave me a new reason for gratitude in the circumstances as I felt a sense of accomplishment with each shift towards acts of integrity.

To think there's someone to blame opens a door that you can be limited by the words and actions of other people. You are sovereign. Your light is too great to be diminished by historical conflicts and misunderstandings with others.

Forgiveness came last with the realization that to forgive the situation set ME free. I forgave it and believed in the Great Spirit's power to make everything whole in love. That forgiveness allowed me to firmly shut that old door and move into a new potential, and new circumstances, that expanded self-love, self-worth, and honor for me and my son.

I visualized letting go of the past like smoke in the wind. I released the ones who were not able to meet me on the solid ground of responsible, truthful, loving relationship. I set them free from unclenched jaws. **No longer did I need to change their perceptions, or their need to cling to a story that diminished my self-worth.** I let it go because I realized all I needed to focus on was my own healing. I made space for blessings in the wake of my grief.

Through the process of extricating myself from the seductive Blame Game, I realized that engaging in blame, shame and judgment actually lower your human consciousness and vibration. In many energy healing sessions, as I peered into people's ancestry and energy fields to understand this dynamic, I saw that there were forces at play inciting the Blame Game because it produced food for them; these forces fed on discontent, disharmony, and destruction.

What I became aware of in my inquiry illuminated the Native American folk tale of the white wolf and black wolf: which wolf will you feed? Do you want to continue feeding war, separation, anger, and human suffering? Or do you want to become savvy to the instigating forces of this drama and choose to not let yourself be played by dark forces that endeavor to distract you into lowering your vibration in this way?

Now whenever I feel the seductive pull of the Blame Game, I raise my vibration to a more clear space of contemplation using this mantra from Paul Selig, and I welcome you to try it:

I know who I am, I know what I am, I know how I serve
I am here, I am here, I am here
I am free, I am free, I am free
I have come, I have come, I have come
I am in the upper room
Behold! I make all things new

From this elevated energy and perspective, sit for a few moments for a realization about the situation, and open to a new possibility. As a sovereign being, how can you respond to the challenge to bring more love, light, and healing? By taking response-ability for your own thoughts, emotions, perceptions, and actions in this way, you liberate yourself from the Triangle of Disempowerment and claim your birthright of sovereignty.

♥

Denial To Response-ability

Denial creates a great deal of human suffering. Denial can be deluding yourself or outright lying to others. The ultimate denial is the refusal to admit Great Spirit (God/Source/Creator/your word) is All That Is. And so all forms of denial serve to shut out the light and keep you in darkness.

Denial is an egoic program that creates conflict between people, because no one likes being lied to. The person who lies is kept in darkness through the denial of the truth which may happen through obscuration of the truth in the person's consciousness, or may happen through the person's stubborn refusal to admit the truth and subsequent decision to blatantly lie. The person who judges the lies, engages in the lies through seeking to prove the lying person has lied, and is hurt by the lying, is also kept in darkness by entanglement in the denial program.

A painful form of denial is gaslighting which seeks to confuse you with intentional distortion of 'reality' that contains a grain of truth. The denial program is what is causing a person to lie and gaslight; underneath that program is a Soul doing his or her best to rise up in consciousness and see the truth through the veil of denial.

It's very hard to see in the dark. It's very hard to hear when your ears are plugged up. It's very hard to understand what another is saying when your brain is contorted with the deceptions of the denial program. It's very hard to move yourself out of denial when you are also afflicted by stubbornness.

As I was 'waking up', I had an experience after a healing of being lifted above that veil of denial. Suddenly I could see out of my own eyes, and I realized that up until that point I had been submerged somewhere deep within under a cloud of darkness, unable to see out of my own eyes. I realized that I could speak more easily and be heard, and that up until that moment I had a hard time being heard, feeling like I needed to shout from down there in the darkness.

We are at the beginning of the Great Awakening. Is it any wonder that we have epidemic of narcissism in the human collective that has been identified and talked about in growing volume alongside identification of the 'empath'?

The narcissist pattern is characterized by extreme denial and self-involvement that does not have genuine care or interest in others—unless that other can give him something to raise his self-esteem or image of success.

The empath pattern is characterized by other-involvement that overwhelms a sense of self, and depending on the outer circle's patterns, she either feels lifted or burdened; everything feels personal.

The narcissist pattern includes not knowing how to connect to others from behind a hard shell exterior wall of protection, and the empath pattern includes not being able to stop connecting with others because she feels at such an expanse that she does not know where the edges are to put a boundary.

Neither pattern supports a person to know who they are in truth. The narcissism-afflicted person thinks he is the external success that defines an image that he thinks is him; the empathic person feels she is the messy soup of sensations and emotions tangled up inside of her and cannot form an external image of herself to think about.

The narcissist pattern makes a person deny responsibility for even the tiniest 'mistake', and the empath pattern makes a person feels responsible for everything. The narcissist pattern leads a person to confine and control and bring his world in tight so he feels safe; the empath pattern leads a person to feel smothered and suffocated being confined in this way, feeling all the members of the family in overwhelming depth, and makes her long for freedom and space to breathe.

This narcissist/empath pattern seems to be the prevalent configuration that the human collective has called forth to help us to awaken. Of course, men can experience either the narcissist or the empath pattern, as can women, and a person can have a mixture of the two patterns as well.

Underneath both patterns is codependency and the primary question: How do I get what I need from the world? The narcissist pattern calls a person to manipulate overtly or covertly to get what he needs from another person, and prevents him from 'feeling' bad about it; he blames or shames to evoke guilt in the other person that leads to a behavior shift in his favor. The empath pattern calls a person to take on the blame and shame, take it personally, and drag herself down with it into self-injury which is used to guilt the unfeeling narcissist for causing her pain; a backwards manipulation to get him to change his behavior out of being exposed as a 'bad' or 'toxic' person...a perpetrator. The narcissism-afflicted person then reacts to being labeled as 'bad' because it smears his preferred image, and so manipulates again to redirect responsibility through projection back to the other person.

It's a never ending cycle of Denial of Response-ability perpetrated by the narcissism-afflicted person and enabled by the empathic person; both people feel like victims of the other's perpetration.

To break the cycle, the empathic person must extricate herself from the configuration, discover her energetic boundaries, discern what's hers and what's not, and firmly push out everything that is not her response-ability. She must learn that her NO is just as powerful as her YES, and use it appropriately. She must bare everything with vulnerable transparency and surrender to the Divine, and let herself be supported and healed and reprogrammed into a sovereign being.

From sovereignty, the empath finds her true power: the ability to know in a very nuanced way the consciousness of another person while staying completely present to herself, and to serve as a conduit of healing and transformation for the other who is willing to become response-able by lifting beyond the veil of denial.

It can feel heavy and overwhelming to face the shadows; however, if you ignore something it has power over you from your resistance to it. If you face it with love, you vanquish it and reclaim your power.

Why does the empathic person have to make the first move? Because she is able to take the shadow journey far sooner than the narcissism-afflicted person. She wakes up before the narcissism-afflicted person because she is in touch with her feelings, and the burden of those heavy emotions leads her to seek help far sooner than the narcissism-afflicted person who has walled off feelings and lives largely from the thinking mind. The unhealed trauma within the narcissism-afflicted person can provoke him to aggressively deflect responsibility and intensify past normal denial, which is a subconscious protection mechanism, to outright lying—knowing the truth and lying about it.

We see examples of covert aggressive narcissism with corporate executives who authorize fracking, knowing that fracking forever destroys the water supply and the crust of the Earth for a short term profit gain that largely benefits a handful of 'powerful people'. In lightworker communities, this kind of heartless greed is attributed to 'reptilian' people whose behavior exhibits sociopathic and destructive tendencies. Using power over others, and leaving a path of destruction on the Earth in a quest for 'power' and 'wealth', are the hallmarks of a narcissistic personality concerned with egoic gratification and material wants. Our planet has reached the limits of this form of narcissistic abuse.

We must say NO with fierce love.

Many experts in the psychotherapy world say that narcissism-afflicted people do not change because they cannot overcome the inner resistance to claim personal responsibility. In other words, they cannot move beyond the denial program which was initially used to overcome trauma through bypassing it, and now has become the primary means for dealing with any uncomfortable awareness in the person's life. The bigger the ditch they dig for themselves with actions that lack moral integrity, the harder it is for them to pull out of the spiral by admitting it.

As you're building self-worth, you can set boundaries to protect yourself from destructive watch dogs. When you know your worth, you will be unfazed by their ploys because you know the attacks of a wounded person are never about you—always about them.

With strong self-worth you trust yourself, can take risks, and can support yourself through setbacks. You don't crumble under attack from critical naysayers. You see them for what they are. As such you're not defensive and can receive course corrections gracefully that support your expansion toward your desires.

With strong self-worth you have a courageous heart that stays open and vulnerable and loving in the face of whatever comes your way.

Strong self-worth is an essential ingredient for powerful alchemy and forward traction as you follow your courageous heart.

If you're conflict averse right now, and find yourself always in the position of falling on the sword to create win-win-win outcomes that protect others from the outcomes of their decisions, stop and question yourself. Is rescuing everyone by diminishing yourself really for the best and highest good of all concerned? What would happen if you held a boundary instead? Can you be with the discomfort of holding your position and refusing to fall on the sword to make peace? What are you really afraid of? What's the underlying motivation for throwing yourself under the bus? Are you afraid that people will talk badly about you, or cast you out, if you don't accommodate them by 'fixing it'?

The only way past the pattern is holding through the discomfort of not doing the pattern. Do nothing, stand firm, and let the energies settle. Notice any discomfort you have with not providing the solution. Be at that uncomfortable edge and feel everything. Sit with all the fear and discomfort as you tune into your own heart and honor your truth and the commitment to your Soul's directive. Decide that you will no longer step over your own truth to please others, or to make it easier for them when there is a conflict. Do not say "I don't care" when you really do, or "it's not important" when it really matters to you. Do not turn your back on your true inner guidance because of external pressure to do what's best for the others involved in the situation. Martyrdom is another aspect of codependency and a way that the ego holds you back from letting your Soul guide the way. When you act from martyrdom, you send a message to your inner child that what others want has more value than what your own heart is telling you. Have your own back for a change. **Stand firm and let Spirit give each person the lessons they need for their personal evolution.** Realize your only job is to know your truth, listen to your heart, and follow it.

Rather than let yourself spin out mentally about conflicts in your life, choose to cultivate a garden in your heart. Make the choice to water your heart and open up the sun within you to grow beauty, rather than giving attention to the weeds that suck your energy and crowd out the sunlight. Open and listen to Spirit for inspired actions, and if that action is let it be…well, let it be.

And take good energetic and emotional care of yourself. When you're a highly perceptive and empathic person, an angry or frustrated retort from someone can feel like a blast of hot stinging air. The person who is angry may not even realize they are spewing toxic waste like a firehose in your direction. If they do not yet have psychic awareness of their own energy and impact, they may just think their thoughts and emotions are contained within themselves.

Let it fall to the Earth.

Nothing you said or did 'deserved' to be smeared with sludge. You did not need to figure out how you 'caused' them to be upset. You are not responsible for someone else's feelings, words and actions.

Let it fall to the Earth.

Do not ruminate over it, wondering how you could have done it differently so as to not provoke that person. Twisting yourself up in knots trying to keep from 'making' people upset is a full-time job, and you really do not want it. It's not very fulfilling.

Let it fall to the Earth.

You are whole. You are blessed. You were just being 'you' and shining your light.

Have you ever considered that maybe you're shining so brightly that some people's eyes need adjusting to see you clearly out of all the darkness?

Keep on shining lightworkers. It's time to wake up, and some people want to pull the covers over their heads and go back to sleep.

What does your mom do in that situation? That's right. Turn the lights up brighter, pull the covers back, and make some noise.

It's better if we do it before Mother Earth has to.

Projection and Discernment

With the highly intense energies prevalent in the world today, people will be doing their best, but not operating at their best because of being burdened by the sheer volume of intensity in the human collective during this 'great purge' of what no longer serves. You may experience an increased tendency for people with less emotional capacity to project pain outwards onto others in the vicinity, typically those who have greater emotional capacity.

Have you ever gotten an angry email from someone and felt the toxic fog before you even clicked to open? When people project onto you, it's like they bundle up the uncomfortable emotions they don't know how to process into a box, light it on fire, and then ring the doorbell as they run away.

The projection is an attempt to 'hot potato' the pain off themselves and onto another person, making the other person to 'blame' or 'at fault' so that it is now that other person's response-ability to 'fix' the situation. Typically people at this level of emotional capacity will also engage in rumination (in their mind or out loud) which activates a deeper psychic connection with you; if you feel this energy, you can feel their underlying need to make you responsible for their pain.

The more empathic you are, the harder it is to discern projections because you often feel so much in others, it can be challenging to isolate what is yours, and what is the other person's. What is helpful in this situation is to take a pause before reacting to any energy that feels like a projection. Practice restraint and give it the space you need to let the energies settle, to tune into your own station, and to discern what (if any) aspects belong to you for processing.

Avoid taking the bait and getting hooked into a greater escalation of drama. Notice that if you respond too quickly in these situations even a congenial response will be misinterpreted and used to deepen the projection and conflict; the person with less emotional capacity will send another volley of toxic energy to you to unburden themselves and leave you another 'box of toxic' at your doorstep. As you give the toxic exchange your attention, you also give power to the provoker of the projection; thus, you end up feeling drained.

Because projection energy can be delivered in such a way as to throw you off guard, you may not be able to immediately discern how to handle it. Engage or ignore? Feel into it to understand if there is a legitimate concern to address, or very neatly dispose of it without opening yourself to it?

As a response-able person, you may get pulled into projections more often than not out of a sincere desire to claim responsibility for 'your part' of a situation, and then walk away with far more than your fair share. To further complicate things, sometimes projection energy masks itself with an outer membrane that resonates as your energy, and so you think it 'belongs' to you.

The more intimate a relationship, the more tricky the projections between you, and the more space is needed to unpack and process before engaging with a response.

Fill Up On You. To avoid inadvertently assuming ownership of projected energy that is not 'yours', it is important to give yourself time and space to tune into your unique vibration and fill up completely with it. Knowing intimately your own vibration will help you spot imposters more quickly, and a regular practice that helps this self-awareness is to fill up your auric bubble with your unique vibration, and then add a flexible membrane as a shield to strengthen your bubble. The more you know your own vibration, the easier it will be for you to discern when someone is projecting something onto you. Drop into that familiar vibration with some deep breathing, and then unpack and assess this projection energy to see if any aspects of it are truly resonating inside of you for investigation and healing.

Shift the Focus. You can also practice shifting your placement in relationship to the toxic projection energy. In the original scenario, you can think of the volley as a straight line between the person projecting the energy and you. The energy is projected at you, and the intent is to make the energy your fault and responsibility. Because of the direct line from the other person to you, it can feel like a personal attack. Now in place of 'you', visualize that there is a ball of perception and conditioning hanging in the air where you were standing. That ball of perception and conditioning is not 'you', it is not 'them' — it is beyond both of you and part of both of you. In your mind's eye, move yourself away from the ball of perception and conditioning that is hanging in the air as the recipient of the projection energy; move yourself closer to the other person. Notice how the other person may try to put you back as the focus of the projection energy. Keep redirecting the projection energy to the ball of perception and conditioning that is hanging in the air where you originally stood as the 'target', and keep moving yourself closer to the other person. The goal is to stand side-by-side with the other person, witnessing together the ball of perception and conditioning as well as the projection energy sent as an 'attack'.

The movement is from opponents being manipulated by perception and conditioning to attack one another, to allies witnessing the perception and conditioning together and unpacking it to restore harmony and understanding. Allies can look each other in the eye with respect as they acknowledge 'this is some big storm we're in'…the conditioning and perceptions being the source of the 'storm'. To get to this place of being allies 'fighting' the conditioning, you must no longer take the conditioning personally nor make it part of your identity. You must know the true vibration of your Soul, and let that help you to be more neutral in witnessing the conditioning that separates human beings. Coming from Soul alignment, it is easier to keep your heart open in a spirit of comradery when perceptions and conditioning seek to separate you from others.

We Have Unique Perceptions. The idea that there is 'one reality' we are all sharing is untrue. Our unique perceptions create individual realities that may overlap a little or a lot, leading to a sense of there being a shared reality. People tend to gravitate towards others whose realities overlap more with their own as this feels reassuring. And people tend to create conflicts with others whose realities do not overlap with their own because it feels unsettling that it's possible for people to exist who perceive nothing of what we perceive. If this has happened to you, you might feel that person is lying; surely, their perception cannot be 'right' when you know what really happened. How can they be so earnestly saying they thought it happened that way, when you perceived it differently? For whatever reason, this has been the cosmic setup between my mother and me for most of my life, always perceiving things in incompatible ways.

I had a powerful moment of realization about perception, conditioning, and realities near the end of writing this text when I received some channeled support from Paul Selig during an online training. What I was able to witness was the likelihood that my mother was feeling hurt and confused, and that she was not aware of her role in leading me to the place where I would accept the job of writing this book to heal the Mother Wound. I know what I have experienced, and the inner work I have done over my lifetime to heal; and I can respect myself and my journey while also honoring that, for whatever Divine reason, my mother's memory is wiped clear of it or simply in a reality where she did not perceive it as I did. I realized in this moment that it was fruitless to ever expect an acknowledgement from my mother of anything I have experienced in my reality and perception. I wept heartily, feeling another level of healing seep into my heart to create right relationship. Because as the Guides said during the channeled message for me, the important thing is for me to heal my own Mother Wound. Then it will not matter my mother's reaction to the teachings in this book because it's not really about her; it's about the Mother that lives within me. My desire or need for her to understand my perspective is an aspect of my Mother Wound, and I have the power to heal it by accepting that the Divine plan, up until now, has made it so that she lives in a completely different perceptual reality from me. By accepting my Soul's curriculum, and embracing the validation of my own heart and wisdom, I release my mother from being response-able for doing for me what she is not able to do. Only I am able to validate my own heart and wisdom. Certainly, I feel jealous of those mothers and daughters who are able to understand one another's perspectives and share a common reality. Yet, that is another aspect for my own healing: to accept my Soul's curriculum and raise myself to gratitude for the gifts of this lifetime that have been claimed directly because of the relationship I have with my mother. This is the life experience that I chose, the incarnation goals I selected and agreed to. I trust there is a purpose to it, and I surrender to the wisdom of my Soul.

❤

Criticism To Confidence

Confidence is an inner surety of one's ability to navigate a challenge successfully. When the spark of confidence is present within a person, she can take a leap of faith to do something she has never done before. Confidence is an inner "yes!" that gives a person the fuel to make the first few steps into unknown territory. Successfully navigating a new experience expands a sense of confidence through the personal 'proof' of having prevailed.

The more a person acts from confidence, the more she can lean into the discomfort of new experiences with forward momentum. Built into confidence is the trust that she will have what she needs to be successful, and that if she is not successful, that she can learn lessons from the attempt that improve her chances of being successful the next time.

Confidence is a muscle that you must cultivate within from the initial spark. No one can give you confidence; you must work the muscle of confidence for yourself, proving to yourself that you have every reason to be confident in yourself.

Clearly, the way a child is parented has a big impact on her ability to feel confident as she grows up into an adult. If the child is controlled and suppressed to 'protect' her, and she does not get the chance to make mistakes and recover from them, then that child can grow into a risk-averse adult who does not have the confidence to venture outside her comfort zone. If the child is criticized for every mistake, and mocked for wanting to pursue interests outside the family's approved activities, then she could either rebel to exert her unique expression, or she could turn inwards and repress herself into an unfulfilling life of conformity.

Sometimes those who have grown up with critical, naysaying, or overprotective parents find both of these patterns within themselves: the one who rebels and follows her heart, and the one who beats herself up if things don't work out since her inner critic knew she would fail. There's a sense of amazing potential that never really took flight, and intense frustration that she 'lacks' what it takes to be successful. She feels the gifts locked up inside her without the confidence to shine her light.

Would she have been more confident and successful if her parents cheered her rather than mocked and criticized her? Supported her rather than bullied her? Seen her as exquisite rather than labeled her as crazy because they couldn't understand her genius?

Since you will never know, because you got the parents you got, turn your attention away from 'what if' and towards 'what now'. Recognizing that you vacillate between confident and critical, or just struggle in general with confidence, find your way to self-confidence by learning to parent yourself. Educate yourself about how conscious parents teach their kids self-confidence, and then apply those techniques to yourself.

You have to reprogram your mind towards patterns that produce self-confidence. You have to re-parent your inner child to heal old wounds and traumas, and instill healthy patterns. You may literally have to start with baby steps, giving yourself small wins and celebrating them so that you strengthen your confidence muscle. Acknowledging the wins is important for establishing the 'proof' that you are capable of tackling challenges. Leaning in to 'failures' to harness wisdom and then recommitting yourself is important for dismantling the crippling effects of harsh criticism.

Be mindful to only allow supportive and encouraging people in your intimate circle. As you are growing your confidence muscle, it's important to not keep weakening it by letting a naysayer tear you down. Find safe spaces to share your progress and challenges that witness you without judgment so you can heal and grow.

The impact of years of subtle and overt abuse is profound on a person's psychology. It can twist you up in knots, make you forget who you are, lose all your confidence, and spend years of herculean effort to achieve a measure of success that is a small fragment of what you're capable of. Give yourself all the support you need to rewire the disempowering naysayer and strengthen your confidence muscles so you can live the life you truly deserve.

♥

Self Doubt To Certainty

In my personal growth work with George Kansas and Tracey Trottenberg, I learned that in any conversation, it is certainty that leads. The person with the most conviction directs the flow of the conversation towards their ideas and perspectives. People listen and believe those that have the most certainty about what they're saying. People with certainty have a quality of authority about them. Combine certainty with being a natural authority, like a mother, and you've got a lot of power to choose the conversation that others engage in.

When your mother leads the family with certainty about her perspective of you, and that perspective is contrary to your own perspective of yourself, then you have a difficult situation, don't you? I experienced this myself. I have always had a great deal of initial certainty within myself whenever I receive inspiration. But then if my certainty did not match my mother's, I would experience a sense of self-doubt because her energy of certainty overpowered my own sense of certainty. Her authority as my mother contributed to the weight of her certainty to make me think maybe I didn't really know what I was talking about.

Complying with my mother's certainty and world view felt like a cage. I was terrified to challenge the cage. Innately I think I knew that if I challenged my mother's certainty by having my own certainty, that there would not be room for me in the family. And my mother and Dad was all I had, being raised primarily as an only child. The few times I bust out of the cage, so to speak, there were consequences for doing so.

For a good part of my life I struggled in the tension between initial certainty, and the erosion of that certainty into self-doubt and confusion as critical thoughts expanded. During my time as an entrepreneur, my career decisions had a pedal-to-the-metal and jerking-to-a-halt pattern. This is because inside I was a jumbled mess of certainty and self-doubt. In weekly psychotherapy sessions, I faced feelings of being 'crazy' and a problem to others—which were messages from my childhood that formed the foundation of my early mind. Even though I was able to rouse people to engage in all kinds of community projects, I felt like people didn't like me or were annoyed by me. Whenever my ideas didn't quite have the stellar outcome I had envisioned, I denigrated myself for failing miserably because my idea didn't rock it the first time out.

If I was to boil down this pattern it's that I always had a jet engine inside of me, but I kept it hidden under blankets and constantly apologized for it because I have lived with a fear of conflict and rejection. I people pleased to stay in the family, and I stuffed my thoughts and feelings out of sight until I could not do it anymore because of the self-harm it began to perpetuate.

As it turns out, my early assessment about challenging my mother's certainty was correct. When I finally challenged her rendition of my identity at 50 years old, and started pointing out some of her behaviors that had led to my lifelong struggle in psychotherapy, I found myself on the other side of a wall…a wall built of family members who rushed to my mother's side as the person certain she had been attacked by her daughter. Within a family where there is a person of authority that needs to maintain that authority by being 'right' and having her perspective affirmed, there's no room for competing perspectives.

In other words, to claim my personal certainty on my journey to the level that I could be effective in my life with relationships and business, I had to let go of self-doubt and step into my personal certainty, even though it meant being excluded from interaction with a good part of my family of origin because my certainty challenged the certainty of my mother.

I recognize that I am in the middle between two paradigms: one paradigm that requires there to be a loser so there can be a winner, and a new paradigm that (I hope) honors many differing perspectives all at once as equally relevant and true. **Unconditional love holds the space for all perspectives to be true at the same time**. I have witnessed that holding the vibration of unconditional Love allows staunch positions to melt away what is false, revealing something more true underneath.

As a mother myself, I have learned that certainty is best applied to my own life. **When interacting with my sons, I have found it is most respectful of their life journeys when I adopt curiosity rather than certainty.** They evolve every day, therefore every time I see them there is a very good potential that I no longer know who they are. I give my sons permission to reinvent themselves in every moment, to become a newer better model of themselves. To do this, I must let go of the history I think I know about them so that I can learn something new. **The mother is a powerful leader, and I choose to use my power to gift my children the certainty that they can find their own truth within themselves.**

"It's not important how the world defines you, it's how you define yourself."
– Stedman Graham

No one can tell you who you are. That's up to you to decide. Of that, I hope you can be as certain as I am now.

❤

Discrediting To Trusting Your Intuition

Growing up empathic, sensitive, and aware with a mother from a generation that valued secrecy over transparency, I learned that there were two realities occurring simultaneously: the surface appearance reality which is how people want you to believe it is, and the deeper truth reality with some ugliness that people would rather you not be aware of.

A profound example of this in my life was my shrouded-in-secrecy paternal origins. To protect me, I was told that my natural father was the man I knew at 5 years old who my mom divorced to move in with the man who became my life-long Dad. This man that I was told was my natural father was actually my first step father who we lived with from the time I was 1 until I was 5.

Inside of me, I knew it was not true. I felt that there was an elephant in the room. And when I turned 14, my mother revealed that, indeed, there was an elephant in the room. I was given the real name of my natural father and a synopsis of why I had not been allowed to know him as I was growing up.

Feeling into the situation (what I now know was my ability to sense the karma of the relationship between my mother and natural father), I chose to delay meeting my natural father until I was in college and more mature.

This ability to feel the karmic weight of a situation from the past, in the now moment, was my intuition at work. My intuition also showed up whenever I said something to a friend that was obvious to me, and then the friend recoiled and denied the truth of my statement. I always seemed to pick friends that were highly resistant to my deeper insights, which served to make me question what I 'knew' because I did not have evidence, data, or outside expert opinions to back myself up—the kind of 'proof' that these friends valued. The strong reactions my friends would have against my insights made me feel like I had to prove myself whenever sharing something; perhaps by finding someone more knowledgeable than myself to say the same thing I was saying so that my friend would listen to the point.

Being aware of a deeper reality with my empathy and intuition, and being surrounded by people who denied that deeper reality and reinforced the surface-level reality was confusing. Also being somewhat naive I would take people at their word, thinking that everyone was being honest (although I have since realized people's capacity for lying when influenced by the denial pattern).

The constant criticism and denial that I perceived from those closest to me made me doubt myself and my inner guidance, and left me feeling confused about what to believe. **It was hard to go for the big dreams in my life when I was riddled on the inside with doubt and confusion.**

What was extremely helpful was being surrounded by people who were also practicing intuition skills during training at The Four Winds Light Body. Being able to listen deeply with my empathic and clairvoyant skills, and then have my intuitive hits validated, helped me to start trusting myself. This trust strengthened over years as I practiced listening to clients during healing sessions, and relaying the messages and perceptions I was receiving which matched the experiences my clients were having. **It was such a relief to be around people willing to be open, transparent and honest; and it allowed me to explore these powerful intuitive gifts so I could trust them.**

When I explore intuition at the level of the collective experience, I see how secrecy and denial are aspects of healing the Mother Wound. The powerful intuitive gifts of women were shamed and condemned by patriarchal institutions to disempower women's knowing, and humans were trained to live at the surface level of the mind. From the surface level, we are operating in egoic self along with all its paradigms including dishonesty and denial; and people even lie to themselves, ignoring their bodies and sense of knowing that is warning them not to believe what they perceive at the surface level. The reinforcement of evidentiary mind-generated proof as the only way to believe something is another aspect of this patriarchal disempowerment of the intuitive feminine gifts.

Geniuses have all known that the most profound truths lie outside of our mind's capacity to grasp them. Einstein very famously said that "We can't solve problems by using the same kind of thinking we used when we created them." In fact, 'thinking' does not lead to genius. **Genius insights come from intuition and opening up your psychic gifts to perceive consciousness that is greater than the capacity of your mind to understand it.**

The patriarchal conditioning is to assume that you are 'crazy' and 'illogical' and 'woo woo' if you trust your intuition more than your thinking mind. The conditioning is also to deny the insights harnessed from intuition because powerful intuitive gifts expose lies and untruth very easily; therefore, the egoic mind has a vested interest in keeping you from exploring intuition.

Only when you are ready to heal are you grateful for the keen intuitive gaze of a well-practiced psychic to help you to see into your shadows. Until then, it is likely a person who is still grappling with egoic stranglehold will feel threatened by someone whose perceptual skills are finely honed.

Mothers have tremendous capacity for intuitive knowing about their children as we are forever connected with our progeny through consciousness links. Mothers can 'tap into' their children at any time to feel how they are doing in that moment (at the deeper level of reality), and to receive messages. **It's important to use this gift respectfully and consciously to honor our children's sovereignty.** And it's a really useful tool for being in service to our children's growth as they grapple with their own egoic consciousness that would like to keep them living trapped in their minds at the surface level of existence.

I remember when my own mother intuition opened up; I felt the Soul of my baby joining with my physical matter in my belly. It was early on in my pregnancy when I felt his Soul descend into the physical baby growing in my womb. I was not a 'psychic' then, and yet I 'knew' he had arrived on a Soul level. I could feel his presence. It was a very unique feeling because up until that point there had only been me inside of me; now there was him and me inside of me. I was aware of him being aware of me. He had a different frequency than the way I felt inside of me. He did not merge with me; his frequency stayed distinct while growing inside of my frequency.

Now my son is a young man and I can still feel him whenever I choose. And because I know that feeling him activates a little cord that he also feels, I do my best to be respectful to not 'knock on his door' too often. Tapping into him to check on him helps me to know he is safe so that I do not need to intrude upon him in the material surface-level of consciousness; in other words, it keeps me from calling him too much.

As a woman, I have at least double the nerve receptors of a man, which gives me access to more sensory data than a man. For example, on average, women have 34 nerve fibers per square centimeter of facial skin while men average just 17. Having double the nerve receptors means having double the perceptual abilities, and our sensing and perceiving muscles are what make strong intuition.

What can fog up women's intuition is the emotion and pain that are part of having double the nerve receptors of men. It's important to let emotional energy pass through (as discussed in a later section, "Feel It To Heal It") and to clear up any repressed energy or emotions stored in the body. The clearer your vessel from the 'crust' of life, the more honed and finely nuanced your intuitive abilities, and the less prone to projecting your 'stuff' onto others.

A good goal is to be the 'hollow bone' that Spirit passes through effortlessly to deliver healing energies and wisdom to your human self. This means that a psychic worth her salt is constantly on a path of self-awareness and digging into her shadows to bring the light and hollow out the bone even more.

When you strengthen your intuition muscles and start leaning into them with faith and trust, what opens up before you is exactly the insight you need in the moment to make a positive impact. I've learned to listen attentively for what is happening for a client, as well as the best way to open that client to discover it for herself.

Being able to see into a person's shadows does not mean that the person is ready to see everything you find there. After all the years of training I now have in accessing and interpreting intuitive guidance, I see in retrospect that the resistance I met before from friends was likely due to their not being ready to know what I just shared with them. Their denial of what I said to them did not mean the intuitive hit was wrong; it often meant it was delivered too soon and without invitation. **Invitation is a really big key to successfully conveying intuitive insights to a person; ask them first if they want to know what you're about to tell them.** Get permission to deliver the message. Respecting people in this way makes your psychic abilities less threatening.

Lastly, we are fulfilling the prophesy of the Eagle and the Condor flying together in the sky. The Eagle is a metaphor for the mind, forward progress, logic, and the individual path. The Condor is a metaphor for the heart, the Soul, intuition, and community. **When we bring the mind and heart together we are unstoppable.**

So as you unlock your Condor gifts of body sensing, heart knowing, and intuition from your Soul, you can integrate this wisdom by running it through your mind's logic and discernment to chart a practical course of implementation on a human level what your Soul is telling you. Many times I find that the insights I receive through channeling sessions are so profound that I stop and repeat them to understand them; this is my mind grasping what just came through from my Soul. If there is a beneficial alignment, it is to open to Condor wisdom and then use our Eagle mind to understand it.

Strong intuitive muscles allow you to be in a space of knowing, which offers many benefits:

- Knowing facilitates proactive decisions without doubt or confusion.

- Knowing allows you to resolve relationship issues without drama.

- Knowing helps you sleep better at night without senseless worrying.

- Knowing helps you trust yourself, even if no one validates you.

- Knowing increases a sense of safety and positivity because you know what you know.

- Knowing is fun when you're 'tuned in' and others also know because they're hearing the same messages.

- Knowing helps you reclaim your power through self-validation.

♥

Conforming To Embracing Your Truth

Sometimes to do what's best for the tribe, you have to stop conforming to it. Conforming is a pervasive human domestication of the patriarchal system of control and domination. You are trained to conform from the moment you are born; you are taught all the behaviors that will earn love and acceptance, and you are warned about the behaviors that will get you punished or (biggest fear) tossed out of the tribe.

A little conformity is useful for setting standards of human behavior that make it safe for every person to live a healthy productive life. Beyond that, conformity becomes a cage that limits individual exploration and expression, and can create a lowest-common-denominator effect that constrains genius in favor of the comfort of the majority. (Every person is capable of genius when he takes the journey to live guided by his Soul. It's just that the majority, up until now, have not chosen to take that journey.)

Consider the ramifications of conformity when there are systems of belief and behavior that harm people. By adhering to these systems of belief and behavior, you are perpetuating human suffering. And this is the place we find ourselves at the turning of the Age of Aquarius. There have been generations within families perpetuating certain systems of conditioning that it is now time to heal and transform so that we may foster a new way of relating for New Earth. Family secrets and suppressed voices and public facades covering up messy truths—all of this is up for a big reveal right now. **Someone has to choose to be a pioneer and disrupt the systems.**

Pioneers are those who break free from the expected way of living; they choose exploration in place of conformity. In the last few centuries, being a pioneer was a literal physical movement; potentially moving across the Atlantic ocean to a new world called America, or traveling by wagon across thousands of miles of wild country with Westward expansion.

The new pioneer is a pioneer of consciousness. It's an inner expansion, an elevation of thought and deed, and an opening to Soul-guided living. It's a disruption of the status quo through love and compassion and demonstration. It's a redefinition of what it means to be 'safe' from being accepted through conformity into your tribe, into being aligned with your Soul and the consciousness of the planet to shine your unique magic.

What keeps you from shining your light? It's likely there is a primal fear of being cast out of family and tribe. If you explore past lives, you might find lives where you were persecuted for bringing in new ways of thinking that challenged the prevailing authorities. When you hear the calling of your Soul, and you continue to cling to the comfort and security of blending into your family by conforming to outdated structures that you know are holding you back from your destiny… it's time to realize you are prioritizing temporary comfort over an eternal prize.

Fear of conflict, fear of rejection, fear of retaliation—these are all reasonable fears because they do happen to pioneers who challenge the status quo by choosing to not conform. And these fears are temporary aspects of an evolutionary process that we are all in the midst of fulfilling.

True allegiance is to Source, the Mother Earth, and your own Soul— not to the temporary people, places and things of this material incarnation. **Conformity to your fellow humans is not unity.**

You have a unique thumbprint. You have a unique Soul plan as laid out in your human design chart and gene keys. You are completely unique in your Soul lessons this lifetime and in your gifts to share with the collective.

Unity happens when each person is led by the Divine which can then orchestrate all the unique parts to play a symphony. Conformity based on conditioning is false unity based in egoic fear and need for perceived safety and control that the ego believes it has when groups of people conform to ideas, rules, behaviors, and so forth.

When you break out of conformity to transition your life to align with the Divine, your human life does get messy; false structures must fall apart so that the true foundation for your life can emerge. False things fall apart so true things can fall together.

The clearer your inner guidance, the more you may feel misaligned with the humanity that surrounds you. This feeling of misalignment is your invitation to dissolve false structures. You may feel especially out of alignment with groups you belonged to when you were less clear in your Soul connection. The desire to belong to these groups, even though you realize you are no longer resonant with them, is a very real human experience; and you must be stronger than this pull to realize your Soul-level potential. Wanting to fit into spaces where you no longer fit can cause the conformity of the group to pull you backwards in your development so you fit again. Wanting people who knew you 'when' to see who you are today is like seeking the Holy Grail; people often have a hard time letting go of historical perceptions of you and embracing your evolving Soul alignment, especially if they are not on a transformational path themselves.

Sometimes the reason you resist embracing your truth is because you believe cultural or familial lies that diminish your wisdom and sovereignty. You may have been conditioned not to stand out, to call attention to yourself, nor to be bold. You may have felt like you were a burden, or too much, or in the way. You might believe the story that you're the problem, and somehow you are to blame for the conditions of your loved ones' lives because you began walking a spiritual path that led to your personal autonomy. You may feel responsible for your loved ones, to lift and support them in this lifetime; and this strong need to rescue can be tempered by restating **you are here to guide and encourage those who are willing to evolve**.

One morning I woke to a sleepy dream where I saw a vision of a shepherd walking in a field with a huge sack on his back. As I got closer to the shepherd, I saw that the sack was wriggling. I looked inside the sack to see dozens of sheep. Then I heard White Eagle say "Sheep can walk."

I realized in this moment that although there is truth that I am here in service to my family of origin, and to many other humans on the planet, I am not here to carry everyone on my back. Sheep can walk. I am only here to guide and watch over those I serve with compassion, understanding, and love. The job feels a lot less oppressive that way because actually, it's sized appropriately for my human-ness.

As you go through this process of re-wiring, the least helpful energy is self-judgment, and the most helpful energies are curiosity and compassion. You did not get 'here' overnight; it took thousands of years of ancestral practice to learn the human drama. You must be patient, loving and kind as you retrain yourself to think, act, and relate from Love.

♥

Power Over To Power Within

A pervasive aspect of the Mother Wound is the Power Over paradigm of the patriarchy which seeks to control and subjugate people into hierarchies of power, rather than uplift and empower people horizontally. The goal of the Power Over program is to keep you entangled with others, fighting over power, money, status, 'rightness', and so forth. As long as you prioritize things that you get from the outside world, you'll be lured into power struggles with others. For example, if you allow yourself to value being 'right', then you will find yourself in many debates with others who also value being 'right.' If you must hold others accountable for their wrongs toward you, then you will be locked in a showdown with a person who may never admit the wrong, nor apologize as you desire. If you require someone to validate your beliefs or behaviors, then you are putting your power on hold as you await their opinion; you are diminishing your own light in favor of another's perspective.

Any time you believe that you need something from someone else in order to survive, you've given that person power over you. If your sense of peace is dependent upon holding a certain title at a company, or living in a certain neighborhood, or being married to a certain person, then your power is entangled in things over which you have no control, and you have therefore disempowered yourself.

If someone does not give you what you feel you deserve, now you can be locked into a cycle of shame, blame, anger, resentment, judgment, and punitive behaviors that only serve to drag your consciousness down into an old matrix that has enslaved humanity for thousands of years.

Do you understand that the entire way you've been led to believe is the 'way it is' or 'how life works' is a lie created by a small group of people that desired control over others to gain 'power'? This lie rippled forth through generations subjected to torture, enslavement, war, persecution—the fear of which lives on in the ancestral DNA of the very body you currently inhabit.

When one or more people leverage Universal Law and the power of co-creation to place themselves in Power Over other beings, that is called sorcery. You can be an unwitting accomplice to sorcery when you are unaware of your Power Within, and have the underlying belief structures that lead you to agree to give away your power, allowing yourself to be dominated, or repress your free will out of fear. Rebellion is still an act complicit with believing someone has power over you, and gives the sorcerer power.

Why do people willingly give up their power to sorcery? Our minds are sponges as children and we believe everything we're told, so we are unaware there is any other possible reality. And once the truth is realized, it can be shocking; it seems easier to stay with the known disempowering reality rather than face tremendous resistance to overturn the fear matrix and reclaim sovereign power of co-creation.

The truth is that everyone on Earth has access to the only power they require: Power Within. The power within is what Jesus was demonstrating to humanity, and it is within you, lying dormant yet ready to be activated. You awaken this power within by doing exactly what you were falsely warned against: commune with your Mother. Honor your Mother. Worship your Mother.

The Great Spirit encompasses all that is...including you. Mother Earth helps you bring your Spirit into a physical form so that you can feel, laugh, sing, dance, play, and create in the material realm. 'God' is not a bearded white man sitting on a cloud out there somewhere. You are an aspect of the Great Spirit expressing itself in physical form through the collaboration of your material teacher, Mother Earth.

Mother Earth is at the end of allowing us hurt ourselves and destroy her forests, animals, oceans, mountains. Like any mother who sees her children intentionally and blindly choosing to suffer, she wants us to wake up and see the truth. We are living in a beautiful garden of infinite possibility that is here to help us discover, grow, learn, evolve, and expand human consciousness. She doesn't prefer to set it all on fire, but she will if that's what she must do to get our attention.

To help humanity raise its consciousness, Mother Earth invited help from across the galaxy. The Second Wave is now, and its mission is to uplift human consciousness by embodying in human form and healing it from the inside out. Members of the Second Wave are old souls and ascended masters who have assisted species on other planets to raise consciousness to the level that they can be full participants in galactic consciousness. Up until now, humanity has been too violent to have access to other lifeforms, and has been isolated until the evolution we are now undergoing.

In whatever way possible, you must make the shift to Power Within and commune with Mother Earth to unlock the tremendous potential of your humanity. To do this, you must untangle from the false programs of the last thousands of years, heal and transform ancestral patterns to purify your vessel, and practice self-mastery to heal the Mother Wound within and elevate to a new level of consciousness.

Essentially, you must let go of the things you are holding others accountable for, otherwise known as karma. When you hold another accountable for their actions, you involve yourself in their karma. For thousands of years humans have been playing the game of who is more righteous than the other and who is more to blame. To play the game of accountability is to carry a burden of remembrance of hurt in your energy field that reminds you of how this person has hurt you for lifetimes.

In other words, to play the game of being the accounter of someone else's sins is to carry a burden on yourself that actually does not belong to you because that job belongs to Great Spirit.

The game of accounting is a losing game because the cards you are holding are a history of wrongs that you will only allow to be resolved by making another person pay. The only payment you accept is that person must admit their wrong to you and apologize. But when you admit your wrong and apologize in this game, you are no longer righteous, you have now admitted you are wrong and so you lose the game.

No one playing this game wants to lose and therefore everyone playing this game refuses to be wrong and remains believing falsely they are righteous.

In fact, no one playing this game is righteous because it is never righteous to hold another accountable to you in place of the Great Spirit. The true teacher is the Great Spirit, and in form, Mother Earth. To make yourself the accounter of another's wrongs is to replace yourself as the teacher of that person which is a lie, and a lie is a burden on your Soul.

If you hold onto anger, resentment, and a requirement that another person repay you for this burden that you created from feeling wronged, then you make yourself the teacher of this person which is false, a lie, and you become burdened by your own lie.

Wanting another person to pay for their wrongs that you perceived is making that person pay for what is your responsibility: to surrender your judgments back to Great Spirit and ask for clarification and teaching so you can continue your souls curriculum illuminated.

To forgive another person is to realize that you were playing teacher and burdening yourself with lies that were causing great hurt to yourself. You can certainly discern when a person has gone astray from a teaching of Great Spirit, and yes, help this person in the way instructed by Great Spirit in that moment to illuminate them with realization. This is your gift. This gift operates in higher consciousness. It does not operate in the game of holding others accountable.

Attempts to illuminate or make people realize spiritual truth in the game of holding others accountable will fall on deaf ears. Attempts to hold another accountable will never result in that person's realization. The ego is too stubborn to admit wrong doing; it prefers pain over being wrong and will endure the most excruciating pain in an effort to deny wrongs and 'win' by being righteous.

Being righteous is playing a losing game because the burden of lies on your Soul prevent the realization that would help you truly 'win' by ascending your consciousness with realization.

The only answer is restore the lies to truth by relinquishing your imagined 'debts' and putting down your cards and saying 'you win' and walking away from the table of the game of holding others accountable.

In this way you receive the far greater gift which is the realization that you were invested in a false game that was burdening your Soul and closing your heart and stealing your joy.

The way to win is to give the Great Spirit every judgment you hold against another, lay down all the cards from former lives and this life where someone owes you an apology or an admitting of wrongdoing, and walk away from the table.

You do not, in fact, owe anyone an apology for anything they imagine you have done to them. You only must unburden your own Soul for anything weighing you down as a way you have wronged another. Untangle yourself from others by releasing these karmic 'debts'. And then the apology is given to release yourself from the burden you created for yourself.

This is the inner work to cultivate inner power and let go of the paradigm of power over. In the Power Over world, you can imagine that humans are like trees who have wrapped their roots around each other's trunks, squeezing each other tight trying to get nourishment where there is none to be had. In the Power Within world, humans are like trees whose roots sink deep into the full reservoirs of Mother Earth, drinking up plentiful nourishment from unobstructed pathways, and allowing their brothers and sisters to be as they are.

As you claim your Power Within, you will still be operating in a world where others are largely operating from Power Over. You can become aware of unawakened people grasping for control through whatever means they can, and also be aware of the Power Within, the I Am Presence within you, that is eternal and beyond control. Remember to access your I Am Presence for guidance; it will lead you by breadcrumbs past control traps set by unawakened minds.

Nurture your body and mind with Love to allow it to rest into your I Am Presence for support. We are in the shift. The egoic structures of fear and control lash out and come back with an empty fist. The Divine light is beyond grasping. **As you access the Power Within, the I Am Presence, you spread the light as a beacon of the frequency of Love, calling people back to remember their Power Within.**

♥

Comparison and Dissatisfaction

Comparison is an act of violence against the self. —Iyanla Vanzant

The patriarchal systems of conformity and hierarchy have created the false idea that there are one-size-fits-all pathways to a successful life, and that our success depends on how well we measure up to others along that pathway. We must compete with others for limited resources, limited hierarchical positions, limited prosperity, and limited recognition.

Women have been trained that the 'good men' are rare, and we must compete over them since living a successful life includes having a man. There are ancestral traditions of valuation of women for matrimony by beauty, family, status, education and so forth. These systems make it seem like some women are more a 'prize' than others in a general sort of way; as if any man would see this woman as a prize because of her pedigree.

While these traditions have faded somewhat with women's empowerment, the lingering effects of comparison and dissatisfaction remain. Just notice the way we elevate certain ideals of beauty by featuring some female actresses often on the covers of magazines. Are there lots of magazine covers with Meryl Streep? Or is it more likely to see a cover with Angelina Jolie? If magazine covers indicate 'success', it seems like the competition to get there is pretty steep; how many people have the 'flawless' beauty that an actress has (especially with some Photoshop touchups)?

The comparison to these societal 'ideals' create a perceived 'us' and 'them'; 'us' the regular people with irregular skin tone and asymmetrical features and 'them' the anomalies of beauty put on a pedestal as a 'normal' ideal that you should be aiming for. Do you feel good about yourself when you see these covers, or does some little part of you say something like 'that will never be me'? In other words, does a part of you critique yourself for not being 'on the level' with a woman like that? Or do you just write it off with 'I don't want to be famous' and wonder how much plastic surgery she's had?

Notice how derisive even that little paragraph of exploration is, and consider the larger daily framework of comparison to others, and dissatisfaction with self. Comparison to others sends a message to your subconscious that you're missing out, and that you want to have that fullness for yourself; your self-assessment determines whether you think it's possible for you to get what you perceive she has. Have you ever thought you wanted what someone else had, and then you actually got it and were disappointed? Have you ever followed the recommended pathway, done all the right things, gotten all the accomplishments, and still ended up hollow and unfulfilled?

Or have you gone for it like your friends and colleagues, and not been able to succeed? Why can't you get what they have? Why do you struggle to receive the bounty? It's right there in your hands and then it slips through your fingers on the way to consuming it. It's not substantial, or the moment of receiving it is fleeting. Your taste buds tingle, and then the sensation is over and you're empty again and want more so you seek more.

It's like your insides can't absorb the gifts of your accomplishments, your family, and your life. The wealth passes right through without being received. You try to fill your cup but it seeps out as you're filling up and so you're constantly seeking and caught in an endless cycle of not having enough or not being enough. You cannot seem to rest into a sense of *havingness*.

Do you ever feel the fullness of gratitude for what you receive? Or do you feel the temporary relief from scarcity and emptiness? You have just long enough to take a breath in relief before the cycle of acquisition or perfection begins again to fill the emptiness. You see another having a success that now you want to have so you can be as successful as she is. You're back on the quest to compete and obtain another marker of success.

What blocks you from becoming full and deeply nourished with what you already have? What keeps you empty so you have to climb back on the wheel to run faster and harder to get more and look better?

Comparison leads to dissatisfaction and disappointment because when you build your life around having what others have, and comparing yourself to others to assess your level of 'success', you're tuned into false measures that will never be deeply nourishing because they have very little to do with who YOU actually are, and what makes YOU happy.

All that outward focus to assess your success leaves you blinded to the gifts inside of yourself, and the gifts that the Divine has brought to your doorstep. **To discover your inherent wealth, you must look within yourself and honestly assess what brings you joy and fulfillment.** Understanding your unique human design helps you to see that you are unlike others, so it is fruitless to compare yourself to them. There is not one measure of success, there are billions. There is not one pathway to a successful life, there are billions of pathways to lives that look very different from one another.

Get to know yourself and be courageous enough to build a life that feels successful to you, even if it looks really different than what you see in the world around you. This is the shift into sovereignty: to honor your own knowing as your first priority. You can certainly still be inspired by others as you open to a life that feels aligned with your personal truth; just do what you do because you want to do it, not because it has anything to do with other people's ideas and expectations.

Choosing your own measure of 'success' based on your own visions and ideals is the ultimate sovereign authority. Claim it.

♥

Expectations To Detachment

You are conditioned from birth with expectations for how 'good' people behave, and then rewarded for behaving like a 'good person' and punished for not behaving as desired. You have learned cultural expectations for how 'good children' act—quiet, respectful, obedient, conforming to rules—and when you start to wake up from that societally-conditioned dream you may ask yourself whether the 'wild child' was actually a strong independent thinker expressing herself.

As a mother you have expectations that your children will respect and honor you, communicate with you, spend holidays with you, and include you on their life journeys. If that does not happen, you get an incredible opportunity to explore the suffering created by your expectations.

There have been several Mothers Days, birthdays, and holidays where my eldest did not feel inspired to connect with me, to send a message or card, or to acknowledge the significance of the day in any way. I demonstrated 'correct protocol' for honoring people in your life at holidays over the course of his two decades of life, so he 'knows better'. The first time this happened I was deeply wounded. I took it personally and that dredged up suppressed feelings of resentment for the daily sacrifices of motherhood over decades...the unacknowledged and unappreciated efforts to give my son a good home.

Was I making all those sacrifices over those two decades with the expectation that my son would reciprocate with thoughtfulness?

Many spiritual teachers have shared that expectation leads to suffering. Indeed, I can confirm that it does. When you have expectations that things happen in a certain way, and then someone does not come along with your vision of how it should be, what do you do?

The old version of me resorted to control, manipulation, judgment, guilt, condemnation, and any other tactic designed to get my son back into line with the culturally significant ways of demonstrating his appreciation of me as his mother. I was just repeating what I had experienced from my mother if I had ever forgotten to acknowledge her importance on a special day. What I realized after my awakening was that if you don't mean it, it's actually far less juicy then doing it when you mean it. Bottom line: his card on Mother's Day when done as an obligation, and not a truth in his heart, feels like crap.

There was one Mother's Day where I felt like I was literally dragging my sons along with me to 'celebrate', and they were so completely disinterested and disconnected that I just felt lucky to get a few pictures with them that made it *look* like we were enjoying ourselves together. Obligatory cards and gifts are just a pretense that let you off the hook from exploring your real feelings, and your children's feelings, about how you showed up as a mother—so you can spiritual bypass self-evaluation.

After facing that self-evaluation and pain, I got the first glimmer of not taking it personally that my son's heart was not generous enough in the moment to be grateful and express it. Am I going to take it personally that someone whose self-awareness is just beginning to open up, someone who is in the self-involved phase of existence we all go through, is not able to lift himself out of himself to consider the feelings of another person? Taken another way, is a math teacher going to feel like a failure because his student does not yet understand the math lesson? Or is that math teacher going to find another way for the student to finally 'get it'?

Am I going to wait to be honored as a mother until someone else chooses to see it and tell me that I deserve it? Because if I choose this path, I am choosing codependency; I am choosing to defer self-fulfillment and honoring until something outside of me shifts me to provide it. This opens the door to disingenuous honoring.

I've also faced my expectations and entitlement as a daughter. As long as my Dad was alive, I felt I had a safety net to take risks in my life. I felt that no matter what happened, I had a family that would help me through it. When my Dad died, I discovered that my mother did not feel the same way. I had expectations that she would be my mother, my ally, no matter what. I found out that my choice to express myself through books and podcasts was not automatically compatible with having a relationship with my mother, and I felt my mother withdraw. By accident, I discovered my family having gatherings without me. It was like a knife through the heart, and it was an opportunity to explore my expectations.

Did I expect financial support or a promised inheritance from my Dad after his death? I was led through a series of events where I realized that my empowerment lay on the other side of releasing this expectation and sense of entitlement. I replaced this negative attachment with trust in the Divine to lead me to prosperity that was cleanly, clearly mine.

Anything that you are attached to, or feel entitled to, can be used as a weapon against you in the human drama. It can be leveraged to cause you pain by withholding love. **When you operate in the human drama, you are exchanging love for conditions.**

And so the antidote to expectation and conditional love is detachment. **Detachment means you are not attached to the outcome, you are present with what is currently unfolding, and you are curious about how this benefits your growth.** You trust the Divine and the process you are being guided through for your evolution. You allow yourself to be realigned to a more true way of being in the world that gives you the freedom to authentically express your Love, and to give your Love freely without conditions. And you commit to the process of this realignment which presents many little challenges that provoke places of expectation within you so you can explore them and make new choices.

I have learned to differentiate between expectations and desires. I no longer expect my sons to do behaviors that give me a sense of being honored. I do clearly express to the Divine my desire to feel honored as a mother in any way that is available to me. In expressing my desires, I let the Divine factor my preferences into its magical recipe of synchronous fulfillment that takes into account all other sovereign desires and then alchemize to deliver to me what I desire (or even better) in right timing through authentic channels.

By sharing my desires and allowing the Divine to align me with any source for fulfilling them, I get to witness the consciousness matrix at work while simultaneously honoring the sovereignty of those closest to me which gives them the freedom to authentically express their own hearts and desires (and not feel caged by mine).

When we let go of expectations, we can open with curiosity to be delighted at how our desires are fulfilled. We can celebrate the magical matrix for its cleverness and astounding sensitivity to all sentient beings to match everyone up for co-learning and co-creation. The vibration of celebration helps you enjoy the process as it's unfolding rather than holding your breath waiting for what you want to materialize, or someone to do something you want, before you acquiesce to happiness.

♥

Competition To Celebration

Something that many women of my generation have experienced is the feeling like you are in competition with other women, and at the root of this is a feeling of being in competition with your mother. It can feel as if your mother is a jealous sister, battling within herself to be happy for you and your successes. This experience is in direct opposition to the image of the perfect mother: cheering you on at the sidelines of your game, talking highly of you to her peers, taking time off work to celebrate your accomplishments, having heart-to-heart conversations where she lets you know just how proud of you she is.

When you have a mother who competes with you, it feels as if nothing you do is ever enough to win her praise. She says she wants you to be successful, but then when you are, she dismisses it with little more than a nod. She criticizes you when you go for a goal and don't succeed, and she diminishes your accomplishments by making no comments and by not celebrating them. She may even make it seem as if your success was at her expense somehow and you owe her something to make up for it.

In early childhood you may have experienced a mother that seemed proud of you, and then as you began to blossom into womanhood the problems with your mother sprouted like weeds in the garden. This is because you start to become a threat to a competitive mother's territory when you step into your moon cycles.

You may have experienced a subconscious competition over the attention of the man of the house. If you start getting too much praise and attention from your father, then your mother jealously steps in to exert her authority as the Queen and let you know that your time is up. Usually there is a redirection toward 'adult' time and you're summarily dismissed to your room to entertain yourself. I have some clients whose mothers actually overtly addressed this underlying sexual competition with statements like "Why don't you put it out there? I'm sure he'd take you up on it." The natural love between a daughter and her father thereby gets tainted by the fear of sexual impropriety.

If this resonates with you, a potent inquiry is to look within for where you still want your mother's validation or approval before you feel you can go for it in your life. Do you lower yourself to fit under the ceiling of your mother's 'level of success' so as not to compete with her and make her comfortable by being less successful than her? Is there a paradigm in your family of a hierarchy of importance that firmly places your mother at the top of the ladder, just by virtue of being the mother? In this hierarchy, are you forever required to stifle your own voice and dreams so as to not outperform your mother and trigger her insecurities? When you start to break free from the suppression, and you begin expressing yourself as a sovereign being, does your mother shut you out of the family? When you begin to exert your own power and voice, does your throat tighten up like it is being squeezed?

If you experienced competition with your mother or the women in your family, you will very likely bring that dynamic into other areas of your life. You might notice yourself seeing the success of a female friend—maybe she has a new love relationship or a success in her career—and instead of feeling happy for her, or inspired by her, you feel jealous of her and go into self-judgment about your own life. "Why am I not experiencing that same success?" "Why don't I have a partner like she does?" And from there, the stories can spiral downwards, depending on your current level of healing the wound of competition.

While writing this book I discovered that a fellow spiritual teacher, a woman I considered to be a sister of light, had been speaking badly about me in her program to her students. When I called to talk to her about it, she sent me to voicemail. When I looked on social media, I saw she had removed me; in fact, blocked me. Why? I do not know because she never had a conversation with me. I was not aware of anything I had done to her to cause her to react in this way, and it remains a mystery.

How often do women choose to berate one another and speak behind each other's backs rather than be courageous and have a difficult conversation? How often do these same women smile and pretend to your face that everything is ok when really, they have something to say and lack the courage to speak?

This is another way the dynamic of competition caused by the Mother Wound divides women. You must see this pattern for what it is and choose to be fearless enough to speak with love to the person with whom you have a hard thing to say. You must see that the Mother

Wound was put there to divide women and to disempower us by making us compete for resources.

Women: we don't need men to tear us down. We do it to ourselves.

These patterns of competition come by way of ancestral traumas and the conditioned behaviors women adopted to protect themselves in a world that subjugated and abused them. Where does the fear that your daughter will take your husband come from? Past history. It has happened in our ancestry. It is best not to take it personally, the competition from your mother that left you feeling unloved and uncelebrated. It is not personal, it is a pattern in humanity that is expressing itself through your individual life. It certainly feels personal, and the pain of it in your heart alerts you to its presence so that you can leverage the tools of transformation to extricate yourself from historical patterns of suffering and discover peace through becoming a person in right relationship to her world.

Up until now we have let conditioned patterns and ancestral thinking guide our actions, and it is time to stop slamming doors and throwing away sisters, mothers and daughters like disposable trash. Our generation has big work to do for the turning of the ages.

Not only must you become aware of these patterns of competition from your ancestry and childhood conditioning, but you must heal yourself of them and reach for a more loving archetype of mother who celebrates her children and lifts them to rise higher than you have. You must give what you have not received. If you want to feel powerful next to your sister, let her inspire you to rise. If you see a mistake your sister is making, share your point of view to help her become stronger. It takes a great deal of inner awareness to make the invisible visible, and self-mastery to comfort your inner child while you give more than you ever received to your own children, your sisters, and your mother. **The more you heal the Mother Wound within you, the more you can stand beside your mother, sisters and daughters as a unified front for Love.**

The first step of healing is to open to the bigger mother: the Divine Mother. In this way you become a sister to your biological mother and her top-down power matrix crumbles. As you receive love and support from the Divine Mother and the Great Spirit, you can begin healing your inner child and reassuring her that there's a new sheriff in town that has her best interests at heart and the power to back her up. As your inner child begins to trust you and transition her loyalty from your competitive mother (who has her own interests at heart) to you (who has your inner child's best interests at heart), you will find yourself able to create forward momentum and traction towards your own goals and dreams with greater peace and certainty.

If your mother is threatened by your power, expect there to be a situation arise in the family where people are forced to take 'sides'. This is your opportunity to trust your own process, trust the Divine Mother, and be an unwavering champion of your inner child and your own Soul. **You get to become the supportive cheerleader of yourself that you always wanted from your mother.**

The more you take steps into your purpose and truth, the more power and self-love you gain. The more power and self-love you gain, the less you feel your mother is withholding something from you that you require to be happy. The less you need love and approval from your mother, the less power she has to manipulate and control you to fit into her power matrix so she can feel powerful. And when you finally break free from the power struggle with your mother, you can feel compassion for your mother who is ensnared by a historical ancestral pattern that led her to believe she was powerless unless she had power over you.

You've got to take the courageous journey step by step, facing all the inner and outer obstacles to embody the truth of your personal sovereignty, to know in truth what I have shared here. Otherwise, it's just words and the compassion you say you have for your mother is actually a spiritual bypass which attempts to avoid the pain of separation from your mother and family by jumping to the finish line.

Many times I thought I would just put a lid on it and not say anything real about myself in front of my mother to 'keep the peace'. This did not work because she began watching my social media and then, from her fear, creating family allegiances for protection as I stepped deeper into my purpose work. For me, there has been no other palatable option than to be fully sovereign and activated on my purpose path. My mother put up a wall because she did not want me to talk about her or the family. This poses a unique challenge for me when I know my Soul purpose is to disrupt ancestral patterns of suffering and to heal the Mother Wound that each of us carries, and then to be a messenger and share with others what I have learned. **When you ask a beloved to choose between honoring your fears, and honoring their Soul path, that is a very difficult impasse.**

I cannot speak for my mother, I can only speak to my perceptions and experience of growing up with the generational mother/daughter paradigms of which she was an unwitting accomplice—and that is the tightrope that I walk as I write.

In the closing of this section, I'll share a story from when I was eighteen and a senior in high school. I had gotten a new car with my own money, and bought a keychain with a curly telephone cord twisted into a rope. The keychain was tight and curled up, and when pulled on it could stretch a foot. My mother and I had gotten into an argument and I grabbed my keys and purse to head for the car. She grabbed the other end of the keychain and got into a tug-of-war with me over the keys. She pulled and pulled until the keychain broke free from my grasp and she 'won', a dark gleeful smile of victory spreading across her face. This exchange made me feel that I had no power, and that she had all the power, and she was willing to do anything to remind me of it. I ran out of the house, down the street to my neighborhood friend, and disappeared for several days without a phone call home. So that was my answer as a teenager, to disappear.

During the writing of this book, that memory resurfaced during a healing session. I realized that I was still held back by that moment in my history where my mother exerted her authority over me. I decided to let her have the curly-que keychain and her victory, which had turned into a 'taking sides' family situation in my current adult life. I simply let go. I chose non-engagement, one of the principles taught by the Four Winds Light Body School.

Non-engagement means seeing the dynamic that is happening, and choosing to not participate in it. Not participating in it means not holding out for a better outcome, not trying to convince anyone of my perspective, not talking about the details of the situation to win people over to my point of view, and not thinking about it. Every time you think about a person that wants to have a power struggle with you, or you think about the situation itself and tell it to others, you're engaging in the power struggle. Some people create power struggles simply to get energy from the other people they're involving in the power struggle; whether they are aware of it or not, they're feeding off the struggle.

So I let go of the keychain and all that it symbolized. I am capable of being happy, loved, and supported without coercing my mother to participate in my life to bring me these feelings. I found my Source, and I maintain awareness in presence of my sovereignty and the Love that I am. This fills me up and gives me what I require to live a happy, peaceful and fulfilled life; I simply need to remind myself of this truth whenever I feel the longing for my mother's love.

Further, I recognize that my mother is ensnared by patterns of suffering that are generational and learned. The light that is my mother is underneath all that crusty painful stuff. I often send Love to the light that is my mother, to the Soul that is my sister. I witness both of us tussling with tough patterns, and discovering many lessons about power. Maybe she'll realize she doesn't need a power struggle to be in relationship with me, maybe she won't. It's not for me to say.

In the meantime, I focus my attention on the people who cross my path that desire to be liberated from past suffering and discover what's possible as we step out of the power struggles and into sovereignty as beings equally loved by the Divine Mother. Women who have power within can easily celebrate one another's accomplishments because we know that each individual's healing becomes a new pattern for the collective human consciousness to expand and benefit from. So thank you sisters for doing the work to shine. I celebrate you. And I ask you today to make this pledge: **We will not allow anything to divide us!**

♥

Seriousness To Playfulness

I've witnessed a paradigm in Western society whereby being a boisterous child was unacceptable, and even embarrassing to the parents. Have you heard the message that you must 'behave' yourself and not 'act out'? Were you encouraged to 'grow up'? I've witnessed parents, and done the same myself, try to project an image of success that did not include children running, playing, yelling, and laughing loudly. When flying on a plane with my babies, I felt the pressure to keep them from crying, and felt mortified whenever my tiny sons did not comply. Where does this need to suppress a child originate?

As a child, I knew growing up that the world belonged to my parents, and I had better behave if I wanted to stay a part of it. I remember many times where I was feeling upset about an admonishment from my mother to 'behave in adult company.' If I started to cry she would apply more pressure and tell me to stop 'making a scene'. I would be sent to my room if I could not comply. This kind of punishment was common in my mother's generation, and much milder than the type of punishment they experienced from their mothers. This pattern of punishment was so unconscious for my mother that she did it as a matter of course until I got too big to do it.

Did you overtly get the message that being a child was an inconvenience to the adults in your life? Or did you notice more subtle and pervasive attitudes toward 'misbehaving' children in public? If you were raised by parents versed in parenting by control, you may have perceived that demonstrating big emotions around adults was poor behavior and not to be tolerated. You may have learned to be a chameleon to bring yourself into alignment with others' feelings. You may have learned how to 'contain yourself', stuff down your laughter and joy when it was 'inappropriate', and lower your vibration to match the person in your environment who is feeling pain to be 'respectful' toward them. It's a system of repressing natural emotional expression to match yourself to an expectation of being neutral or 'under the radar'.

Repeated punishment in childhood for expressing natural joy and playfulness leads to an unconscious belief that joy and playfulness are embarrassing. Repeated punishment in childhood for expressing anger leads to an unconscious belief that you don't have a right to feel angry nor speak up about it. Often the person who has experienced these messages in childhood will pick a partner who adopts a consistent attitude of seriousness so they will have to keep bringing their joy down to fit under that ceiling. Controlling your emotional state is a protection mechanism to avoid punishment in childhood, and it is a lie people tell themselves long after its efficacy for survival.

It's actually painful to hold back your natural feelings. Suppressing your feelings is how the crust is formed around your heart and after a while of forcing this unnatural system you find yourself unable to feel nor believe that anything greater is possible. When a person conditioned to restrain joy sees someone outwardly exhibiting joy there's resentment of that person and distrust: "They're lying. No one is that happy." That level of happiness in a paradigm of not-feeling seems impossible. But what if the happy person is truly happy? What if they managed to break through the inner barrier of seriousness that was suppressing their joy?

And as if to make the point, right at the moment I was finishing the last sentence a big brown dog bounded out of nowhere as I sat on my front lawn writing, and began lavishing my face with kisses. The pure joy and playfulness emanating from this dog refused to be pushed away or denied. It was as if Love itself forced its way into my heart and expelled layers of resistance with every determined lick of that dog's tongue upon my cheeks. I began weeping and laughing all at once realizing the profound message being sent by the Divine Mother through this animal.

You never really got to play and be a kid and be silly, Kerri. But it's never too late. It's right here in front of you, inviting you in the most blatantly obvious way.

And now I'm remembering my rescue dog with her adorable white fur and one eye surrounded by brown fur. She was sweet and playful even after surviving being left with her mother and four siblings in a fenced yard in the Texas heat without water and food for weeks. The animal rescue named her 'Trouble'. I rejected that name as an insult to her character. I asked her what her name was. I heard the word 'Faith'. And so we named her Imani which is Swahili for Faith.

In just the same way, I was often called Trouble by my mother. My true nature was Faith. Faith is what we need to cultivate when Love is not present. Love has not been present for thousands of years except in a few rare cases of the enlightened ones. We live in a world that has been conditioned to think that the greatest accomplishment is to have Faith that Love exists. We are about to discover that the greatest accomplishment is to Know that Love Is All That Is: including us. We're not bad children that need to earn love (lowercase). **We are Divine beings that get the privilege of practicing self-mastery to unleash Love (legit Love) into a world that has been starving from the lack of it.**

There's not some imaginary being in a cloud that's going to grant you Love after you've earned it by suffering from your sins. You are waking up to the Love that you already are by choosing to become aware of the mental conditioning from human history that has told you otherwise, and firmly deciding to move through Fear to release patterns of suffering that shut the Love out.

What diminishes your ability to feel joy, gratitude, Love and awe is your mental conditioning that you are unaware of. If you were aware of it, you most certainly would make a different choice, right? Well maybe you're unaware of it most of the time, and when you begin acting from it you might become aware of it but then feel stubbornly obstinate about changing it.

You've got to exercise a few muscles to feel Love and its friends: stillness, awareness and determination to change.

For example, I've come to experience true grounded Joy. Grounded joy is what happens when you honor your stillness and tap into the deep waters within. Earlier in my life I experienced frantic happiness which is different than grounded Joy. Frantic happiness is pushing the energy upwards by using mental games and mantras and dance: it's really 'working it' to shift your mind and mood. It works but it's not sustainable. The more profound and longer lasting feeling of Joy is possible once you are present with the deep waters within which requires facing the not-so-wonderful feelings you banished there during the time in your life when you were forcing your happiness and shunning anything that was not happy. **Getting to true grounded Joy is a messy process of clearing out your inner closets where all the things are buried you never wanted to face.**

Which leads me to the muscle of awareness. You often repeat the same patterns as your parents without even realizing it. There's extra resistance to seeing these patterns when you do not want to 'be like them.' The muscle of awareness is being courageous enough to see into your shadows to reveal the unconscious behaviors you're doing, and when you get a fish biting the line: pull it up out of the water and investigate it. I didn't say berate yourself. I said investigate it. Bring curiosity to what you find under the surface of your consciousness.

Patterns from the Mother Wound run deep and are hard to see sometimes. I had to admit at one point that I was acting from a pattern my mother had of being unhappy with my Dad's disorganization, and overspending, and losing his wallet and keys, and so forth. It seemed to me that she often focused on the negatives rather than the greater truth that my Dad was a kindhearted loving person with incredible patience and wisdom. Then I caught myself in the pattern I learned from my mother! I found myself criticizing Akeem for losing his wallet and keys, and being disorganized, and overspending.

Luckily I reminded myself of a quote from Don Miguel Ruiz "If you cannot love your partner the way she is, someone else can love her just as she is. Don't waste your time, and don't waste your partner's time. That is respect."

Lastly is the determination to change. Most people are stuck in the same patterns as their parents, and their parents before them, because they either refuse to become aware of the unconscious, or do not have the determination to change the things they find. Changing your consciousness requires a moment-by-moment decision to reframe your language, redirect your attention, and refocus on your intention.

An example is my awareness that in my consciousness up until the writing of this book, I often revisited historical scenes from my life and replayed them in my mind. In this way, I lost myself to the present by focusing attention on the past. As I began to unravel this pattern, I brought awareness to the sensation of historical viewing in my mind. I realized that it felt like a pulling to the left, and that I would actually draw my eyes up and to the left when I was about to do it. So I chose to become aware of the behavior of drawing my eyes up and to the left, and consistently redirect myself back to the present moment by gazing straight ahead. It's a small shift that, taken consistently, has vastly improved my presence and awareness of the Now moment, which is where all true power resides.

As you shift from seriousness to playfulness, tune into how you feel on the inside and avoid the external comparison game discussed earlier in the book. Social media is a place that can ensnare you in a feeling of not 'being there' yet when you see pictures of people living total joy; it can make you want to tuck away your less-than-joy like a shameful secret.

Realize that it is not an all-or-nothing destination to playfulness and joy. **There are moments of elation sandwiched right next to moments of despair.** You get to hold it all as a human being. If you deny the moments of not-joy then you're involved in self-delusion, and if you're dwelling in the not-joy then you're addicted to the suffering.

Instead, notice the moments of not-joy, breathe through them, and listen to what's underneath so it can express itself and release. Then practice a tool to lift yourself to peace, to contentedness, and ultimately to joy. Expand the joy without trampling the shadows.

Welcome the joy to take her place next to peace, fear, anger, happiness, and pain.

♥

A Burden To Being Cherished

Ultimately many of the unloving patterns you may have experienced as a child, when distilled down to a root cause, is that the primary adults in your life felt encumbered or burdened by your child-ness. Children are so tapped into their parents, and sensitive children can feel every nuance.

I remember feeling my mother's irritation rising up when she had enough of me resting my head in her lap; I loved the feeling of nurturing as she gently stroked my hair, and I dreaded the moment that her willingness to nurture me would turn into irritation and she would push me away. It became a pattern in my life to distrust closeness with partners because I was always waiting for the shoe to drop: for them to push me away. To avoid this pain, I would often be the first to push away whenever I felt the intimacy feeling too nurturing and loving. In this way, I denied myself the deep nurturing connection I truly desired for most of my life up until I met my partner Akeem.

Because of my dedication to awareness and spiritual practice, I was finally in a place to hold myself through the discomfort of crossing the threshold into vulnerability and love and staying there past the impulses to flee or disconnect. In this way, I expanded my capacity to experience loving connection which helped me to stay in the loving vulnerability even if something not desirable arose (like disagreement).

Were your parents stressed out about money, working hard at full-time jobs, or overwhelmed by other situations in their lives (like mental, emotional, or physical illness) when you were a child? Perceiving the heaviness of these burdens on your parents may have made you not want to be one more problem; or your parent may have overtly indicated that your presence, in fact, added to the sense of overwhelm.

Even a small remark made over and over—"you're such a pain in the neck"—can stick with you as a pattern into adulthood. Because I received this repeated message over decades in my early life, I tended to carry a lot of tension in my neck whenever I was feeling burdened. On my healing journey, my partner patiently spent hours massaging this place on my body to unpack trapped feelings and negative self-concepts, and to fill it up with the new reality of being loved and cherished. **Having greater body awareness is a key part of healing trauma stuck in the tissues from these early reinforced messages.**

If you somehow received the sense that you were a burden to your parents (through any number of nuanced messages and perceptions), you may notice that you apologize for yourself, almost as if you're apologizing that you are alive and taking up space. You may find it hard to ask for what you want, knowing that you're already tipping the scale towards being burdensome and now asking for something you desire pushes you well past the point of acceptance. You may have felt the need to compensate for your burdensome self by over-giving to others out of a sense of apology.

You may not be sure what exact aspect of you is the source of the burden, so you may have spent a good deal of time tightening yourself up to be impeccable and beyond critique. Although, it doesn't seem to work because you realize you are like an elephant in a china closet, and even with the best intentions you seem to send someone else's valuables crashing down by simply breathing...so can you breathe a little less conspicuously please?

The child who feels unwanted, unseen, and unheard grows into an adult who feels burdened by herself and her emotional needs.

The adult has learned to 'step over' these childhood feelings and 'get on with it' using the will center, yet typically feels burdened by the responsibilities of her life. The child who feels she is a burden grows into the adult that knows she is a burden who then has children who she feels burdened by. Except there is a tiny voice inside her that reminds her how awful it is to be a child who feels like you're a burden to your parent, and now there's all the research to show how a loving parent does not make her child feel like a burden, and so the woman who has not healed the inner wound of burden not only feels all the burdensome conditioning, but judges herself for it. The mother who judges herself as being a burden, and feels her children are burdens upon her, holds back her love from being fully expressed because, in some way, she feels her love is a burden.

Consider the possibility that ancestral patterns contribute to the sense of children, and women, being burdens. A quick look at your ancestral history may reveal ancestors who struggled to make ends meet with the income of a father who had to provide for the wife and children as the sole breadwinner. For a large swath of human history over the last several thousand years, providing wealth to a family has been the job of the man of the house. If the man provided a good income, the family was elevated above basic survival and higher needs on the hierarchy could be satisfied.

As the responsibility to provide income has shifted to include women (since the 1950s), and even rest completely on the shoulders of single-mothers, there has been a learning curve as women embody the masculine provider traits along with the nurturing feminine traits. Mothers during this last 70 years of Western civilization have been stretched into a quick learning curve as they've expanded to 'have it all': career, children, and self-care.

It's quite likely that very stretched mothers felt overwhelmed and burdened by trying to 'have it all', and their children may have taken on that sense of being an additional burden on their mothers. Therefore, we do not need to go into the 'Blame Game' here; we can simply acknowledge this cultural paradigm and do the necessary healing work to reclaim the Divine Mother nurturing that we each need to remember how cherished we are.

Shifting yourself from feeling like a burden to remembering you are cherished is a slow process of witnessing and bringing compassion to yourself. You must be willing to listen deeply to subconscious messages, and pay attention to signals from your body, so you can unpack the repressed feelings and beliefs that keep you in a cycle of feeling like a burden. You must expand yourself outside your comfort zone by asking for help, being vulnerable, expressing your feelings, and taking actions to support yourself in claiming your desires.

As you take the actions that help you feel cherished, and you embody the truth that you are cherished, you develop the capacity to cherish your partner, children, and other loved ones. **Only when we cherish ourselves can we give the gift of cherishing others.** You cannot give what you do not have. If cherishing the moments with your children is what you desire, then you must begin by cherishing the little one within you and training her to trust that she is not a burden to you.

When the little one within you throws a temper tantrum, and the adult you is mortified at how 'you' behaved, remember to soften that judgment, realize 'who' was throwing the tantrum, and bring love and compassion and listening to that aspect of yourself. As you see, hear, and want your little one—especially in her worst moments— you will release the repressed tensions of feeling like a burden, and relax into a space of grace where you can be yourself no matter what. When you learn to love yourself no matter what, you can open the next door to learn to cherish yourself as the unique expression of the Divine that you are.

Giving yourself loving, cherishing, nurturing attention, and receiving fully, heals you and fills your cup so that you have an overflow to give to others (without depriving yourself to give it). Fully cherishing yourself allows you to take up all the space you need to become a fountain of light and love and giving to your beloveds. **You become the Giving Tree, and people truly, deeply cherish your fruit.**

♥

Apologizing To Acceptance

A well-worn groove in the female psyche is to apologize for anything you say or do that 'causes' another person to be upset or have a negative outcome. It's normal to make mistakes, and then to apologize for those mistakes once you realize them. However, for many women and mothers, we apologize so much that it's almost like carrying around a broom and dustpan to sweep up the messes we know we're going to make just in the course of being ourselves.

Making excuses or explaining why or endlessly apologizing are micro negotiations that drain your power and leave you feeling used up and disrespected. There are people who consider it 'having the upper hand' to refuse to accept your apology, which can create your need to apologize again and again until you can close the loop and have your apology accepted. In this way, your need to have your apology received subjugates you to the power of another person's will to forgive you, or not forgive you. You're really counting on that person to have integrity when you make your acceptance of the situation dependent on their ability to receive your apology.

The real issue underlying the apology is a lack of acceptance of yourself, or of something you did that you feel has hurt someone. Let's imagine that you have a trigger that whenever someone touches your feet, you instantly kick out of reflex. This is a biological unconscious response that you do not want to have, but it happens every time. If you are in acceptance of this reflexive kicking, you will warn people in advance that it happens, and if people want to test that theory, you allow them to have the consequence of getting kicked. If you do not accept this reflexive kicking, you will spend your life apologizing and preparing people to stay away from you because you do this terrible thing that hurts people and it's out of your control, and you completely understand why they do not want to be around you, and why they don't feel safe, and why they want to shun you, and you're so sorry that you're made this way, you just simply cannot apologize enough for being a person with reflexive kicking. Can you see the difference that acceptance makes?

When you accept yourself, as you are, you can honor your flaws and respect yourself as a student of life learning unique lessons around those flaws. You don't need to turn up the volume and be defensive about your flaws to make sure others stop judging you; and you don't need to apologize endlessly and drain your vitality by judging yourself and sweeping up your perceived messes. You can accept your flaws and express your lessons with grace and gentleness.

If you are empathic, and feel very big emotions that overcome you periodically, you can gracefully hold yourself as a person who needs space to process her feelings, and honor yourself even as you realize that for some people, your feelings are like a tidal wave in their pond. What if your emotional expression unblocks the repressed emotions of a person whose conditioning led them to wall off and deny all feelings? Is it a blessing that the person is now feeling something (and blaming you for it), or is it negative that 'because' of you this person is feeling painful things they stuffed way down inside?

Intent is another aspect to consider as we evaluate apology and acceptance. Sometimes flaws drive us into wounded behaviors that either seem appropriate to us given the lens through which we are viewing the world, or seem terrible to us but we can't stop ourselves from doing it. In both of these cases, it is not the intent of the person to harm another through acting from the flaw. In the first case, it is ignorance that the flaw is causing a wounded behavior, and in the second case it is addiction to the suffering caused by the flaw.

You can certainly apologize for your ignorance, and dedicate yourself to the adage that once you know better, you do better. And you can apologize for your addiction, and dedicate yourself to learning how to be stronger than your addiction so you can overcome it and live as the person you want to be. In both of these cases, it is not necessary to bend over backwards apologizing for yourself, even if you keep repeating the mistake, because you are dedicated to learning from your flaw. Keep applying yourself to learn the lessons that will help you move beyond the negative outcomes created by your flaw. That's what you're here to do in Earth school.

A toddler does not apologize for himself because he fell down the first dozens of times he tried to stand up. He just kept trying again to learn the art of standing up. The same is true of every flaw given to you by your innate human design; you are here to grapple with these flaws and part of that is experiencing the negative outcomes of not handling them well. **Accept that you are in the process of learning your Soul's curriculum, and honor yourself for digging into the challenges.**

Beyond these potentials is a third where we knowingly act from the flaw with an intention to cause suffering even though we have the inner power and knowledge to not do this. This scenario provokes a genuine need to make apology, which may happen down the road when the person's heart opens to realize the mistake. And this scenario also produces karma, which means you are now entangled with the other person to resolve the karma.

Realization comes in layers, and so self-acceptance and apology also come in layers. When you are in the middle of an addictive behavior, and learning how to resist its seductive pull, your attention is quite absorbed in that challenge of fighting the addiction. You are less aware of the effects of your addiction on other people in your life, or even on the little child within you.

As you overcome the addition through self-mastery, you now are open to realizations about the effects of this addiction on your inner realms and your close friends and family. These realizations can be painful, and lead to more self-judgment which is why self-acceptance is necessary.

Self-judgment is a bottomless pit; self-acceptance helps you keep realizing and evolving as well as opening your heart to hear your loved ones, and heal the relationships through witnessing. Once you really hear and feel the pain of those you love about your prior addiction, you are able to give a sincere apology that heals the wounds (when the apology is received fully).

The tool of 'painting with a new brush' is particularly helpful here in releasing the stories of the past with acceptance, and inviting in the perception of what is here now with curiosity.

Once you've given a sincere apology from a place of understanding your flaws, accepting what has been as part of your path to self-mastery, and witnessing others for how your flaws have impacted them, it is done. You accept yourself as a student of life, you understand the path you have walked up until now, and you apologize for the wreckage along the way as part of the Divine design of teaching you and others.

This is how you respect yourself with the tool of apology.

♥

Suggestions

Practice Deep Listening There is a practice I learned from HeatherAsh Amara whereby you close your eyes in contemplation, and imagine that there is a deep well of water in your heart. Now imagine that you can ask a question of your heart and drop a pebble down into that well. Wait for the answer to bubble back up. When you hear an answer, let that inspire a deeper question which you now drop down into the well of your heart with another pebble. Keep going until there is no more need of questions.

Neuro-Squeegie Before taking the bait to slide into an argument with someone, stop and breathe deeply into your belly until it expands and then slowly exhale. Repeat two more times. Use this breath to cleanse your brain of its reptilian response and open to a new way to handle the situation. I learned this technique from George P Kansas and Tracey Trottenberg, and use it liberally.

You May Be Right When someone challenges you with their perspective and you feel triggered to engage in the Right Vs Wrong Game, take a breath to bring yourself into neutrality and say "You may be right." Stop and breathe and do not fill in the space. Notice what happens inside of your body; do you feel tightness, fear, release, or relief? What happens to the other person? Does the energy shift? Remember that perspectives are fleeting and that all perspectives can be 'real' at the same time. It all depends on the vantage point from which you're viewing things.

Suggestions

Raise the Vibe! When you notice yourself getting drawn into the Blame Game or self-criticism and self-doubt, take a moment to raise the vibe; you can use the Paul Selig mantra if you wish. Now view the situation again and see with fresh eyes. Are you saying "What if" instead of "What now"? What can you claim as your response-ability? What gift or wisdom is being unlocked for you via this situation?

Let It Fall To The Earth When you feel smeared by a toxic energy dump, blow it into a stone and then let it drop to the Earth while saying "I let it fall to the Earth". Practice tangibly releasing in this way until you can just do it.

Practice Confidence and Certainty If you have struggled up until now with self-doubt and a feisty inner critic, give yourself practice to build confidence and certainty muscles by speaking about things you can be confident and certain about already. For example, "I am certain I have gained wisdom in my life, and I am confident I apply that wisdom to keep growing." Pick something you can absolutely be confident and certain about. Once you get strong, you can branch out into more tenuous statements.

Self Compassion In The Mirror Stand and gaze softly at yourself in the mirror with one hand over your heart and the other over your belly. Speak gently "I see you. You are important to me." Try different supportive phrases and notice how you receive the loving support.

Quotes

"My mother told me to be a lady. And for her, that meant be your own person, be independent."
— Ruth Bader Ginsburg

"Raising a child gives us a second chance at completing our own childhood. It's an opportunity for us mothers to nurture and meet the needs of our inner child so then we can intuitively connect with the soul whom we've been assigned to rear and launch. Knowing what my needs are first allows me to clearly see what the needs are of my son without projecting my wounds. This awareness has been a gift of nurturance that keeps on giving for everyone in my family lineage, past, present and future."
— Caitlin Peterson, LCSW founder of the Soul School

"Most things will be okay eventually, but not everything will be. Sometimes you'll put up a good fight and lose. Sometimes you'll hold on really hard and realize there is no choice but to let go. Acceptance is a small, quiet room."
— Cheryl Strayed

"Sometimes it's a win if all you 'get done' all day is a shower for yourself by midnight."
— Adrianne Hicks

"The phrase 'working mother' is redundant."
— Jane Sellman

"Motherhood has a very humanizing effect. Everything gets reduced to essentials."
— Meryl Streep

You must overcome conditioned judgments of feelings and emotions being 'bad' or 'too much' or 'too sensitive' or overly dramatic. Being uncomfortable with your own feelings, and being taught to suppress your emotions, is what keeps you from being emotionally clear and healed enough to be present in the moment. This societal expectation that you process your 'stuff' on a therapist couch, and then show up with a smile on your face as if nothing had affected your composure, is part of what is out of balance.

Having to 'hold it together' to appear happy for other people is an underlying cultural expectation that, I believe, is what has led to the narcissistic syndrome we are witnessing in the collective. Keeping all these secrets and compartmentalizing and stuffing down real feelings is burdensome. From that state of being, is it any wonder we are so self-absorbed as a culture and do not seem to have the energy to consider the lives of people outside our own family and friends?

Being able to be in service to the world in a greater way requires expanding your emotional capacity. You need a safe space to learn how to hold the gigantic overwhelming feelings without judging them, and without collapsing under them. You must learn how to hold yourself through emotional turmoil, letting the clarity come before speaking; and this emotional capacity helps you to be courageous enough to have difficult conversations directly with the right people (rather than resorting to gossip). As you face your own emotions and heal, you'll create the spaciousness within yourself to be able to hear other people. Feeling what is stirred up within you from another's perspective helps you to develop discernment about what's yours and what's theirs, which serves you in creating clear boundaries for relationships.

Having strong emotional capacity allows you to show up for others, even the people closest to you, with a wide open heart and ears to listen. Sometimes what they say will hurt, you may take it personally; and then you'll remember you have the tools to process those feelings and put things into right relationship so you can keep showing up. **When you no longer abandon yourself by ignoring your feelings, you can be there for others truthfully and authentically.** Paying attention to your feelings lets your inner self know your life matters, you value your voice, and you have compassion for yourself. When you know your life matters, you can be a mighty ally for others.

Becoming this mighty ally, and bringing yourself back into harmony with yourself and the Earth, requires you to learn to embrace your feelings and the information your body is sending you through sensing and pain. The learning on Earth is experiential through your senses and feelings. When you resist sensing and feeling you resist learning from Mother Earth. To hear Mother Earth you must tune out the brain and into the heart. Enter the realm of sensing and feeling.

Your body is a hologram as well as a vast network of intelligence, a web that captures experience for you to digest and process through silence and contemplation, sensing and feeling. The intelligence of the body is far more comprehensive than language can capture using the mind. Song is vibration and is more closely aligned to the truth as you feel the song resonate through your body.

Your body is the record of your accountability in Earth School. Nothing can be hidden from the Divine Mother because she listens all the time to your consciousness held in your biological matter created from her materials and designed by her as your vehicle of learning. All the things you hide from yourself, she knows. She tries to help you see it by sending you messages in your body and environment. If you're not listening, you'll develop ear problems. If you're insecure about stepping forward in your life, you'll get a twist to your right ankle. If you need time to integrate your lessons or are not letting go of something toxic in your life, you'll develop digestive issues.

It's all very simple and straightforward. She gives you ample supply in very obvious ways what you need to live better in harmony with yourself. It's typical to ignore the obvious clues because the mind believes the solution to problems is elusive and complicated. So you keep searching for what is hidden when the answers are in plain sight. Dandelions are a good example of this: they are everywhere! Their medicine helps with detoxifying the liver and kidneys and improving digestion, as well as supporting healthy immune function with its antimicrobial and antiviral properties; and what do we humans need right now? Exactly that!

When you want to heal – yourself, your ancestry, your family – you've got to listen to your body and notice its messages; and you've got to listen to your environment and notice the synchronicity. Realize that your body is a temple of the divine. It is the sacred union of material and spiritual. The human begins with energy and includes emotions, thoughts, subconscious, ancestry, spirit/Soul, chakras, meridians, auric field, and the physical body. There are many non-physical aspects of the human that Western medicine largely ignores which is why illness is typically detected late in the game when it has become highly painful and in need of an immediate solution.

Feeling it to heal it means being willing to patiently peel back the layers one by one to discover what your body is revealing to you. At some point you realize that the problem you sought to resolve is gone; you do not know exactly 'how' it is gone, and you cannot identify the one thing that resolved it in the end because it was not one thing…it was a process of healing. Once it is healed, it does not return; it's only when you're chasing it through thought tunnels in your mind that you get twisted up and find yourself right back at the issue at a later time. Feeling it to heal it resolves issues at the level of your body and energy, and creates wholeness from which there is forward momentum. I remember being worried that the gains I made during healing sessions would not 'stick', that I would slide back into a prior state of consciousness; what I learned is that if you continue to be aware of yourself, and continue to practice healing with yourself as you notice the pebbles, you do not 'go back'…you evolve.

The human mind wants to prove everything, and feeling it to heal it means humbly accepting the mystery. The human mind wants to find the cure, set it as a rule, and then go back to autopilot; feeling it to heal it means staying awake and present to the shifting nuances so you can course correct long before a 'problem' manifests that could become a disease by ignoring it. The human mind wants the recipe for success that can be applied to everyone; feeling it to heal it means choosing to dedicate to daily practices of wellness and heightened awareness, and realizing that your best health is a unique blend of solutions. To find it you must navigate your own journey with practitioners and experts as guides and resources.

As you take personal responsibility to restore optimal health for yourself, you become a healthy cell operating in harmony with Mother Earth. Disease is caused by being out of harmony. When you are in harmony you do not require something to realign you to it. Mother Earth has been out of harmony and so is now detoxing what is causing distortion; thus, the virus that we have collectively experienced in 2020. Your body is made of Earth, and therefore as Mother Earth is detoxifying herself, it is futile to try to escape or hide from this process.

What is being detoxified? The lungs. What is stored in the lungs? Grief, karma, unforgiveness, and repressed feelings, abuses and traumas that you did not want to face. Notice how quickly the virus mutates; it's almost as if Mother Earth is saying "Catch up with me if you can." The virus came in 2020, the year of reckoning and 20/20 vision. It's time to face yourself, fess up and forgive. Fear is a distortion and love is harmony. The closer you are to love, to health, to alignment with Mother Earth…the less difficult your detox will be. Take good care of your spiritual home: your body.

Feeling it to heal it is a process, and you're invited to have grace for yourself to move through it. Strengthen your ability to stay present with yourself through discomfort to expand your capacity. Expanded capacity to be with discomfort helps tremendously if you reach the part of your spiritual evolution where you experience an ego death. I have gone through a few of these big purges of emotional content, and they literally feel like death, and made me think thoughts of death and suicide. Because I had strengthened my emotional capacity, I was able to stay present with myself through the storm of intense feelings, ask for help from my support team, and keep breathing until the energy lifted and passed.

Going through an ego death feels a bit like the end of the "Raiders of the Lost Ark" movie where Harrison Ford is clenching his eyes shut and shouting warnings to everyone to not look at the spirits emanating from the Ark, no matter the temptation. Except in this case, the advice is to witness all of it without acting—just keep breathing.

One of my ego death experiences was catalyzed by reading a handbook for a 12-Step Program. The line where you have no control because God is ultimately in control of you; yep, that triggered a big moment of ego death for me as I felt that statement and let it resonate through me. So much fear rose up within me as I sat in my Lazyboy chair reclining, blanket and doggy in my lap, that I actually texted my mentor "I think if I just sit here through this fear attack, that I will not die." She confirmed that statement, and about 30 minutes later I was on the phone with another friend, forehead planted on the earth begging for help as I felt the tectonic plates of my brain shifting into a new configuration. That's the best way I can describe the experience. It was intense; and I survived it and even thrived because of it.

In another ego death experience, I had been extremely depressed and lethargic for a couple of days for no good reason. It was hard to get out of bed, suicidal thoughts flipped into my mind continuously, and I sobbed relentlessly. My husband was genuinely concerned when I told him he needed to change the key code to the gun safe so I would not know how to get to the guns. He managed to get me out of the bed and into the car, and brought me to a safe house in the woods where I slept for days, only venturing out to stand and look at the lake outside the cabin. Having gone through this experience, I am aware that sometimes the sheer volume of old programs being purged at once creates a feeling of death that is overwhelming to experience. While it is happening, unprocessed life experiences come into your awareness that you have not yet forgiven or released so that you can do that, and be done with it. You feel like you're going crazy, or possessed by something trying to punish you. But really, I believe it is just aspects of your egoic self that are ready to die so that you can be rebirthed at a deeper level of Soul guidance and embodiment.

To prepare for these kinds of experiences, flex those muscles of facing your feelings and being with discomfort. Expand your emotional capacity to stay with yourself without taking action when your inner world is in turmoil. Get accomplished at asking for help with the smaller things so that you can overcome the resistance to getting help when you need it most. Surround yourself in community with others who are walking the spiritual path and know how to best support a person going through big emotional processing.

Consider the intensity of birthing a baby into the world, and realize that practicing how to feel it to heal it helps you to be ready when your own rebirth process arises in perfect timing. **You are never given more than you can handle, and you'll be given that amazing rebirth when you've proven you've got the emotional capacity to hold yourself through the process.**

Aside from simply learning to feel your feelings as they arise, you can learn some tools for shifting through big feelings and repressed emotions more gracefully.

Emotional Freedom Techniques (EFT) – You can perform EFT on yourself when you are feeling intense emotions. By tapping with your fingertips on the same energy meridians known by acupuncturists, you can release the emotional blocks from your body's bioenergy system, and restore yourself to balance. You can use EFT while thinking about a specific problem—whether it is a traumatic event, an addiction, or pain—and help shift it in the moment.

The Emotion Code – A widely used technique for emotional clearing these days is The Emotion Code that was created by Dr. Bradley Nelson (D.C., ret). The Emotion Code helps you to alleviate physical discomfort, ease emotional wounds, and restore love to relationships. Dr. Bradley Nelson has also created a special clearing for our hearts to remove the Heart Wall that you unconsciously protected yourself with after heartache.

Suggestions

Immerse and Breathe When you are overcome by a 'negative' feeling, such as anger or fear or grief, rather than deflect away from that feeling…**immerse in it and breathe to expand it.** This recommendation is counter to how you have been programmed to suppress your feelings. When I studied with Alberto Villoldo at the Four Winds Light Body School, I learned the distinction between feelings and emotions. Feelings pass in moments as you allow the experience to happen. Emotions are feelings that get trapped in your body and can last your whole life. An example of this is feeling resentment for your former partner. When you begin the healing journey, situations occur to trigger the release of trapped emotions from earlier parts of your life; the wisdom is to recognize it is happening, and allow yourself to finally let that trapped emotion go by immersing in it and expanding it with so much compassion and love that it finally dissipates. The key here is to have no expectation of making it 'go away.' Accept that it's there, explore it, and understand its reason for being. It will release itself when it is ready.

Name It After being conditioned to deny your feelings, you must build a new vocabulary and nuanced awareness of feelings that allows you to make emotional intelligence your new superpower. When a feeling emerges, sample it as you would a fine wine, and match it to the name that describes the experience. What you resist, persists. What you embrace reveals gifts and becomes your medicine. Naming the emotion acknowledges its existence and can reveal its reason for being present in this moment.

Quotes

"We cannot selectively numb emotions. When we numb painful emotions, we also numb the positive ones."
— Brené Brown

"Unexpressed emotions will never die. They are buried alive and will come forth later in uglier ways."
— Sigmund Freud

"When you shut down emotion, you're also affecting your immune system, your nervous system. So the repression of emotion, which is a survival strategy, then becomes a source of physiological illness later on."
— Gabor Maté

"Repression creates the unconscious. The more repressed you are the bigger unconscious you have."
— Osho

"Running a marathon with a backpack is tough and may hinder you from winning the race. Don't let the baggage from your past—heavy with fear, guilt, and anger—slow you down."
— Maddy Malhotra

"When our emotional health is in a bad state, so is our level of self-esteem. We have to slow down and deal with what is troubling us, so that we can enjoy the simple joy of being happy and at peace with ourselves."
— Jess C. Scott

"The deeper that sorrow carves into your being, the more joy you can contain."
— Khalil Gibran

Surface Living To Deep Waters

Most of humanity is living at the surface level of consciousness, operating in the shallow depths of mind with awareness that does not go lower than the head and throat. This is the outcome when the masculine mind dominates people's experience of life, and it is an aspect of the Mother Wound in its denial of the profound power of connecting with the Divine Mother, the embodied Spirit, through your entire body and down through your feet into the Earth.

Social media notifications, appointments back to back, constant interruptions, responsibility to be on time: all of these prompts from the construct of Time keep people enslaved to surface living from their minds, and leave no space for them to go deep within themselves to access the inner wellspring of Soul through the Divine Feminine.

If you won't go to your depths, to the void within like a bear, you'll deplete your resources with surface living. If you stay in the fast-paced distracted state of the shallow mind, you'll be scatterbrained and miss out of the truly relevant messages and opportunities for your growth and fulfillment.

To access the deep waters within, and to live from those deep waters, you must decide to extricate yourself from the Time matrix and collective agreements that bind you there. You must face the fear of not 'belonging' to the collective consciousness of Time. **You must be willing to 'lose' the physical world status, reputation and possessions that you think you own in favor of a greater presence and reward of Peace from the realm of the Infinite.**

What keeps you from going deep are collective agreements about Time and 'responsibility' and the measure of perceived safety you derive from these constructs. Of course, the safety you perceive from the material realm is an illusion because you cannot get anything tangible from something that does not exist. The material realm itself is an illusion based in collective Soul agreement to present itself in certain ways, thereby providing a training ground for you to learn your Soul's curriculum. The more 'real' realm is the realm of your Soul which is infinite and connected to all that is.

Have you ever noticed when you are in the flow how time seems to stop and you accomplish way more than you thought you could, effortlessly, and the resulting product was brilliant? That is because you accessed your Soul and it guided you to enter the realm of Soul where all things are possible outside of Time.

It is necessary to bring yourself to the deep waters of your Soul often if you wish to have vitality and presence and be in the flow. If you restrict yourself to the shallowness of surface living with Time, it is like you are holding your breath to stay in an illusion where you have to keep going, and going, and going and doing, and doing and doing, in order to survive.

Confining yourself to the mirage of Time and the temporary playground it creates for the benefit of you and your peers is like cutting yourself off from oxygen. Sooner or later you will turn purple and die from a heart attack. Or go into a deep depression because you are missing something very important that keeps you alive and vibrant. Ahem...your Soul.

All you have to do is slow down and take a breath. Say Yes to your Soul.

There is one aspect of you that would very much like you to continue dreaming the false dream of Time, and that is your ego, which is also a temporary illusion created for the purpose of your Soul's curriculum. And so your ego leverages the one strength it has to resist your Soul and that is free will. You see, this game of Soul's curriculum was created by your Soul to be a puzzle to solve worthy of its infinite wisdom. **Your Soul willingly strips itself of its knowing to enter into this artificial realm of shallow Time living with an ego that can tell it 'No' so that it can practice its own self-mastery as to how to bring itself back together in Love.**

On Earth there are many Soul pods learning their own collective lessons, simultaneously co-habiting the Earth School. The collective lesson of one Soul pod may be to experience what happens when the Soul allows the ego to stubbornly resist Love and starve itself of the deep ocean of Soul. The collective lesson of another Soul pod may be to experience what happens when the Soul lovingly guides the ego to relinquish its perceived control through its Time-constructed small world in favor of a greater majesty and wondrous flow of synchronicity delivered by its Soul.

Learning the dance between Soul and ego is the kiss of the Divine, the crème de la crème.

When you are born into the Earth construct, you sometimes choose to allow a Soul of a very different collective lesson to birth you into being and domesticate your mind so that you can bring your Soul's self-mastery to a new level of refinement. That's how powerful your Soul is. It can experience the harshest of conditions growing up, and still bring itself back to Love.

Helpful tip: when you notice yourself surrounded by people who choose to operate within the shallow space of Earth dimension, starved for Love...don't diminish yourself to fit into that world, thereby depleting yourself so you can also starve for depth and meaning in your life. That's like having a PhD and deluding yourself into thinking you belong back in kindergarten. The 'love' you would gain from diminishing yourself to accommodate a shallow space cannot possibly be worth the loss you suffer by preventing yourself to access the deep ocean within yourself to commune with your Soul's wisdom and unconditional Love.

Depression, anxiety, hopelessness, listlessness, resentfulness, numbness, worry, fear, scarcity, lack, and all related feelings/experiences are a symptom of staying too long in the shallow space. Bring yourself into the depth of your Soul, outside of the false illusion of Time, to replenish and restore yourself to Truth and Love.

Can you dance between the worlds? **Better yet, can you bring your deep waters to every moment of the shallows, experiencing the**

illusion of Time while knowing it is an illusion? Have you ever experimented with asking your Soul to wake you up at a certain time in the morning, and then gone blissfully to sleep knowing you would be woke at exactly the 'time' you requested? It's only through fear that there's nothing 'helping' you that you doubt you will be woken 'on time'. And it's through control that the ego even asks to be woke at a certain time; why not become curious about the Soul's plan for you today? Because you're still enmeshed in the collective agreement to Time and 'responsibility'. You don't want to miss your meeting or be perceived as irresponsible because you were late for the agreed-upon meeting time. So you think you have to control this by using imaginary items like alarm clocks to set the illusory 'Time' to wake so that you can show up to the meeting, perhaps even early.

Yet, the Soul is able to make many events occur effortlessly and synchronistically. All you must do is follow. When you relax into the depths of your Soul, and let go of the collective constructs of 'Time' and 'responsibility', you find yourself in a flow of events that happen for you, to which you can respond. **When you are in Soul, you 'hear' when something needs to happen and you 'tune in' for the message about what that is.** It might be a message that you need to be somewhere or do something, you've lost track of Time (which is good), and now you need to become aware of Time again to respond to the thing you're committed to do in this moment. You feel the urge of your Soul, and you're aware and empty enough to notice it. When you're in shallow busy mind, you totally miss these urges and messages, or dismiss them in favor of whatever distraction is happening for you right now.

The 'But...' in your mind is there to pull you back from a new understanding by bringing forward into the Now some historical evidence of why it's not possible to operate this new way that is being shared with you Now. History does not apply to Now. Now is a new moment, full of new potential. **If you want your life to be different, YOU have to be different. To be different, you must relinquish certainty that what you have experienced up until now is absolutely the Way It Is.** It is not the Way It Is, it is only the way you have experienced life up until now because of the conditioning of your mind and your attachment to operating within the shallow waters of collective agreement to Time and 'responsibility'.

Whose responsibility is it? Is it yours as the small self? Whose dream is this you are living? Is it yours as the small self? Or has this entire life experience been laid out for you to experience by your Soul, and for your Soul to guide you through a series of lessons back to the eternal knowing that has always been present, and was only obscured for a while to have this illusion of separateness whereby the ego could say 'No.' **The ego can only say 'No' through the grace of its Creator, its Soul.**

The consciousness of Earth that has facilitated the illusory dreams of billions of egos is moving herself into a new phase of consciousness where the game she wishes to play is a dance of ego and Soul. If we want to continue playing on Earth, we must play by her rules. And so it is time to wake up dear ones. Move into the deep waters of your Soul. Surrender to the dance between ego and Soul, and receive the Divine kiss.

From the space of dance we can experience all new potentials within Time and without, within physical space and without, within illusion and without. We can balance the hemispheres and weave it all together into one consciousness.

We are moving from "No" to "Yes And."

In 2020, we all collectively experienced the effect of discord and fear, grief and loss, uncertainty and confusion. The tumultuous thrashing is akin to being at the surface of the waves where you get pounded by shifting life circumstances. Trying to lead your life or others from the surface chaos is like throwing powerful punches that never land on the real opponent. Are you exhausted yet? Maybe you feel like you're talking yourself blue in the face trying to change things at the level of the ego mind, and now the only place left to go is a slide down into name calling and entrenchment because other ego minds won't listen or understand.

There is another solution and it's the deep ocean of your Soul. This is not a spiritual bypass. Rather, this is immersion deep within to tap into your peace and presence so you can bring it to the chaos. **When our hearts are full, and we are tapped into peace within, we have the expanded capacity to do something that is required for building the bridges that create peaceful outcomes: listen.**

A conversation is between two people, two aspects…within yourself and out in the world. The energy with which you hold that conversation is the key. If you hold that conversation from the egoic surface-of-the-waters self, you get engaged in debates that have no resolution. If you hold that conversation without actually listening — only waiting for your turn to prove you are right—you have missed an opportunity. If you hold the conversation pretending to listen and empathize, but underneath discrediting the speaker, you have missed an opportunity. If you speak to share but actually hold the energy that the other person is too stupid to get it, your speaking falls on deaf ears.

At the surface level is judgment, criticism, blame, projections, scarcity, fear, shame, and survival needs that get in the way of a true exchange of ideas and perspectives. Leading from the deep ocean, the Soul guidance and wisdom, offers a balm of peace and love to everyone you meet. It's like a glass of cool water on a hot summer day; a restorative and beautiful gift after the thrash and burn we collectively create when we interact from the egoic shallows.

♥

Codependency To Sovereignty To Interdependency

The only person you can now or ever change is yourself.
The only person that it is your business to control is yourself.
—Melody Beattie

The point at which you enter the spiritual path is the paradigm of codependency and its failure as a viable structure in your life. I spent twenty years in a marriage where I was a victim to my perpetrator, and felt powerless to speak my truth and stand in it. It was a never-ending barrage from my former partner that poked and prodded at my most vulnerable fear—the fear of conflict. So I twisted and turned and ran away and said what he wanted: anything to get him to stop the barrage.

Funny thing is, if you heard his version of the story, he was a victim and I was the perpetrator. All the things I did to avoid conflict with him, he saw as lies and manipulation and a way to hurt him deeply.

The first spiritual teaching that really sunk in for me was the Triangle of Disempowerment: victim, rescuer, perpetrator. It is this triangle that keeps you locked in codependency, never feeling your inner power, always feeling tangled up with others' needs, wants and expectations. At all costs, you avoid being the perpetrator because that role means being to blame for the suffering of others and being a bad person, a villain. The victim is a much more lucrative spot to hold on the Triangle of Disempowerment because it's never your fault which means you don't have to clean up the messes you help to create, and usually there is someone that comes along to validate and save you from any feelings of responsibility: the rescuer.

The dark underbelly of the rescuer is the belief that no one in the situation is capable of doing the right thing, so the rescuer swoops in to save the day and claim the glory for vanquishing the perpetrator and leading the victim to safety. The rescuer needs to be seen as superhuman and above reproach, and that automatically creates the need for a villain and a victim. Western society is addicted to the Triangle of Disempowerment as evidenced by all the superhero movies we consume annually.

It's a very black and white way of looking at people: good and bad, right and wrong, villains and heroes. **And it's spiritually immature.**

When you desire personal freedom, you must extricate yourself from the Triangle of Disempowerment which is an energetic process and a spiritual practice of awareness and consciousness choice. You must cut the cords with everyone from whom you believe you need something, and then deepen your roots to provide it to yourself. You must be aware of any sense of powerlessness, and look within to heal the source of the wounding that led to this lie. You must listen inside and follow the guidance of your own heart which often leads you into conflict with people with whom you used to be tangled up in codependency; leaning into this discomfort with love is how you heal those parts inside that were told you were powerless so you can reclaim the truth of your sovereignty.

You most certainly have to face the ways you blame your parents for the conditions of your life, and claim your power by realizing the gold nuggets of wisdom and ability you gained from the way you were raised. And you must tap into a bigger source of power as a guide for your life's choices and a framework for understanding the events of your life: your Soul. **From the Soul perspective, you can learn to see unexpected challenges as the initiations leading you to claim the desires of your heart.** You can outgrow the victim mentality you were programmed with and see the bigger picture of your Soul's evolution. The path to sovereignty strips you of entitlement and gifts you with gratitude, replaces obligation with an authentic Yes, upgrades manipulation with the 'open invitation', exposes unhealthy relationships and patterns, transforms lack into generosity, and reveals unwanted events to be initiations into greater wisdom and power.

As I have stepped more and more deeply into my sovereignty, I have become more and more free. I have liberated myself from things I did not even realize were prisons until I found the edges of my 'box' and ventured out beyond it. **Until I discovered new horizons, I never knew how much of a slave I previously was.**

When you become sovereign, you enjoy many freedoms:

- Freedom to take risks with confidence and see what happens

- Freedom to say No and Yes according to your heart's guidance (without obligation)

- Freedom to release critical thoughts and worries and restore your mind to peace within minutes

- Freedom to self-validate and allow others their own point of view (no more Right vs Wrong tug of war)

- Freedom to show up exactly as you are and let others react as they choose (no more walking on eggshells to please people)

- Freedom to fully express your truth and feelings vulnerably (no more choking back your truth or hiding your feelings)

- Freedom to try new things and discover what makes you happy (no more worrying what others think)

- Freedom to harness the wisdom in your wounds and make new choices (releasing guilt and shame)

- Freedom to create spaciousness within yourself in any situation (no more feeling trapped)

- Freedom to connect to your Soul for reassurance and guidance (no more feeling lonely, isolated or abandoned)

- Freedom to navigate and reorient your life as needed from Power Within (no more external control)

A sovereign Soul is able to be a great contributor to humanity and does so through interdependency with other sovereign Souls. **Interdependency recognizes that each Soul is uniquely designed to fulfill a purpose for the family, tribe, or global community.**

These special Soul gifts are useful to others who do not possess those gifts because they possess other gifts that are also special and useful to the collective. In this way, each Soul is special and useful to the collective, creating a web of interdependency that allows everyone to feel useful and also recognize the usefulness of others. **Life on Earth becomes a symphony, a divine orchestration, when we reclaim our sovereignty and surrender it to the Divine Mother so that our gifts shine in service to the collective in exactly the right timing where our gifts are most useful.**

The mechanism of discovering your special sauce and realizing how it plugs into the collective consciousness is inherently employed when you become sovereign and tapped into the divine Mother Earth for guidance. When you know your Soul's blueprint there's no more need to compete with others over anything. Competition becomes an outdated paradigm that can be released. Full embodiment of your gifts is the paradigm for New Earth which means that you know who you are as a sovereign being, you are connected with the greater consciousness for guidance, and you fully align yourself to your role and purpose for the good of all.

A place to get started for understanding your specialness is the Human Design Chart and the Gene Keys. I personally find great value from Chetan Parkyn's book "Human Design: Discover the Person You Were Born To Be" and Richard Rudd's book "The Gene Keys: Unlocking the Higher Purpose Hidden In Your DNA".

I Am ... We ... expressed individually as unique voices and collectively as one orchestra playing an infinite song of life.

♥

Suggestions

Get Off The Triangle To become sovereign, you must rewire codependency which means getting off the Triangle of Disempowerment. Explore the shadows within yourself to find out how you diminish your power as a victim, perpetrate for power over others, and play the role of rescuer or hero. Once you cognitively understand the ways you unconsciously engage the Triangle of Disempowerment, you can clear the energetics and more consciously choose sovereignty. Extricating yourself is a matter of discerning 'what is mine' and 'what is theirs' in situations until you have clear boundaries and sovereign wiring. I offer meditations to support you in becoming aware and healing yourself of the Triangle of Disempowerment and codependency.

Soul Design Discover your unique soul design by looking up your Human Design Chart and Gene Keys. Listen to the contemplation audios from Richard Rudd for your Gene Keys to understand the shadows you are navigating through your life's challenges to unlock the gifts of this incarnation. You will gain a soul-level perspective of your life through this investigation. Next, look up the Human Design Chart and Gene Keys for your mother and children. Do you see the larger context of your relationships and how they intertwine to offer everyone growth opportunities? How do your shadows and gifts relate to the shadows and gifts that your mother has been working through in this life? Considering the intersection of your shadows and your mother's shadows, can you identify the underlying points of friction as you each work your soul's curriculum?

Quotes

"The relationship of a mother with the child growing within her has the potential to change the face of society. It is through this relationship in the crucial stages of development in utero, that the child is acknowledged and received with joy. This connection is beyond an emotional attachment to the child. It is about the attitude with which we relate to everyday life. It is about the link between thought and creation. For when we ourselves are willing to live life from a place of joy, then the birthright of our children is ensured. When there are enough of these children born into the world, those who from birth are recognized as the creation that they truly are, then it is the world itself that will grow to reflect this transformation."
— Laurie Seymour, Founder/CEO The Baca Institute

"The mother-child relationship is paradoxical and, in a sense, tragic. It requires the most intense love on the mother's side, yet this very love must help the child grow away from the mother, and to become fully independent."
— Erich Fromm

"There is no way to be a perfect mother, and a million ways to be a good one."
— Jill Churchill

"When I stopped seeing my mother with the eyes of a child, I saw the woman who helped me give birth to myself."
— Nancy Friday

Shaming To Honoring

"Shame cannot survive being spoken. It cannot survive empathy."
–Brené Brown

Shame has been a major part of my journey as a woman in this incarnation. I began at just a year old taking on shame from my mother when she found me in the tub with my naked biological father who was being 'inappropriate' with me; code for molesting. As a little being of light, I did not know what was happening was wrong; until my mother walked into the room and had a big reaction of shame. I took the shame within me, and my innocence departed my beingness.

After this event as a toddler, I began to bite my hands and arms. I left huge red bite marks in my flesh. I was trying to bite off my hands and arms that did the 'bad thing' that made mommy mad and made my daddy go away. My mother took me to a child psychologist to help with this trauma, which was compounded by the fact that she had moved us in with a physically aggressive alcoholic man (who had appeared to be a nice professional).

Most of my recollection of this early event comes from my first spiritual healing session where my mentor at the time, Gerry Starnes, did a drum journey to see the root cause of my suffering as a 42 year old woman. As he worked on me, he removed shame from my heart and my hands and arms. My whole life I felt an aching around my heart like a pulsing and contracting black energy; Gerry removed this energy of shame and it has never returned since. This session healed my original wound of shame. It helped me to understand how my mother's shame became my own and unfurled for me a life being ashamed of being a woman, and ashamed of my sexuality.

It's normal for children to explore their body parts and to be curious about the sensations they can produce; however, my mother was on the lookout for abnormal sexuality because of what happened with my natural father. Speaking from experience, when normal curious exploration is stunted, or made to feel shameful, it's likely that healthy adult sexual expression will be compromised.

I remember being in second grade in the tub with a friend and exploring the way the little wind-up motor dolphin felt when I put its flipping tail against my 'hamburger' (clitoris). When my mother found us in the tub in 'the act', I was immediately pulled out of the bath and shamed for playing with myself in public. I got my first urinary tract infection, and got the message this was payback for my naughtiness.

After this uncomfortable moment of being bad, and not understanding why, I left my vagina alone. Unless I was riding my bike, in which case the bar was a harmless rubbing tool; like a scratching post for a cat. I only did it discretely though, because by now I figured out that was probably 'bad' too.

Life went on like this, only acknowledging my private parts when going to the bathroom, until I got my first menstruation cycle at 13. Upon which I was unceremoniously told I had now entered a certain hell that women shared and was given a pack of pads. I remember the day it happened; I had just pulled down my panties to go to the bathroom and saw a stain. I immediately called my mother at work, certain I was tremendously sick to be bleeding in my crotch. This was my initiation: invisible. So different than what I have come to learn about how indigenous people celebrate and honor girls becoming women with their 'first moon'.

A year or so later I had attempted to use tampons, could not figure out how to do it, and asked my mother for help. She refused to help saying it was my private matter. Our family friend, my 'aunt', brought me into the bathroom, pulled down her underwear, and showed me how to insert the tampon. That was so amazingly helpful. I felt cared for, and have always been grateful for that moment, as embarrassingly awkward as it was at the time.

Very soon after this I learned that my vagina was something that boys wanted, and then I began the series of lessons promiscuous girls learn in high school. Your vagina is pure and desirable until you have sex with a boy, and then your vagina is dirty and desired by sex-hungry boys who lust you (but not love you). My desire to be adored and wanted was so great that I fell for the 'romancing' boys do when they want a girl to give it up. Behaving in this 'inappropriate' way satisfied my rebellious side who fully knew having sex was against house rules; so in other words, sex was rebellion that reaffirmed I was bad, rather than curious exploration that affirmed my right to explore my body.

Almost to drive the point home, I chose one of the few African American boys as my first boyfriend in high school which served to deliver a hefty dose of shame from the blue-collar white community that was just at the beginning of exploring what racial equality means. I was called 'nigger slut' to my face and behind my back on a regular basis; especially when my next boyfriends were also black. I was in love with my first boyfriend, and the love included shame. I had a lot of sex with multiple African American partners in high school, rebelliously immersing in the shame of being openly sexually active. Arguably all of my partners simply wanted to prove something to the people in the town that had discriminated against them due to the color of their skin by having sex with a pretty 'white' girl. I was aware I was being used as a political statement. I developed such a reputation that no one 'white' would date me.

My parents were mortified with my choices. I was an embarrassment. After a few years of this pattern, my self-esteem was decimated. I didn't have boyfriends who had sex with me because they loved me. I had boys have sex with me because they wanted something for themselves. Sex was about pleasure for the masculine, not about my own pleasure.

After a bout of rampant promiscuity I decided that I wanted to be seen as pure and desirable again, so I stopped having sex and experimenting with multiple partners and I waited for the 'boyfriend'.

Because my reputation preceded me in my town, I found a boyfriend in a neighboring town who became my best friend and partner from the last year of high school through college. Apparently, a committed relationship makes a woman's vagina pure again. I tightened everything up, closed my legs, and made sure it was clear that no matter how much of a 'slut' I was before I had now switched to being a prude and above judgment and gossip.

My boyfriend was incredibly supportive, loving, kind, and generous. He knew my history and he saw me as a champion of causes he also believed in like racial equality. I flipped the switch from bad girl into good girl and struggled to feel sexual.

In 'good girl' mode, I was reluctant to explore my clitoris and was unable to orgasm no matter how patiently my boyfriend tried to help me out. The shame ran deep. I was ok being used for a man's pleasure, but my own pleasure was cut off. The only pleasure I allowed him to give me was massage, much to his sexual frustration (and mine). I wore sack dresses like the girls on Little House on the Prairie to cover up my figure. I did not want my sexual beast getting loose and ruining my pristine pure relationship. He did all the right things, and I battled myself inside to relax and receive pleasure. Letting myself be loved was hard. Having a partner that dedicated himself to making me feel good made me feel unworthy and selfish, and so I compensated for that by being demanding and entitled.

When I left that relationship and met the father of my children, I thought I deserved to be mistreated. And so I attracted a partner who vacillated between putting me on a pedestal and tearing me off of it, because that's what I was doing to myself.

When I became a mother the stakes got bigger: moms can't be sexy. They're supposed to be frumpy and lack all sexuality except behind closed doors.

I relate all this history to set the context for the beginning of my spiritual awakening which could arguably be the moment I bought my first sex toy at 38 and had an orgasm. That orgasm unleashed the beast within that had been repressed my whole life. I wore out vibrators like a ninja wears out knives. I went through so many AA batteries I should have bought stock in Energizer. Then I moved onto the hot tub leg jets because the little toy just wasn't cutting it anymore…I needed more power.

And then it was back to black men. Porn at first and then the real deal. I was so crazed after a lifetime of sexual repression that I literally could not stop myself from hunting down a man and getting freaky. I needed to know all the ways that orgasm could happen with my body, and I discovered quite a few. Was I a total 'slut' by societal standards? Absolutely. Was I empowered? It was very liberating and empowering, yes. Somehow embracing being 'dirty' made me free to explore myself.

When women begin to express their truth it's not very elegant at first. It's fierce and violent and powerful. My primal desire demolished everything that stood in its way; including my marriage.

Looking back at my first book, *Awakening To Me: One Woman's Journey To Self Love*, I'd like to erase the subtle apology that winds its way through the text. As if my primal requirements were something to be ashamed of, and my new adventure as a spiritual mentor can't hold space for this woman's journey to self-love—which includes the pinnacle of divine expression in a female body—the orgasm.

Without ego and without apology, I claimed my sexual partners like a jaguar hunting in the dark. I knew exactly what I wanted and I got it. As an adulteress, my relationship to sexuality was clearer than it had ever been before.

Yet I was still tangled up in societal expectations and judgments about female sexuality. I discovered this entanglement after my marriage ended when I desired a new committed relationship. Being 'dirty' and sexually liberated worked really well for one-night stands; but that's not the kind of woman you bring home to meet you mother, right? Right about this time, the raw porn that had been getting me off started seeming demeaning to women and like it shouldn't get me off. *Which was really frustrating, because I liked getting off and that was a well-worn pathway.*

I kept having sex with men that could not commit to me, and my addiction to the attention outweighed my self-respect. I was so seduced by sex that when a spiritual teacher invited me to do a 100 day celibacy experiment, I balked. There was no way I could last 100 days without sex. Can't we just do a week? I talk about this struggle in *Awakening To Me*. I did eventually complete the whole 100 days straight of celibacy, and this reset my patterns to have more balance with my sexuality and choice of partner.

Within a year of this realization I had a spiritual experience of integrating an ancestral energy of a Cherokee medicine man on the Trail of Tears into my consciousness. I describe this profound experience in *The Second Wave: Transcending the Human Drama*. The integration of this man of integrity made it even more obvious to me that I was disrespecting myself by fantasizing about being used by men for sex. The awareness of this medicine man and his quiet observation of my addictions made me uncomfortable whenever I fell for a man who just wanted sex, and didn't want *me* to go with it.

Women have systematically been disconnected from owning their sexual power and energy through the sexualization of the female through pornography, shame, shunning, and judgement. The woman who claims her sexual power is regarded in demeaning ways through these structures, and the woman who does not want to be demeaned abandons her sexuality in favor of being morally superior. All of these responses are operating within the paradigm of controlling women through their sexuality, and leveraging their sexual power for male satisfaction.

I was working my way through this maze of unhealthy sexual conditioning to find my own truth. Needless to say, sexuality, shame, and violence were interlinked in my brain. If I was being a 'good' girl, my world did not involve sex. If I was being sexual, there was a component of shame and violence to it. I wanted to be in a new, healthy relationship with my yoni.

I began to experiment with making love to myself with my vibrator, and trying to simply notice the sensations rather than create the visualizations that had gotten me off for so many years. I tried to find a new pathway for relating to my pussy that honored me as a woman. Awhile after I let go of my addiction to fling sex, and replaced it with self-pleasure, I attracted my life partner who loves my body, never makes faces of disgust about my private parts, and enjoys communing and sensing and relating to me and my body on all levels. It took a bit of sincerity on his part to convince me he was for real that he enjoyed my body and honored me at the same time. I tested him A LOT with pretty disgusting behavior…just to be sure he really meant it and would stick around.

What strikes me now, looking back over the journey, is how I had to embrace being 'dirty' and 'slutty' and 'disgusting' and 'shamed' in order to move through that energy to reclaim my sexuality for myself. I had to become aware of all the false structures about sexuality and shame in my consciousness so I could dispel that energy by flagrantly enjoying my yoni. I orgasmed my way to spiritual enlightenment. It's when I get concerned about what others might think of me that my sexuality tightens up and it's harder to 'get there'. Throwing all caution to the wind and embracing the wicked within is what creates the spaciousness to just be me, as I am, with my body as it is.

In retrospect, my mistake was not my sexual liberation. It was trying to wrap romance and conventional structures around primal urges. My mistake was to try to avoid other people's shaming judgments by shaming myself first.

Shame was a part of my sexual journey from birth, and continued as I became a mother. On the heels of my healing journey, I witness that I grew my sons in a womb filled with shame and insecurity, and that vibration has been part of the formation of their consciousness and shaped my struggles to guide them while I was feeling unworthy and disrespected. I fully believe that the healing work I have done on myself, to honor and respect myself, has been witnessed by my sons and the energetics have begun dissolving generational mother wounds within them. It takes some time for energetic work to be revealed in the manifest world, especially when considering personal choice to receive that healing or not. The healing is right there at the edge of their auras, waiting for their YES to witness a mother fully in her power, self-respect, and self-honor.

Starting off as a mother who disrespected herself means that my sons witnessed patterns of behavior from their father, myself, and my family of origin that demonstrated disrespect for the mother figure. As I have reclaimed my self-worth on the spiritual path, my own behavior and choices have changed and that has strained the existing structures in my sons' world.

When one person undergoes spiritual growth and changes what they will accept, and not accept, all of their relationships must now adapt or die. My consciousness upgrade created a recoil in the existing family structures that looked like gossip in front of my sons, clinging to the old identity of me, unforgiveness, disbelief, and for a while, excommunication from the family. Families often cling to narratives that keep them in the familiar patterns; the familiar is more comfortable, and so the old narrative will be enforced even if there is all the evidence in the world to the contrary of that story.

The shift from shaming yourself to honoring yourself as a woman and mother requires deep roots into the Mother Earth for support as you weather the storm of your family catching up to the new and true you. Often the people closest to you will test you with some pretty darned difficult behavior so you have to prove your spiritual merit by holding steady in love and compassion. The more you hold the higher vibrations of love and honor for yourself, and compassion for your family, the more the light seeps its way into the shadows of unconsciousness to reveal it as false, and the harder it is for them to keep lying to themselves by holding onto old stories of you.

All of this is good practice for honoring yourself and knowing that the shifts in you are real and permanent. To close the loop and truly honor yourself, you must love and accept every woman you've been along the journey to becoming the *you* in this moment. All of those versions of you were necessary to learn the lessons that led to the new choices that ultimately became your new way of being. You would not be you today without all of the you's that came before. **The most**

'shameful' and 'dirty' and 'slutty' you deserves a space of honor in your heart; her pain became your evolution.

I remember a moment of clarity I had one day shortly after my soulmate walked into my life. Akeem had taken me to dinner and I was feeling awkward inside as I felt the presence of 'Pinky'. At the peak of my sexual reclamation, I had been donned the name Pinky by a man with whom I was cheating on my husband who I called 'Daddy'.

To my spiritually superior self that attracted my soulmate as I stood in my power leading a firewalk, it seemed like Pinky was a shameful aspect that should be hidden in the shadows created by my current light. Being the sensitive and perceptive man that he is, Akeem asked me if there was an aspect of me that I was hiding in that moment. I confessed that it was Pinky, and that she felt ashamed of herself; she did not want to ruin this opportunity for love.

He looked me right in the eye, directly down into the shadows at Pinky, and told her he loved her. "Without you, I would never have found Kerri. I love you completely, and you deserve to sit at this table with me and be honored." I wept tears from deep inside of me, tears from this unloved shameful woman that I was, and I allowed love to pour into her heart...my heart.

That was the beginning of honoring my life journey and all the women I was that led to the woman I am. It was the beginning of loving and having compassion for all my selves. It was the beginning of integrating back into my Self these aspects that I had disowned because the burden of shame was too heavy to hold at the time.

We've all done things that we are ashamed of, and often we become ashamed of ourselves. This splinters off a part of yourself into the shadows where it hides its face from the world, which means you can only show up for others to the degree that you have welcomed home these shameful aspects back into your love and grace. **To fully reclaim your power and honor yourself, you must be willing to forgive your mistakes, have compassion for yourself in learning**

your lessons, and make the choices that lead to being the person you know in your heart you want to be.

Hold steady as others catch up to the new you, and practice loving and having compassion for yourself as their old stories of you haunt you and poke at deep wounds and places you're still ashamed of yourself. If a story someone else tells about you hurts you, it's because you hold that same judgment of yourself unconsciously; this person is just making you aware of your own self-judgment. When you've really reclaimed all the splintered pieces of you, your dedication to honoring yourself will have strengthened you to the place where you can allow others to tell whatever stories of you they want, knowing those stories are told by a person grappling with their own unhealed shadows.

From a space of honoring yourself, you can allow yourself to explore with curiosity your life, your body, your relationships, and the world. You gift yourself the freedom to try new things without knowing what is going to happen. And because you are present with the totality of yourself, you become a safe space for others to share their judgments, fears, shames, and insecurities. **When you've really accepted yourself, you can hold your heart open without fear because you've already gone down into the deepest shadows within to bring love to the pain.**

Love is always present. The work is opening to perceive and receive it. You are worthy.

♥

Suggestions

Release Your Judgments What judgments do you have about your sexuality? What judgments do you have about your mother's sexuality? If you have a daughter, what judgments do you have about her sexuality? Write down all the judgments without thinking nor holding back. Get it all out of you where you can see it. As you consider each judgment, notice how it makes you feel. Blow that feeling into the paper (yes! Use your breath to transfer your feelings into the paper). Open sacred space to invite support from the Divine Mother to help you heal. Declare out loud "I am releasing these judgments and claiming a healed relationship with my sexuality." Then hold the judgment pages over a fire pit and burn them to release. Notice if you feel a shift. You can repeat this process in a week if you wish; be curious about what arises as a judgment now, and what has been erased from your mind. As you repeat this ceremony, watch the list of judgements decrease as your acceptance of your sexuality strengthens and rises.

Love Your Body Create a personal ritual to honor your body that includes gentle, intimate touch. As you caress your belly, speak words of gratitude to your womb for its gifts of wisdom you receive. As you gently run your fingers along your body, speak softly to each part: "You are so beautiful, thank you for helping me sense and feel, I am grateful to feel you beneath my fingers, I love you." Say the words that rise to your lips without thinking. If there is awkwardness, allow it to be there as you continue loving your body and expressing your thankfulness.

Quotes

"If you put shame in a petri dish, it needs three ingredients to grow exponentially: secrecy, silence and judgment. If you put the same amount of shame in the petri dish and douse it with empathy, it can't survive."
— Brené Brown

"Someday every woman will have orgasms - like every family has color TV - and we can all get on with the business of love."
— Erica Jong

"There is unbelievable power in ownership, and women should own their sexuality. There is a double standard when it comes to sexuality that still persists. Men are free and women are not. That is crazy. The old lessons of submissiveness and fragility make us victims. Women are so much more than that. You can be a businesswoman, a mother, an artist and a feminist-- whatever you want to be--and still be a sexual being. It's not mutually exclusive."
— Beyoncé

"If sexuality is one dimension of our ability to live passionately...then in cutting off our sexual feelings we diminish our overall power to feel, know and value deeply."
— Judith Plaskow

If you consider a woman less pure after you've touched her, maybe you should take a look at your hands.
— Kaija Sabbah

Staying In The Conversation

When I walked into my mother's house unexpectedly and saw the entire family gathered around the table having dinner, a dinner to which I was not invited, I felt numb shock. I felt the rug ripped out from under me, and I sank my roots into the Earth for support.

There had been family disagreement since my Dad passed away, and for the first time in my life, my mother was in charge of the family. Her house, her rules. And since she was displeased with me for writing and speaking publicly about private matters, her retaliation came in the form of family exclusion. My younger son was at that table as well, being influenced by this example. As my mother's only child, and the mother of my son at this table, this was hard to bear in that moment. I breathed deeply, took the action I came to take, and left them. In the car, I wept all the way home until I could be with my husband for processing.

Rejection has been a constant theme in my life. It is something difficult to move through when you care deeply about others. There's no area of my life that has been excluded from this experience until my relationship with Akeem Sami. What I have come to realize is that it is my Soul's curriculum to love myself profoundly through the experience of rejection from others. The closer the person to me, the more hurtful the rejection feels. Keeping my heart open and being willing to stay with the discomfort has been an incredible spiritual initiation. **Rejection is an opportunity to release all expectations, to extricate myself from all forms of co-dependency, and to stand in total personal sovereignty.**

I get the chance to heal the painful wounds in the collective psyche around roles you 'have to' play as a daughter and mother for your family. It does hurt during the process, and it's my self-mastery to feel all the feelings while releasing the conditioning and resisting the urges to hurt back as I've been hurt. I get the gift of self-mastery to hold myself and others in unconditional love while stepping into a world of zero obligation.

All the places where I have attachment for someone to love me, or treat me with respect because of my role, gets challenged one by one until there's no more strands of co-dependency for me to stand on and demand something of another because of historical rules.

It was hard to experience rejection from my mother in the painful ways she chose to act. It was almost harder to experience rejection from my eldest son as he moved out, and went months not communicating with me. The first time he moved out, it felt like my heart was being ripped from my chest. The pain of it woke me from sleep, and I went out to the front yard to rest my chest on Mother Earth and cry. The second time he moved out I felt like I wanted to die, the pain was so great throughout my whole body. I ran several miles to move the energy, and came home to my husband who embraced me while I sobbed and wailed in primal pain. Weeks later, I was still waking up in the night crying.

This is hard work. It's for the greater good that you make the shift from co-dependency to sovereignty. You have to feel the pain to heal the wounds, and many of these wounds are ancestral and magnified. So keep stepping the steps even if breaks your heart.

It's only breaking your heart free of the crust of human suffering.

What has helped me through these intense experiences of rejection are my spiritual practices of connecting and grounding with the Earth for support, opening sacred space for assistance from Divine allies, letting the emotion flow freely, allowing myself to express the pain, deep breathing, exercise, tobacco clearing, lavender or other essential oils, soothing bubble baths, journaling, and chakra clearing. I also continue to enlist mentoring from my own spiritual teachers, which I advise for anyone walking a spiritual path: you must give yourself ongoing support to face the challenges.

∞

I've witnessed a fairly consistent pattern in the collective of disconnecting from and disposing of people when relations feel too intense, critical, or argumentative. A typical form of disconnection is silence, and when used in a way to gain control over others, or manipulate the outcome of a situation, it is called the silent treatment.

Sometimes people disconnect from others because they feel overwhelmed by the situation emotionally or mentally and do not feel capable of continuing in the conversation without resorting to saying or doing something negative. Sometimes people disconnect from others because they feel 'under attack' and want to protect themselves. It takes a certain amount of self-awareness to see that you are disconnecting from a conversation due to overwhelm or feeling of being attacked, and to realize that you need to give yourself space for emotional processing. In this space of personal reflection, you can bring yourself to a sense of clarity and realize something beneficial to offer that moves the conversation forward in a good direction. You may realize that your feeling of being 'under attack' did not actually come from the other person, but was an old pattern provoked by the conversation; witnessing the old pattern gives you an opportunity to see it and choose to heal it.

Disconnecting in order to gain space for reflection and healing is certainly an understandable need, and healthy when you use that space and silence to do the personal work of becoming curious about the situation and your role in it. The next step is to convey in words that you need time for reflection and space to the person with whom you've been in conversation. **This communication is what keeps the silence from becoming a weapon to hurt the other person.**

Whether or not your intention of silence is to hurt the other person, realize that people have all kinds of reactions to silence and disconnection in a relationship. Some people's minds lead them down a rabbit trail of questions like: "what have I done egregiously wrong to deserve being treated with total shunning?", "maybe they don't value our relationship", "I guess they don't love me." Those are all tremendously painful contemplations, and when silence is prolonged and repeatedly used as a tool of disconnection from a relationship, it wears thin the trust between people and makes bonds more superficial and less substantive.

How can you trust a person who keeps disconnecting and disappearing with your true feelings and vulnerability?

Ultimately disconnection provokes the fear of being all alone and abandoned, or the primal fear of being shunned and cast out from the tribe. It's a foundational program in your reptilian brain and it leads to anxiety, depression, and hopelessness without the right tools for re-grounding yourself in Spirit—which ultimately is the solution for the person being shunned or disconnected from. Connection with a larger presence such as the Divine, Mother Earth, Great Spirit, God— the true, abiding, ever-present consciousness that imbues and surrounds us—is a healing balm for the temporary interruptions of human connection.

The flip side of disconnection is that the person receiving the silence is invited to view this as a boundary, and respect it. **You must respect another's choice to not be in relationship with you.** Even if you feel their reason is clouded with conditioning, or a huge misunderstanding, it remains that in their dream of life they desire to be disconnected from the relationship. If you want to have your dream of life honored, you begin by respecting yourself, and other people's dreams of life. There is freedom in respect; the freedom from trying to control others to conform to your needs, wants and expectations which can feel quite burdensome (especially as they resist control). When you miss that person, send love through the winds to their heart. Time heals all wounds; it is much easier to allow time to heal things, than to try to push and force a healing before it is ready.

And as humans, you can learn to stay in the conversation just like the Divine stays with you. You can cultivate the emotional capacity to stay connected through discomfort, and to open and listen and understand. Emotional capacity is a muscle you exercise through the choice to open and listen, rather than disconnect and disappear.

Ultimately, this is the muscle we collectively must become very strong with in order to heal humanity and our planet.

Right now, the mentality of simply disposing of things (and people) is highly prevalent; rather than stay in engaged in a conversation where there are differences, people simply choose to block on social media, ignore messages and calls, and terminate connection at all levels. It is as if it's too difficult to stay connected with someone whose point of view on one topic of conversation differs from ours.

Obviously there are circumstances where the participants of a conversation become angry and 'toxic', in which case a cooling off period is certainly helpful. And in cases where those engaged in the dialog are entrenched and immovable in their positions, or are targeting each other with hateful energy, it can feel fruitless to continue a conversation. There can be a strong urge to pre-empt the other person's entrenched point of view with an automatic invalidation, or a volley back and forth of critical comments that tear down each other, and it's this heated exchange where neither party feels heard that leads to disconnection through blocking, silence, and severing of the relationship.

If you empathize to understand another's perspective, does that mean you are agreeing with them? Will you become infected with their point of view and led astray by simply listening to understand? What is the fear of putting on someone else's shoes and seeing things from their eyes?

In my experience navigating into this territory, the process of truly hearing another person sheds light into the way you are speaking or behaving that is contributing to the conflict, even if you are not able or willing to change it. At least by listening, you can understand why the other person holds their stance, and be able to choose whether to meet them partway by changing something on your end, or agree to disagree.

Can you be respectful of someone that you do not agree with? Or do you need to change them towards your way of thinking in order to love and respect them? These are some of the questions that get revealed as you stay in a conversation as a conscious participant.

Seeing through someone else's eyes, you might realize a shadow aspect of your own programming that has (up until now) gotten in the way of your relationships deepening. Of course this is vulnerable, to stay open and willing to see your own flaws right in the middle of an uncomfortable conversation with another person. You do not need to throw yourself under the bus to make peace happen. That's not a true peace; that's a tactic people sometimes do to stop a conflict, thereby putting an end to the discomfort they're feeling, and in the long run it does more damage than good.

You have the choice of how far you can stay with a conversation until it feels like it is siphoning your power or sense of self-worth. And in these 'edge' moments, you'll discover subconscious programs that are leading you to believe your power can be siphoned by another person, or that your self-worth can be diminished by a conflict. These subconscious programs can be shifted with love and compassion into greater wholeness that allows you to stay longer in an uncomfortable conversation the next time.

When you feel you have been disposed of, either through extended unexplained silence or through direct communication that a relationship is no longer viable, there can be potent feelings of loss, betrayal, shunning, blame, abandonment, not good enough and not wanted. The surfacing of these feelings is an opportunity to bring healing and compassion to the aspects of your consciousness that have feared exactly this kind of abandonment.

You can lean into the discomfort of the loss, and bring your listening deep within to reveal what your hurt voices are saying. Maybe you discover the little child within you who thinks she must have done something wrong, and desperately wants to fix it so she won't be abandoned. It's your opportunity to comfort that aspect within, and to assure her that she does not need to be punished, and she is still loved even as this disconnection is occurring. Maybe as this aspect relaxes, you'll be open to introspection and discovery of what you may have unconsciously been doing or saying that can be modified for better outcomes of future conversation engagements.

Staying with uncomfortable conversations, and staying with yourself through them, can lead to amazing shifts and growth. It most certainly leads to expanded emotional capacity that allows you to stay present with others in their difficult times of need.

♥

Quotes

"The most terrible poverty is loneliness and the feeling of being unloved." — Mother Teresa

"You cannot convince people to love you. This is an absolute rule. No one will ever give you love because you want him or her to give it. Real love moves freely in both directions. Don't waste your time on anything else."
— Cheryl Strayed ("Sugar")

"Tenderness and kindness are not signs of weakness and despair, but manifestations of strength and resolution."
— Kahlil Gibran

"The only way to change someone's mind is to connect with them from the heart."
— Rasheed Ogunlaru

"There can be no deep disappointment where there is not deep love."
— Martin Luther King, Jr.

"If you're betrayed, release disappointment at once. By that way, the bitterness has no time to take root."
— Toba Beta

"When you're following your inner voice, doors tend to eventually open for you, even if they mostly slam at first."
— Kelly Cutrone

Transforming Your Life

I've never seen any life transformation that didn't begin with the
person in question finally getting tired of their own bullshit.
—Elizabeth Gilbert

Have you ever stayed in a situation past the moment you knew that it was not in your best good to stay? Maybe you felt your situation was 'as good as it gets', and you decided to settle for it since you could not imagine a better potential. Self-doubt and fear of the unknown are likely contributors to being stuck.

If you want to experience a potential even better than you can imagine for yourself, you must move to the edge of your comfort zone and then take at least one step beyond it. That step into the unknown is where you learn to trust yourself, and you find out what you really believe. Sometimes it takes a radical act to move yourself into the flow of change; that first act can be a proving point from the Divine that you are going to be just fine as you take inspired actions. That radical act is what makes everyone in your life think you've gone off the deep end—you have! When you follow your Soul you move into the deep end of life where meaning and purpose reside.

It's the shift from outer 'having it together' with inner mess, to inner 'having it together' and outer mess. Once you take that first radical act, you set into motion a series of initiations that will ultimately lead you to your authentic self who sees change and evolution as part of the magic of life. The most potent and juicy life moments happen after that first radical act to follow your Soul.

As you embrace the Divine Feminine energies of the Age of Aquarius, you move into flow with life. You learn through taking Soul-guided risks that you are safer and happier following Spirit than you were stuck in the so-so situation you thought was 'as good as it gets'. You also learn how resilient you are as the initiations of power begin showing up for you to rise to the challenge, and learn just how much more amazing life can be when you open to the Divine.

The master of transformation—mariposa (butterfly)—knows that to become the beautiful butterfly she must let go of everything...including her identity. She must dissolve into what appears to be a total mess. And then she must open to her innate design, and the masterful orchestration of the Divine, to grow wings to fly. You are being given the opportunity to learn from mariposa to enter the cocoon and transform everything into beauty.

Is it frightening to enter the cocoon? Is it terrifying to lose what you've relied on to feel 'safe'? Yes...and on the other side of the cocoon is something far greater. You have to claim it for yourself by saying Yes before you really know what you're saying Yes to. Trust that your Soul has amazing things in store for you as you follow. Because I went into the cocoon with mariposa, I am writing this book for you today.

♥

The Power of Letting Go

It's so hard to let go of the people you have loved deeply, and especially those you still love. Letting go is the ultimate respect for those you care about. Once you have expressed your desires in a relationship, to honor your beloved is to let go and let them make their own choices for how they want to respond to you (or not respond to you). **Letting go is an act of love, and it requires tremendous faith that the Universe is benevolent and has your highest good in mind.**

You can fall so madly in love with a moment in time that you never want to let it go. Yet sometimes relationships reach a point where the highest and best good is to let go, for a while or forever. And the thing is, when you're doing the letting go, you do not know whether it will be for just a while, or whether it will be forever. Sometimes when you let go and set your love free, it returns to you later in Divine timing in a new configuration that better supports you and others involved in the relationship. Other times, you never hear from your beloved again. There are no guarantees for a happy ending.

Letting go of a meaningful relationship can feel like getting the wind knocked out of you. All that time and effort working on the relationship, all those difficult conversations...to have the best solution come down to parting ways can feel devastating.

It might feel so painful that you do not want to feel it. You may want to drown in a bottle of wine, or fill up your life with so many activities and responsibilities that you don't have time to sit still. You might find yourself chewing and stewing on it, looking under every single rock for the solution that will bring resolution and peace, and return your love to you. You might build walls around your heart, decide to 'hate' or blame the other person to push them away, block them socially, or pretend they never existed.

For twenty years I was married to the father of my children and we enjoyed many joyous moments, and we pushed all of each other's buttons. When I saw 'the end of the rope' in a Spirit vision, I knew it was true. I knew that all the suffering I was experiencing was not good for me or the kids; and I felt in my heart that things had reached that point where letting go was the best solution for the family.

The letting go was a process over the course of eight years. Wave after wave of letting go happened as the ocean of the Great Spirit washed me clear of my history one tide at a time. The first letting go was moving out of the home I shared with the father of my children, and moving into my own little house. That first night in the bubble bath with my candlelight and wine, I tasted freedom from unresolvable arguments before bed.

Over eight years, every new painful interaction with him about our sons, or within my family, reopened wounds. I performed ritual, release, and energy healing to let go of the relationship and my feelings about it at deeper and deeper levels. I practiced forgiveness to let the relationship slip into history without trying to clutch it into this present moment.

At one point during a healing ceremony, I realized that I had rivers of Love running through my heart, and that I had blocked off the branches of the river that originally led to the father of my children and to my mother. These rivers that once flowed Love for these two people had gone swampy and putrid in my heart. The toxic sludge from blocking my own Love for them was hurting me, not them. I welcomed my guides to unblock my heart and let the Love begin flowing through these branches once again. At first, it was painful to experience the sludge at the bottom of my heart as it began stirring with Love to flow again. And then, like any swampy river reconnected to a river that is flowing, it began to clear. Tears streamed down my face and my heart was cleansed of feelings of betrayal and pain.

Now that I surrendered control over my Love for these two people in my life, the Love flowed cleanly through my heart. I realized that Love flows wherever it is needed, and right now, it was flowing through me because I was no longer blocking it in an attempt to deny my love to others.

More lessons from the river came as I watched its currents flow past an eddy. I realized that sometimes people need to stay in an eddy to process something painful, and it feels like you're leaving them behind to flow where the river is taking you. You might feel that you are leaving them behind forever stuck in that eddy of your past. But watching the river, I saw how it used currents to fast-track some energy far down the river. I realized the same is true in life. Sometimes life uses special currents to leapfrog people up to where you are later in your life when you least expect it. **Let the Great Spirit do the work of channeling your love where it needs to go, and trust in miracles of healing and Love.**

I am still here after the letting go. And in the space created by letting go, the Great Spirit has brought me many gifts including a new husband, a fascinating career, wonderful friends, and a new sense of family.

Because I have experienced the power of letting go of what you once loved, to welcome what greater love might come your way, I was able to face new moments of letting go. Each letting go feels like the hardest letting go of my life. I let go of my 20 year marriage, I let go of my Dad when he transitioned beyond the veil, I let go of my mom and family, and I let go of my son when he moved out the first time. Each of these letting go challenges broke my heart; I came to understand that I could keep loving through the pain of the heartbreak.

When my eldest son moved out for the second time, he stopped communicating with me which felt so painful. I wanted to escape this pain, to wall it off, to walk away from it, to project it out...anything to not feel it. But how can I deny my love for him? I cannot. The river of love pours through my heart for my son as an unstoppable force.

I came to the realization that it would not serve my son to be tied to his momma in the configuration of being my baby forever. He needed to step into his manhood to fully experience the potentials of his life, and I had to let him go so he could do it. My mother's heart wanted my son to have an empowered life creating his dream like he creates his artwork. I knew I had to cut the umbilical cord and grieve the ending to my son's childhood; I had to let go of my baby. He doesn't belong to me anymore. He is his own person. And so with my heart wide open without expectations, I let my love flow through me cleanly, letting the Great Spirit send my love where it's needed as I cut the umbilical cord with my son.

Time heals all wounds but it's harder to heal when you keep picking off the scab. Trying to speed up the healing does not work well when other people are involved and they need space for their own healing process. You can dive into your process however you want, and you can't force others to hurry up with you. They may not be ready in this lifetime to rejoin you in Love, and you have to find a way to accept that within yourself without hurting yourself with it.

Waiting to connect again is an energetic prompt that other people can feel, and it can be a not-so-subtle message of impatience with their process. **That's why letting go means really letting go: letting go of expectations, timeframes, and personal dreams and visions of your relationship with someone.** Letting go means grieving the loss of what has been, and celebrating the gifts of it.

It was a beautiful gift to serve as my son's mother for 21 years. I did my very best that I was capable of doing at the time. I ran my race, and now that part is done. I have to accept what was, as it was, and let it be.

In the silence of letting go, I remember the ocean and its waves of release and expansion.

The ocean leaps high onto the shore, drowning the sand castles, reclaiming its creations, and recycling the sands as it pulls out to sea. Then there is a quiet lull between breaths of anticipation. A moment of complete uncertainty. And then the ocean rolls into shore replenishing the land with renewed vigor. In the pause can be gratitude for what has been that is now swept away. In the pause can be feeling your heart's yearnings. In the pause can be dreaming visions of beauty. In the pause is the East, the void, the certainty of the sunrise and the anticipation of the dawn.

You and I are still alive, and therefore, there is more to come. To help yourself realize that letting go is a continuation, imagine yourself down by a river that is flowing with grace and ease on a beautiful summer day. You grasp a tree root that is extending into the river, and walk into the waters holding onto the root. Imagine that tree root is something you have a hard time letting go of. Place all your feelings into the tree root with your breath; all your grief at the loss, all your gratitude for the experience, all your fear of letting go and moving into the unknown, and anything else you feel. Now lie back on the waters, still holding the root. Feel the waters supporting and lifting you even as currents move underneath you towards the future. Now let go of the root.

You are moving down the river. And the root is part of the river, so it is not lost; it is just behind you as the known experience of your life. You are floating now with ease and grace towards new blessings, and the river is guiding you. **Let your love of that root pour into the river, and it will find its way to a beautiful destination that can authentically and joyfully receive your love.**

♥

Disorientation Is Reorientation

Letting go of what has been, or of who you used to be, is a big step in the path of transformation because it creates a void into which the Great Spirit can breathe new life. The absence of my eldest son in our home created the space for me to focus on and connect more deeply with my younger son, and this was a beautiful gift to receive.

My husband and I repurposed our living room, let go of the sofa I sat on as a pregnant mama with my eldest son and bought a new blue velvet sofa and loveseat that we adored. We put a family tree of pictures on the wall, got a new sound system for dance parties, and intentionally made our home inviting for all of the members of the family to congregate together.

While my heart still yearned for my eldest son, I did the daily work to invite the new gifts being offered to me by the Great Spirit and to allow myself to be re-oriented. **You have to be willing to let go, and then stay with the feeling of being disoriented as the Great Spirit is re-orienting you to a new chapter of your life.**

Allow yourself to be reprogrammed by the consciousness of the Divine Mother so you can receive something even better than you imagined was possible from your historical perception of yourself and your life. Release attachment to the thoughts, beliefs and behaviors you became accustomed to because you were programmed by human egoic consciousness and your history. Pay attention to yourself and the circumstances of your life to fully engage in this transformation process, inviting re-orientation to better and better potentials. Lean into the discomfort of things not being the way they were, and become curious about the changes you can make to more fully manifest the new potentials that you are feeling come into being.

What are you aligning to? What are you giving attention to? What is your truth? Is your mind revealing your truth, or is the Divine revealing your truth? Can you allow your truth to evolve?

❤

Being Uncomfortable In The Shadows

"You are not a drop in the ocean. You are the entire ocean in a drop."
— *Rumi*

Consider this teaching from Rumi. If you are the entire ocean in a drop that means that within you is the entire human experience. Perhaps this explains why some moments you might feel fear, other moments joy, and then horror at something you've seen which leads you to feel judgment and then rebellious, then powerless, then back to hope. **The entire human experience lives within the drop of consciousness that you are.**

Except we deny it because we do not want to be identified with the darker aspects of humanity. We deny feeling hatred, jealousy, insecurity, retribution, greed, shame; and we do everything we can to avoid seeing the shadows through numbing out, distracting, projecting, distancing, silo-ing, and so forth.

Fear is a difficult thing to feel without going down dark tunnels into despair. Anger, grief, shame, regret...all heavy emotions in fact...are difficult to feel without slipping into a dark hole. That's why so many people distract away from the pain.

Over the years I've had many go-to strategies for distracting away from discomfort: food, wine, movies, television, running, overworking, escaping and hiding, sex, happy pills. Because it was hard to face my own uncomfortable feelings, it was hard for me to hold space for loved ones when they wanted to express uncomfortable feelings. I would find myself multi-tasking or walking away from serious discussions because I wanted to escape the discomfort of it. Can you relate?

Yet this is a time we are collectively being brought to our knees by the Divine Mother through a powerful spiritual two-by-four. It's very intense since the beginning of 2020, and as an empathic person I can feel the stress. I feel myself wanting to find a way out so I can escape, and there is no escape. The whole world is on lockdown.

Do you want to run away to Fantasy Island too? Well, it is time for each of us individually, and all of us collectively, to face our shadows. You must learn to love the totality of your beingness as the entire ocean in a drop.

You are not just here to love the good stuff. You're here to love the aspects of yourself that you wish did not exist. And those of us who are healers must embrace being uncomfortable a good part of the time because we are using our very bodies and lives to heal the wounds of the collective.

As you walk into your shadows, you heal. As you heal, you release layers of crust between your heart and the human experience. As you release layers of crust, you become more sensitive and perceive in greater nuances the energies and emotions of life. Being sensitive, you feel densities with greater discernment and things that others do not notice can feel very uncomfortable to you. These discomforts are your body's way of letting you know that some experience you encountered has touched a wound within that needs healing.

So many sensitive people feel 'negativity' and stop engaging, hide or walk away. Anything that feels unloving is used as a reason to give up. People with 'normal' perception may not even notice the event that led a sensitive person to give up on them, especially when the sensitive person disappears without a conversation.

A question for the sensitive healers and lightworkers is this: **how are we going to heal the world if we are too wounded within ourselves to handle a mild disagreement**? The world around you is filled with conflict. If you are here to ascend human consciousness, then you need to be healed enough within yourself to hold space for greater levels of conflict. You need to be able to lean into difficult conversations rather than judge them as lower vibration than yourself and silently walk away.

What if that 'lower vibration' judgement is really an egoic protection of an old wound of not being included, appreciated, wanted and loved?

My invitation is to get involved with your shadow rather than avoid it. **The shadow is helping you to heal the wounds you carry inside so you can lean into this world as a wisdom keeper.** You can only bring peace to conflict when you can embrace negativity as a sign that it's resonating with a wound inside of you. Start by having a difficult conversation with someone 'negative' that you're avoiding. Open your heart, breathe, speak, listen, and see what happens through the discomfort.

Some people prefer the illusion of being spiritual to the real deal. They silo themselves to only interact with people of their 'high vibration' and keep eliminating anyone 'lower' than themselves who resonates any nuance of 'negativity' or 'toxicity' until they are alone with themselves. This is a huge false projection. **True spiritual warriors get gritty in the shadows knowing that the 'negativity' and 'toxicity' is not just 'out there'…it's 'in here' too.**

If you want to change the world and make it a better place, you must embrace the shadows and do the healing work within. You must courageously take inspired actions in the world to bring new ideas and energies. Hanging out in the bubble of higher consciousness where it's safe and loving is helping to raise the vibration, yet it does not help nearly as many people as getting involved and bringing your light TO the darkness. What if Harriet Tubman had said "It's way too negative and scary in the south…I'm going to hang out with my free people in Philadelphia"?

I've learned that the best way to handle intense feelings and urges is to be present with them. To breathe through them. To acknowledge the aspect of myself that is generating those feelings. To listen to the feelings in my body and the thoughts in my mind. To validate my current experience without resistance. And to then bring compassion to myself.

Often holding presence with myself leads to an emotional release that leaves me feeling so much lighter and better. I'm not talking about simply using meditation as another way to bliss out and bypass your reality. I'm talking about learning to hold peace and pain right next to each other in presence.

There's a world out there of humans who are feeling pain who would love to feel the elevated state of consciousness and lightness of being that you are able to bring yourself to experience.

Remember what it was like to feel like there was no God.
Remember what it was like to feel all alone.
Your light is needed in the darkness.
Your positivity is needed in the negativity.
Your helping hand is needed even more than your prayers from afar.

Bring your courageous heart into the world to be the demonstration of Love. **Your love is more powerful than the resistance of people living in fear.** Instead of seeing the adult as 'toxic', see the afraid little child inside of them yearning for Love.

Realize that as the entire ocean in a drop, you can heal that ocean by claiming your space as I Am. Here is a prayer you can recite to bring yourself to a space of healing when you are feeling the density of the shadows.

I Am the Keeper of this Space.
I Am remembering that all I see out-pictured in my reality is also inside my ocean in a drop.
I Am courageous to see and feel everything that out-pictures itself in my reality, knowing it is only doing so because it is also inside my ocean in a drop.
I Am listening to the voices within my drop of consciousness.
I Am feeling the feelings within my drop of consciousness.
I Am realizing I have created what I am witnessing, as Being the entire ocean in a drop.
I Am remembering that I have the power of choice.
I Am claiming that choice to lift everything to a higher octave.

From the teachings of Paul Selig:
I know who I am in truth
I know what I am in truth
I know how I serve in truth

I am here, I am here, I am here
I am free, I am free, I am free
I have come, I have come, I have come
I am in the upper room
I lift all I see before me to the upper room
Behold! I make all things new

♥

Learning To Parent Yourself

A profound transformation began unfolding after my Dad passed away. When he was alive, he held such beautiful space of unconditional love for the family, that in retrospect I realize that I did not have to fully mature. In his absence, painful family dynamics unfolded that helped me to see that part of my strength up until his death was his strength, rather than my maturity. Actions were taken in the family that violated my sense of trust and fairness, and I had a resurgence of emotional lashing out that I thought I had overcome through my spiritual work.

I sought the help of new spiritual mentors, George Kansas and Tracey Trottenberg, because as my family unraveled, I found myself unable to fill the gap from the absence of Dad's very large presence. With their help I was able to begin seeing clearly the unhealed rebellious anger of my teenage self, the frightened powerless shrinking of my toddler self, and the emotional overwhelm of the daughter within me who had lost her safe harbor.

With the simultaneous shunning from my mother and remaining family members, I felt wounded, disrespected as a mother, and abandoned even as I was experiencing the most loving, supportive and powerful relationship of my life with my new husband Akeem. I was committed to fulfilling the Spirit visions of my purpose work in the world, yet despite 80+ hour work weeks, nothing was really taking flight. My wings had been clipped with all the family drama, and I needed to reclaim them for myself.

The little girl within me felt she lost both of her parents, and she was frightened and abandoned. She needed my love, attention and compassion. The teenager within me felt betrayed by her mother, and all the hurt feelings from a lifetime of misunderstanding and suppressed anger rose to the surface. She needed me to listen, nurture, and support to claim her own voice independent from her mother. The daughter within me felt tremendous grief from the loss of her Dad, her one person she could always turn to for help. She needed me to become that person she could always turn to for help. The mother within me was filled with self-doubt and worry over how to help her troubled son. She needed me to be grounded, resilient, and wise so she could relax into her knowing.

I began to listen and watch my reactions and words intently. Who was speaking? Who was feeling? Which aspect of self was reaching out for help?

Resting into the supportive container from my spiritual mentors, I could let these voices speak, cry, fume, turn beet red—and express themselves, at last. It felt tremendously painful to lose my Dad, and to feel rejected and unloved by my mother. I faced my feelings of self-doubt and lack of worth to do the Soul calling set before me. I committed to healing these voices within as part of navigating and understanding the pathway that, someday, I would hold big space for others to move through.

What I learned was how powerful an illusion can be created by a wounded aspect of self as she releases her pain in a cry for help. **Equally as powerful was learning how to simply hold patient loving space for that aspect to express, without judgment or expectation.** As I was held and supported, I learned how to adopt unconditional love for myself and all the voices within me. The old programming would rise to the surface, I would become aware of it as programming and hold steady through the discomfort of it with love, and it would dissolve. Stories that circulated in my brain for decades would surface with renewed vigor from the latest injuries, and I would listen, hold presence, feel it to heal it, and express what needed to be said in safe spaces.

In my mind's eye, I would see the aspect of myself as I was listening to her; and when she was ready, I would give her a hug. In this way, I rose exponentially in the frequency of Love that I could hold for myself, and I expanded my capacity to hold space for others.

Simultaneously with this spiritual work, I was realigning myself to Mother Earth as my mother to give myself greater support and a sense of stability. I became aware of codependency with my biological mother and family members and dedicated myself to making the inner shifts needed for me to stand in my power. I healed the immature patterns that had snuck into my adulthood, including entitlement and expectation. And I took response-ability for healing dynamics with my sons that were now revealed to my new eyes as unsupportive of their growth and evolution.

Through my greater awareness of my inner children, and by gaining their trust, I was able to divert myself from previous unhealthy relationship patterns with my mother and family. As my inner world felt heard, loved and supported, I could expand myself to perceive situations through the eyes of my mother and others in my family, which helped me to make changes to my own perceptions and beliefs. At some point, I was able to make a hard decision to walk away from the family dynamic for a while so I could focus on my own healing and growth.

My little girl did not want to let go of her mommy and accept me as the replacement; she kept trying to go back and rekindle the attention she was craving from my biological mother. Through patient work however, I was able to shift through this addiction and let go. And it was during this year and a half that my business catapulted into much greater impact, and I channeled and released a book that was over a year as an international bestseller (*The Second Wave: Transcending the Human Drama*). Following on the heels of this success, I began writing this current book and embodying even more profound healing of the Mother Wound.

Becoming my own Mother within has been life-changing not only for my purpose work, but for my relationship with my sons. I was finally strong enough emotionally for my sons to be honest with me about how they were feeling in our relationship, to not take it personally, and to not invalidate their perspectives. In other words, I was finally able to do for my sons what my Dad had always done for me.

Expanding on this huge win, I have been able to make a new home with my life partner Akeem that integrates all our children under one roof as part of a FAMILY. My Dad taught me that family is where you can feel safe and supported so you can go out into the world and take risks. Now I had been able to mature myself through my spiritual work to provide this gift to my children...even if the overall family was 'taking sides'.

More than that, I was able to let my mother know that I am here for her when she is ready to talk.

♥

Rebirthing Yourself

Are you sick of telling your story yet? Are you tired of disempowering yourself with all the inherited patterns revealed by this book? If not, then you are not ready to reclaim your power. Are you ready to commit to self-mastery on a daily basis? If not, then you are not ready to reclaim your power.

Everything you have experienced up until now in your life has shaped your perception of yourself and the world. Until you are ready to claim response-ability for your life, as it stands today, you will keep perpetuating the same conditions that you say you do not want by telling the same story about yourself, your life, and the world around you that has become a familiar blanket of suffering covering up your true essential self. You will make every excuse in the book to avoid having your familiar yet unfulfilling world turned upside down, and avoid the truth tellers who see clearly what you're doing to yourself because you are addicted to your story and your conditions of suffering.

Was it your fault that your mother treated you in an unloving way, and that your brain adopted a world view based on that unloving treatment that has shaped your life in self-sabotaging ways...up until now? It is absolutely not your fault, and completely your response-ability, if you want your life to change. Putting your life on hold waiting for another person to set it right by apologizing, or changing their behavior to make you feel better, is a recipe for the same old patterns you've been perpetuating up until now. Nothing in your life will change until you decide to change everything, let go of trying to get something from other people that you feel you're owed or were denied, and open to a whole new story of you.

The way others have treated you, and your addiction to telling the story about it, can keep you stuck for this entire lifetime in an unfulfilling existence if you choose to hand over your power to create the life you actually desire. **Your reasons why you can't change your life are based in upholding the operating conditions of your current life situation.**

For years I let the underlying programs from my childhood run my life. I attracted a twenty year partner to reveal those patterns to me day in, day out until I was finally fed up with trying to 'fix' myself to win love from another. The patterns in my subconscious mind that told me I was a burden, to blame for everything, 'crazy', irrational, not good enough no matter what I did, and so forth led me to adopt self-sabotaging behaviors. Even though people close to me demonstrated these patterns through their words and actions, the patterns lived in MY subconscious mind and therefore I could choose a different response than to believe and act from them.

When I stopped agreeing to the self-sabotaging inherited patterns, then of course my external world changed to reflect that I was no longer in co-resonance with those patterns and the people who operated from them. My relationship with the father of my children and my mother turned confrontational the more I gained personal power because they were still operating from the historical reality in which I was agreeing to be a burden, to blame for everything, 'crazy', irrational, and not good enough and I was finally in rebellion to that world view. They were still living in past world in which I apologized for my existence and focused all my energy on mental hoops trying to figure out how to get love and acceptance from them. When I finally realized that love comes from within, and that it was a tangled codependency to try getting it from people on the outside, I stopped behaving like a crack-addicted rat compulsively pushing the lever to get a hit. I stopped playing tug-of-war with people who wanted me to play their game to win their 'love'. I found a greater source of love…within.

As I tapped into love within, extricated myself from mental loops and tunnels that had been there my entire life, and detached energetically and physically from those whose conditioning was dragging me back into disempowerment, I gained personal power. The more self-mastery I practiced, the more old stories I stopped tolerating, the more I practiced presence and co-creation with the Divine Mother, the more I filled up with love and self-respect and the more people from my old paradigm faded into the background.

Now when I think of the father of my children and of my mother, I feel neutral. I no longer need anything from them. I've extricated myself from the patterns. I let them be as they are. If I think of them, I allow my heart to feel and send them love.

To rebirth myself, I had to heal the deepest wound: the Mother Wound. To heal this wound I went right into the most painful fear and brought profound acceptance: *My mother does not love me.*

If my mother was to read this statement, would she defend herself by proclaiming "That's not true! I do love my daughter!"? She might love me and her conditioning might prevent her from expressing it in a way I can receive it as love; and she might not love me, but defend herself by saying she does, because it's the deepest taboo for a mother to admit she does not feel love for her child.

"I love you as long as you don't do xyz" is not love. Love stays present and connected through the turmoil of disagreement. Love accepts the journey of your child and keeps an open door and an invitation while, of course, maintaining boundaries that protect one's personal physical welfare. Love also admits one's own faults and commits to personal growth, resisting the urge to blame another for personal wounds.

In accepting my worst fear, whether true or not, that my mother does not love me, I allowed myself to move through the pain so that it no longer had power over me. Facing this fear, and moving through the pain as if it was true, helped me stop the pattern of getting swept up into hope and delusion. It helped me to stop trying to figure out the magic recipe to make my mother love me. It let me learn how to love myself and be happy right now, whether or not my mother is engaging with me in a loving way. It also helped me to focus on what is in my sphere of control (my perceptions and actions), and let go of things out of my sphere of control (what my mother thinks or feels about me).

Applying *The Four Agreements*, I reached into a new level of not taking it personally what my mother was doing or not doing, and being impeccable with my word to myself with not making assumptions and exposing my own conditioned patterns of thought and behavior.

In healing the Mother Wound, I realized how much of my life was spent walking on eggshells trying to make my mother proud and earn love with my good behavior, and conversely, how much of my life was spent in rebellion proving why my mother must not love me. A huge percentage of my consciousness was derived from this one relationship which turned into two when I married the father of my children and repeated the dynamic.

I accept that the majority of my life was spent drowning in self-doubt trying to win the love of a person whose conditioning stood in the way of that love. I claim my personal power in turning this lifetime immersion in the pattern of the Mother Wound into a diamond of wisdom that I share with the world, for the benefit of all.

Your mother's opinion of you is none of your business.

Your mother's feelings about you do not matter in your world unless you make it matter.

How your mother treated you was the fodder for you to create your fuel.

Let her live her life as she chooses.

Give yourself permission to live your life as you choose.

I thank my mother for catalyzing the painful events that helped push me into the best transformation of my life: loving myself and living my life for me. My mother has been my greatest teacher about self-love just by being herself. That's how you know that you've been immersed in your Soul's curriculum. You can't avoid the lesson.

You might wonder whether I love my mother. The answer is yes. I love my mother as she is. I let her be. I no longer expect her to do or say or be something to help me love myself. I claim responsibility to love myself.

The pathway to reclaiming personal power takes dedication and a mentor who is familiar with the territory you are facing in your inner matrix. It's a very tender journey that is most effectively taken within supportive conscious community.

"If you don't climb the mountain, you can't see the view." Once you choose a path and start down it, such as a program for awakening, don't let yourself back out. Keep going until you complete that cycle of learning. You will be uncomfortable, you will want to leave. Stay.

On the other side of the discomfort is an awakening that will restore your personal power. The discomfort is completely your conditioning and your fear of being without that familiar blanket of suffering.

Be courageous enough to be free.

♥

Coyotes Are Your Best Teachers

I remember one medicine ceremony where I was really complaining about my mother, and expressing to White Eagle how hard it was to be born as the daughter of a young Soul mother. It was then that White Eagle said something very surprising to me: "Sometimes old souls can do a really good job pretending to be young souls." Since I trust White Eagle very much in his guidance, I allowed that statement to flip my perspective and then the normal next question is "Why has she been acting this way toward me?" In other words, how is having exactly the mother I have...*for me*?

My mother was married to three different 'fathers' from my birth to five years old; one father who molested me, one father who beat my mother, and one father who was unconditionally loving. This is *for me* because it opened me up to see that not all fathers are the same, in fact, they're radically different. This realization helped me to have a more fluid perspective in my life because my patriarchal foundation was not set in stone. I am not locked into a single ideology; I can be flexible in my views on things. This early beginning also served me because I had a demonstration of a woman who courageously protected her child from harm through dangerous circumstances, and who did not settle for less than she desired in her life, ending up with a man who was generous, loving and kind.

My mother tended to be critical and see the problems in situations or people that needed improvement. This is *for me* because it challenged my Soul's curriculum to overcome the shadows of judgment, opinion, conflict, seriousness, and taking it personally. Because I have tousled with these shadows, I have claimed integrity, perspective, peace, delight, and clear boundaries.

My mother has been my primary coyote teacher. **Coyote teachers provoke your shadows, consciously or unconsciously, to catalyze you into facing the shadows of your Soul's curriculum.** Facing your shadows is an initiation into greater personal power and your Soul's purpose. Often we resist these coyote teachers by feeling victimized and powerless, and shifting the blame for our life's circumstances to the coyote. Speaking from experience, you can spin out decades of your life in an eddy of pure victim energy.

Circumvent the victimization story by consciously using the coyote in your life to release all outer attachments, embrace the shadows within to learn their lessons and harness the medicine, and align yourself to a greater force and truer Source. When you're aligned to your Soul, then you won't be starving for love and you'll gain clarity about the Soul's curriculum that makes your coyote teacher the ideal matchup for you in this incarnation.

The lessons can be painful as the coyote teachers trigger your shadows. As I shared previously, walking into a family gathering at my mother's house to which I was not invited was very painful. The experience triggered my sense of being a victim out of betrayal and abandonment. Because I know to make my coyote my friend, I was able to transform these feelings into a stronger sense of self love, and claim more laughter and joy in my life by embracing the people who wanted to be part of my life in the moment, rather than lamenting the ones who did not. The pain of being 'not loved' became an inner guide of unfruitful attachments, and I brought self-mastery to plug up the holes in my heart by loving myself.

Arguing with reality is another way that we resist the lessons of our coyote teachers. If it is happening, it is here for you. Maybe you think it should not be happening because it does not match your desires, or it is not the same comfortable familiar that you prefer. Coyote teachers often disrupt comfort and familiar circumstances, provoking situations where we can see our shadows, and this does not feel like what we want. But actually, we do want that provocation because on the other side of facing our shadows we evolve and claim more self-mastery and freedom from limitation.

2020 was a huge year of the coyote teacher. Many of us knew that 2020 would be the year of the Great Awakening, and got really excited about the positive aspects of that transformation. Yet, to get to the positive we've got to disrupt all the old structures which can feel very negative, even though ultimately it's positive.

To be awakened is to be reoriented. To be reoriented requires movement out of a stuck place. Movement out of a stuck place often requires an external jolt of some kind. Jolts like accidents, death of a loved one, loss of income, ending a relationship, or any other loss of something that held you in a stuck position.

What holds us in stuck immovable places? Fear of change, fear of being wrong, fear of loss, fear of the unknown—shadows of our subconscious.

You can embrace coyote medicine by recognizing it and leaning into the discomfort of your shadows to face them and bring more light and understanding. When you are being provoked by coyote teachers and feeling the victim energy swelling inside of you, take a few deep breaths and consider your Soul's curriculum. Perhaps review your gene keys or human design chart. **How is this coyote teacher offering you a chance to claim the medicine you came here to get as part of your life incarnation?**

As you heal the shadows and claim the medicine, your relationship with coyote teachers can evolve. When you change, those close to you inevitably change as well, or they fall out of congruence with you and simply disappear. Stay the course and work your medicine, and let the energies reorient everyone to new alignments that are more beneficial.

♥

The Wound Is Your Wisdom

Taking it a level deeper now, realize that inside your wounds is your wisdom. Inside the Mother Wound is actually Mother Wisdom being gifted to you through pain, through your biological mother, by the Divine Mother.

Every wound you have received or perpetrated through ignorance, addiction or malice is wisdom that can be claimed by you *and* by the people tangled up in that wound experience.

To claim wisdom from the wound, you must flip your perspective to realize the event that caused the wound is *for you* in some way.

For example, a good friend of mine in the spiritual community suddenly became Christian and believed that the only path to salvation was through Jesus. Whereas before he co-facilitated firewalk ceremonies with me for healing and intention setting, he now felt it was evil and wanted to be completely disassociated from the events. I felt betrayed, judged, abandoned, and condemned by his certainty in his newly acquired faith. Although I told myself that I was letting him go because he was on an incompatible path, the truth was that his certainty in his path, and his rejection of all we shared together, provoked an old wound within me that was part of my Mother Wound…and the planetary Mother Wound.

My personal Mother Wound was around being able to hold my own truth when confronted by the conviction of my mother in her perspective; so often we saw the same situation in opposite ways, even remembering the event differently. My mother's powerful certainty in her perspective made it hard for my voice and point of view to be heard. So when my friend inadvertently touched my Mother Wound by following his own Soul's curriculum to reject firewalking, it really stung. I could not receive his invitation to remain friends because his rejection of our firewalking history, which we had both embraced from open hearts, hurt too badly.

As I leaned into his arguments against firewalking and Earth-based spirituality, and felt into what is true for me, I gained clarity that now contributes to my ability to speak to the fear that often lives inside a Christian-trained brain. I stayed in the discomfort of my friend's fears, feeling them in my body, asking for help from the Great Spirit to bring truth and clarity, until I finally realized I had no reason to fear the elements of the Earth of which my very body is made. If I fear the fire, I fear myself. If I fear the water, I fear myself. If I fear the wind, I fear myself. If I fear the Earth, I fear myself.

I am made of fire, water, wind, and Earth. Why should I be afraid of myself? Why should I be afraid of my Mother who gave me my Earth incarnation?

What began as a wound of separation, judgment, fear, and projection, turned into a realization of wisdom that unraveled all the fear-based arguments like dust dissipates in wind, like salt dissolves in water, like paper burns up in fire, and like time heals all things on Earth. I can allow my friend to have whatever fear he chooses, and I can claim my knowing that firewalking is a blessing of healing. I can allow my mother to have whatever perspective she has from her unique life lens, and I can honor my own truth as equally relevant in the grand scheme of souls crossing pathways to discover life.

A practice that is beneficial for claiming wisdom from your wounds is to make a list of the wounds you would like to resolve. For each wound, journal the story of that wound so that you can see the patterns of thinking and association your brain is making. Now challenge the assumptions and associations to reveal new ways to perceive things. Breathe through the discomfort of challenging the wound so that you can create space in the tightly woven egoic matrix surrounding that wound, and get deeper into the 'why' it is so triggering. If you suddenly cry or become angry, you're hitting gold; underneath the emotion is the nugget of wisdom you're seeking. **Stay with the discomfort through the storms until you reach clarity and a new perception.** Sometimes it's helpful to have support to move through the waves of suppressed or unacknowledged feelings and beliefs, and so gift yourself help for these vulnerable explorations.

♥

Shifting Identity

You can live a life of pain and suffering, or you can live a life of beauty. Either way, the inner consciousness with which you dream your life into being has everything to do with the nature of the life you experience. So the most direct path to a beautiful life is to shift your identity from whatever has been the story of you up until this moment, into a new dream of you that is even more beloved, joyful, prosperous, kind, compassionate, and powerful—because that is the Divine truth of you.

As humans we are consummate storytellers. **We weave our lives by the stories we tell just as a spider weaves a web and catches flies.** We can catch ourselves in a painful web with our stories, or we can tap into the Divine in our hearts to unfold life for us in an ever expanding kaleidoscope of beautiful moments. The Divine within has the power to shine truth and dispel gossamer story webs, just like the sun rises in the morning and dispels any nightmares that visited us in the dark.

To change the story of your life in the most awe-inspiring way, you must shift identity from your personality self to your Soul. Your personality self is a collection of stories fed over the course of your lifetime by yourself, your mother and father and siblings, your friends and colleagues, and your partner and children. The stories are told over and over to reinforce the personality as your identity. Most people define themselves by the stories they tell about themselves and that are told about them. In other words, most people define themselves by their personality selves.

What you make a part of our personality identity becomes something you need to protect because the personality self lives in the temporary physical world of limitation. A different experience or a story that challenges your perception of your identity feels threatening and leads to conflict. When you are insecure and aligned to external things to define your identity and create safety, and then those transient things change, you have a new opportunity to realign your identity to what is permanent—your Soul—so that what is transient can keep changing.

While you are enmeshed in old stories and patterns, you can't break free to discover who you really are. Evolution requires letting go of these personality stories so your Soul can see the light of day. You can learn to let go of the stories every single day to open yourself to a new potential for the *you* that can emerge in the *now*.

You may need to sequester yourself for periods of time as you liberate from these stories that created your identity up until now. As you release these stories, you reveal the essence underneath that has been starved from the light. At a certain point of my spiritual awakening, I realized that a wonderful ally for releasing old personality stories was the Spirit of Death. Death is ultimately a recycler of energy so that something new can be created. **Nothing that is actually true can ever be taken from you, so you can fearlessly let go with trust that what is true remains.** I realized this was a helpful ally, this Spirit of Death, for clarifying what my personality self might hide from me in its quest to stay alive and in control. While you are letting go of old stories and attachments of your personality self, it can feel painful. You may feel a surge of aching energy through your body, especially around your abdomen and will center. You may feel an urge to flee, or leave your body. You may feel like you are dying. Painful stories may surface in your mind for one last torment on the way out. Hold steady. Although painful to endure, this death process frees up space within you for your Soul to inhabit, which is the authentic essential self.

As the release completes, invite the light of your Soul to more fully embody in every atom, every cell, and every space in between of your being. Welcome your Soul to breathe through your body, to send you loving messages through your mind, and to cleanse and purify your heart to receive even more blessings than you imagined were possible. Invite your Soul to inspire you, to teach you, to elevate you in frequency, and to bring you to an experience of awe and magic. **Touch your will center and say "I trust my Self" which is your Soul.**

Aligning to your Soul to guide your life and bring you wisdom is what makes a beautiful life. No matter the winds of fortune, you can feel at home and content with your Soul. Even with the greatest pain of your temporary existence happening, you can transcend the experience on the wings of your Soul.

It might seem paradoxical, but through transcending the human experience with your Soul as a guide, you can actually deepen into the human experience and feel it more fully. Maybe it is because you feel safe and protected by your Soul, so you can open up and immerse in being human.

❤

A New Foundation

In the first part of my life, I put the material world as a first priority because that's what I was aware was happening. I led my life from my human personality and all the conditioning that came with it. I made beautiful contributions to my world from that place of understanding, yet without a strong spiritual foundation, the responsibilities of my life felt burdensome and I buckled under the pressure. My first marriage began with a wedding ceremony where I removed all mention of 'God', and we could not even agree on a last name to share (since I did not want to take his name). In retrospect I see the forces that combined to corrode our marriage to the toxic place where leaving it was an act of mercy for us all. Even the decades of psychotherapy when viewed through this lens can arguably explain the lack of progress as a result of the lack of involvement from higher consciousness.

In the chapter of my life that began nine years before this book, I welcomed help from the Great Spirit. I opened sacred space every day, prayed at my altar, and sat quietly listening for messages from my guides and Soul. As a result, I received a lot of help, synchronicity, guidance, connections, and support to move through challenges and create beauty. My marriage to my husband Akeem began with agreements we crafted together, the first of which is "We invite the Divine into all aspects of our relationship with humility." In this relationship, we move through challenges from a higher Soul perspective which allows us to release egoic attachments and shift the energy more quickly from fear patterns to Love patterns. Because of our access to our souls, we experience more gratitude, compassion, forgiveness, love, and kindness.

Living your life from a foundation based in spiritual practice helps you to live from integrity. Patterns of manipulation are exposed as egoic constructs that are met with compassion and redirected into opportunities to heal and grow. As you build your foundation to claim your personal power, you'll discover you have new priorities; spiritual classes might become more important than pedicures. Through the discomfort of becoming response-able for your life in this new foundation of Spirit, you'll learn something priceless: your Spirit is all you need to go after your dreams. With this foundation of Love from your Soul, you'll realize you can expand and grow beyond other people's expectations of you. You'll get your feet on the ground so you can tear down the roof over your head.

Be courageous enough to claim your true power and boldly take steps to live the life you were meant to live. Even as you clearly see people living from the conditioned patterns that used to be invisible to you, keep raising your potential by tapping into your Soul. You'll witness others believing the world is unjust or unfair, and you'll walk the road less traveled to become initiated by Spirit as you face your shadows. As others keep living from the passed-down stories of generations of disempowered women, you'll step confidently into the future with your heart open, certain, and trusting in your Soul's guidance.

You must believe your visions of New Earth *before* you see and experience them. It's you, the dreamer who dreams, the Soul who co-creates, that will believe New Earth right into material form by becoming it in every moment from your new foundation in Spirit.

♥

Respect Yourself

You were born on Earth and given a life incarnation. You deserve your opportunity to live the dream of life you desire. You also have the sovereignty to choose how you learn your Soul lessons, heal yourself, and discover yourself. The path you walk is your choice. Respect your sovereign choice.

As you learn to respect yourself and your sovereign choice to live your dream of life, you are able to respect others and the steps they choose to take in their lives. You are able to untangle yourself from judgment and gossip and codependency and manipulation to let others live free.

I have been learning to respect myself over the last 9 years on my Soul's path. I have been learning to respect my heart and listen to its wisdom. I have been learning to respect myself by being loving and gentle and kind to myself, rather than demanding and judgmental. I have been learning to respect myself by letting go of what is not serving me. I have been learning to respect myself by choosing my words carefully to uphold my integrity. I have been learning to respect myself by valuing my breath, my body, and my life.

I thought I was being disrespected all these years by my mother, the father of my children, and others in my life with whom the pattern of respect arose for my witnessing. **Now I see that the world was only reflecting back to me how I had been disrespecting myself.**

You're invited to respect your sacred dream of life, your unique heart medicine, and your thumbprint of a lifetime on Earth. Here is a prayer I share with you that has helped me to deepen respect.

I choose to be respectful of my sacred heart.
I choose to be gentle, loving and kind with myself.
I choose to believe in myself.
I choose to bless myself with beauty.

And because of these choices,
I choose to be respectful of others' sacred hearts.
I choose to be gentle, loving and kind with others.
I choose to respect each person's life, and this beautiful planet we call home.

I send great respect to don Jose Ruiz who shared messages with me on Soul Nectar Show that opened me to a deeper understanding of respect so that I could show up more respectful of myself, my sons and my mother. He comes from the Toltec tradition, a lineage of artists of life, who respect each other's dreams like you would respect another person's artwork hanging on a gallery wall. **You would not bring your own paints and brushes into a gallery to modify an artwork hanging there; in the same way, do not interfere in the artwork someone is creating with their life.**

♥

Forgiving Without Apology

Sometimes the person from whom you want a sincere apology simply cannot authentically give it because that person is unwilling to see the world through your perspective. In that person's dream of life that she has created for herself, she might be the victim and you are the perpetrator. From that storyline, it's almost impossible for the person to acknowledge what you have experienced from your vantage point, especially if what you have experienced directly contradicts the story this person tells about herself, her life, and her relationship with you. **If you have made her a villain in your dream, can you understand why she cannot reconcile your dream with hers?**

Granted, if the person who completely denies your reality is your mother, that is a complex situation to process to bring yourself into a space of true forgiveness. At some level it refutes your perception and your feelings, and denies the hurt and repercussions you endured. It challenges your understanding of your life: "What pain? I don't know what you're talking about. You're making this up. None of what you say about me is true."

There is a tiny bit of solace from knowing that once this person travels back behind 'the veil', she will be unavoidably faced with any truths she denied while in a body. And by the way, so will we all. So as a conscious person, it is wise to take another look in your own shadows to see if there's more you can heal and acknowledge regarding the apology you feel you deserve. Can you see your part in the dynamic of suffering between you and the other person? Is it possible that your view of the relationship has been based in misperceptions and misunderstandings of your own? Have you made this person into a one-dimensional character in your screen play rather than acknowledging her as a complex human being?

If after doing your personal inquiry you still feel you are owed an apology, how can you move forward in your life knowing that there will be no external acknowledgement of the pain you have endured and learned to heal? Can you even be in relationship with a person who denies your pain and their role in it? How can you bring yourself to forgive when you know you'll never receive an apology? What do you do with all of your unacknowledged feelings and perceptions?

When I reached this question on my own journey, what was important was to first acknowledge myself and the path I have walked. I know that I was in pain, and that pain was the impetus for spending so many decades in psychotherapy and spiritual inner work. My pain was real, not imagined, and I took loving actions to support myself in healing from it. The pain I felt, and acted out from, was initiated during a time of my development when I was helpless and dependent. As an adult, the pain became very intense during my spiritual awakening, and I acted in ways that hurt my family; and when I was wrestling myself free of the pain and rebirthing myself, I also acted in ways that hurt my family. The actions I took during my dark night of the Soul and rebirth were from my own pain and carving out a world where I could heal and express my voice; yet I can see in retrospect how my family may have interpreted my actions during these phases of my healing journey to be intentionally hurtful towards them. Through my dedication to healing and evolution, I elevated myself out of the pain and also learned how to soften myself with Love. I retrained my brain with more loving patterns than those I had been conditioned with by continuously exposing myself to people who had claimed more healing for themselves.

At this point in my journey, I had a much more refined understanding of Love than I had previously known. And at some level, I realized the fruitlessness of trying to get someone to see their culpability in the pain I experienced when that person did not share my understanding about Love, had her own reasons to feel as I was a perpetrator in her life, and had created a perception that obscured from her awareness any response-ability for the conditions that led to my life experience with pain.

As a timely support to my process, I was given a unique opportunity to have a well-known psychic provide insight into my mother's state of mind and perception, which confirmed the perspective that I suspected she held: "I didn't do these things you say I did. I am innocent. I don't know why you're saying these things about me." My brain wanted to argue that point with a very realistic truth that people do not generally endure decades of psychotherapy willingly who were not emotionally and mentally abused. Yet then the channel gave me a message that this was an opportunity to bring Love to the situation as a healing for both of us.

A voice within me felt angry. I felt I was the one whose life was set into a direction of pain by an adult who now denied response-ability for it, and I saw it was me who was being invited to bring Love to the situation on behalf of us both. Upon feeling this voice, my Spirit guides reminded me of a story I was recently told about a master teacher who was punched in the teeth by a prince, and did not retaliate; he sent Love instead to the prince. Then the prince realized that this humble person, now missing some teeth, was a master teacher and chose to learn from him, seeing his mastery of Love.

From my personality self, the story of myself from my current incarnation, I could not get to the place of bringing Love to the one who caused me pain. My personality felt angry and unacknowledged and threatened by this person who denied my reality and pain. I was immersed in my storyline and outraged at the villain who had wronged me. I was also operating from a learned pattern of enforcing condemnation until an apology is received.

Only from the Soul self could I bring myself to a high enough awareness of the Soul's curriculum to see that this challenge was an illusion designed to lift me to a new level of self-mastery with Love.

This relationship, with all its pain, was *for me*, to help me evolve and keep loving unconditionally no matter what things appeared like in the material world.

When I know who I am in truth, what I am in truth, and how I serve in truth, I know that this material world is an illusion designed to help me learn Soul lessons about Love. The pain is real, and deserves my compassion for my personality self who feels it and has worked her way through it courageously, continuing to lean into a relationship that denies her pain. And the pain is not real because my mother is only a mask worn by a Soul who agreed to play this role for me, for my evolution, out of her Love for me as a Soul.

And this is where the questions are raised: "It is more important to be right than to be happy?" and "Do you really know what happened?" and "Do you want to change the story?"

As a sovereign being, my mother makes the rules of her 'reality', her dream of life that she creates with her thoughts, beliefs, words and actions. In her 'reality', she may have decided that I am the perpetrator because of the ways I behaved during my dark night of the Soul, or due to the things I spoke publicly on my path to healing from the wounding of my childhood. **To respect her is to realize that I cannot change that dream of life she is creating nor the perception of me she chooses to have; only she can choose to change it.** I can certainly get out of the way of any harm it might inflict upon me.

As a sovereign being, I make the rules of my 'reality', my dream of life that I am creating with my thoughts, beliefs, words and actions. If I want to welcome a potential where my mother acknowledges the pain I have experienced from the Mother Wound and apologizes, I must acknowledge the words and actions I took on my path to healing myself that were difficult for my mother to experience. Then I must let go of my stories and projections about her 'never acknowledging nor apologizing' to create the wiggle room for her to show up differently in my reality…if she chooses.

A very interesting phenomenon to consider is that the way we perceive a person calls forth from within them the aspect of their personality that fulfills that perception. Each of us has multiple aspects of personality operating within our individual consciousness, and these aspects 'lead' at different times to be the outward facing persona. People with multiple personality disorder reveal this phenomenon to us in an exaggerated way, and yet each of us also has multiple aspects of personality. We can be completely unaware of some of these aspects from our primary personality, and this is when we are acting unconsciously...one of these aspects has taken the 'lead'. Perhaps the aspect of your mother who has been 'mean' in your definition is a denied aspect of self; but as you focus on this aspect of your mother, it gets triggered and rises up to the forefront to enact more 'mean' behavior even as the dominant personality denies the 'mean' aspect. Focusing on the energy of the 'mean' aspect brings more of that to you because, of course, what we focus on grows and expands. It takes a very conscious person to become aware of a shadow aspect being activated, and shift the energy to prevent acting from it.

Certainly in most cases, the energy we hold about a person causes a reaction in that person that matches the energy we are sending. If we are holding resentment about a person, and using the power of Word to speak ill of them, that energy is felt at some level and reacted to by the personality self to return the energy. **If we want a different result, we have to change the energy WE are holding about the person, and the words WE are speaking about the person, and create the potential of activating a different Personality aspect within that person that is resonant with the energy we want to receive back.**

In my personal grappling with forgiveness without an apology, the gap to navigate was how to let go and create the space for a new potential, without stepping over my truth up until now, and without disrespecting myself with 'rose colored glasses' lies that previously led me to throwing myself under the bus over and over to make peace with my mother.

And indeed the phrase 'up until now' gives some grace to acknowledge what has been true up until now in my perception of my relationship with my mother. It's like a bucket to hold what has been true, validating the experience of my personality self.

Then the bridge is offered with the phrase 'and now I am in the process of' to give myself an opportunity of saying what it is that I desire to experience, and sincerely hope that Love can deliver a miracle.

An example of the complete bridge looks something like this:

Up until now, I have felt pain from having my feelings and perspectives invalidated by my mother, and now I am in the process of allowing Love to heal these wounds and create the opportunity for me to experience more loving and respectful interactions with my mother. And so it is.[3]

What would it be like to realize that there has been a black fog between you and your mother, hanging in the space between you, generating misperceptions and tensions? What would it be like to realize you could clear it all right out of the air and finally see eye to eye with her?

This is exactly what forgiveness offers: a clearing of the stories and misperceptions and pain so that you can experience a new *potential*. What new potential do you want to experience? The opportunity for that potential lies on the other side of forgiveness. The potential for the apology lies on the other side of forgiveness because it cannot happen from the state of consciousness of denial and pain. The apology can only happen from the space of realization which is an elevation to Soul perspective. There are no guarantees, and yet if you desire the actualization of the potential, you must step over the threshold and forgive (as many times as needed).

This is why you must bring Love to the challenge and allow the frequency of Love to elevate the situation to a space of Soul perspective which is where the potential for healing is created. Forgiveness invites the frequency of Love to fill the spaces that were

---

[3] This formula was shared with me by George P Kansas and Tracey Trottenberg

previously walled off from Love through holding a grudge or resentment. **Forgiveness releases old stuck energy so that the river of Love can flow through and take you to a new place you'd rather be anyways.**

Does it really matter what happened that set the ball in motion for you to become the person you are today? Are you more self-aware, more masterful with Love, and more capable of fulfilling your Soul's purpose? If the answers are yes, then you are invited to feel grateful for the catalyst to your personal growth that has allowed you the opportunity to become the person you needed to be to fulfill your purpose. If you had received different life circumstances, you would not be the person you are today.

Forgiveness is the ultimate acceptance of your Soul's curriculum. You got exactly what you asked for when you were beyond the veil planning this incarnation. Is it tough down here in the flesh experiencing that lesson plan? Yep. It sure is. And that's what self-compassion and self-love are here for.

One relevant insight I received during a medicine journey where I was opening to heal the Mother Wound. I was asking for support from the Divine Mother about how to hold space with love for people who act from wounding or conditioned patterns. What I felt was a neutral patient energy expand inside of me, the patience of the eternal Soul, and the invitation "Try again". This is the energy to hold as a guide and mentor for others once you have awakened to your Soul and are living from that consciousness. A patient, loving, kind and forgiving invitation to "Try again." Mistakes are opportunities to learn, and we learn by practicing and trying again.

So keep moving yourself into the space of forgiveness by contemplating all the points raised in this section, by feeling the stuck emotions that rise as you hear your story of your villain once again, and by releasing your villain and your story and opening yourself for an answer.

When you are finally ready to forgive, you will receive the realization that opens your heart to forgiveness as a soothing balm that heals all the wounds as the stories dissipate into the past. Gratefulness fills your heart for the truth and clarity that lets you move forward into a new potential. **Your villain is transformed into a human being with flaws and blessings who is also Loved by All That Is.**

I worked and worked and worked at forgiveness for my mother for years as I was doing the inner work that led to the content of this book. Little by little there was healing, and yet there would still be a tug towards the familiar villain story and indignation, especially if new circumstances arose that contributed to her identity as the villain of my story (which there had been some since my Dad died). I kept using my tools, processing and releasing, and seeking the path to true forgiveness and then one day it happened. In a profound moment of realization, I saw that my mother had lost the love of her life when my Dad passed away, I had lost the one who helped me feel loved and secure, and we had lost our translator, our bridge. My heart burst forth with the tears of forgiveness, and as that balm washed over me, I knew that the stories did not matter anymore. I finally had the embodied clarity I needed to move forward with Love. It was time for me to learn how to communicate with my mother, to form a new bridge between us. And to do that, I had to realize that the man I loved and cherished as my Dad, loved and cherished my mother as his wife for 45 years. Seeing as my father was a genius, there had to be a few good reasons why he loved my mother, and the invitation I gave myself was to become curious about it. The energy completely shifted with the forgiveness, and a door opened to a new potential I could explore with curiosity. Of course, I knew I could ask my Dad for plenty of help as I learned to speak my heart in ways my mother could hear it.

If you're not 'there' yet, keep going. It's a mystery how many licks it takes to get to the center of the tootsie roll pop. You can only find out if you keep doing the work to open to forgiveness.

♥

How To Deal With Your Family Of Origin

The night before I was to write this section, I woke in the wee hours of the morning with this message: "By the nature of being human, you are subject to the human drama. You can react from your human with more drama, or respond from your Soul with Love."

For those of you reading this book who are part of the Second Wave (read "The Second Wave: Transcending the Human Drama"), you came here on a mission to uplift human consciousness by embodying into a lineage where there was great value from the wisdom and work of the ancestry, but also unhealed trauma and repeating patterns of suffering that needed healing. Most Soul pods come to Earth and stay together lifetime after lifetime, incarnating together and switching roles so they can learn the dynamics from different angles. The Soul pod for the Second Wave came to the planet and then spread out into different ancestral lines. Therefore, growing up you may only have had one other like-minded Soul in your environment or family. This has likely felt lonely, and being different, it may have given your family an opportunity to make you into the black sheep.

When you are sensitive and perceptive and empathic, as most of the Second Wave are, you feel things very deeply and may have gotten confused in your life about who you are, what energy belongs to you, and who other people are. In healing the family lineage (without directly knowing you were doing this), you may have taken on the shadow aspects of the family that were denied, repressed, and unhealed as things to process in your personal experience. You made the invisible – visible – by making these shadow aspects your personal wounds to heal, and having these patterns exposed to the light makes everyone else in your family dynamic uncomfortable because these things were denied and shoved into darkness. It's like your family members have blinders on, unable to see themselves acting from the unhealed patterns, but perfectly able to see it in you.

At some point, you gain enough inner healing to cast off that shell of family wounding and reclaim your true identity. It's at this point that you may find your family of origin completely rejecting you and battening down the hatches against you and all of your light. It can be confusing, because in your healing communities you feel totally accepted and loved for who you are; yet with your family of origin, who is 'supposed' to love you, you have the opposite experience of being the big problem of the family.

For decades I assumed my role as the problem of the family, going to psychotherapy to fix myself, and accepting the labels that made me 'broken'. I did not understand what was really happening; I thought I *was* the problem. It took a great deal of inner healing to remember that the wounding that saturated me for a good part of my life was not just mine—it was ancestral wounding that I came here to heal. The more I committed to this deep ancestral healing work, the more I felt the love and gratitude of my ancestors beyond the veil, and the more resistant my living family of origin became against 'seeing' the transformation in me.

It was so curious to me why my family of origin would want to trap me in diagnoses of 'broken' and 'crazy' when many others in the world were acknowledging the blessing that I was becoming. Family members took actions that felt like personal attacks, and when I expressed how it made me feel, the shunning worsened; almost as if I was a terrible person for pointing out how these wounded behaviors felt to receive. One of my family members shared with me, from her training as a psychotherapist, that "When everyone has a problem with one person that person should take an inventory of themselves and not everyone else." Having been engaged in psychotherapy sessions for over two decades, plus another decade of spiritual work, I knew that not only had I taken an extensive 'inventory' of myself, I knew that relationships involved two parties. It was never just one person that was 'the problem'. Relationships require all parties to look at themselves and do 'the work'. That is, if they're committed to the relationship.

What I have come to realize is that I was holding a great deal of suffering and trauma from my family's lineage, and as I released that burden off of my shoulders, the natural dynamic would be a redistribution of what was left to heal onto the rest of the family members to help in the process that they are part of. As it turns out, and what you see in the statement shared above, is that the family may not be ready in their Soul's curriculum to become self-aware and response-able to heal family dynamics; and so it is temporarily easier to extricate you from the family to avoid the issue. For example, my family member who was trained in psychotherapy never once asked for a therapy session to work things out, which seems to directly contradict the work she has claimed for herself in the world. Refer back to the section on "Denial to Response-ability" to understand this dynamic; those in my family of origin who were particularly strident about shutting me out of the family system were also the individuals who had experienced the most severe forms of childhood trauma. Severe childhood trauma leads to a very entrenched denial program that is hard to overcome to accept personal response-ability. People who are not ready to heal the traumas underneath the denial program will likely avoid the issue so they don't have to face uncomfortable things about themselves and the family.

If you are facing a similar dynamic, here are some insights from my own healing process that you can explore. At the personality level, it really hurt to be abandoned and shunned by my family of origin. I shared earlier the story of walking in on family dinner where everyone from the family was present except for me. **Family shunning is a control tool to remove the influence that is exposing underlying patterns and traumas that need healing.** Although you may intellectually understand this, there are lots of hurt feelings that the personality self generates from this experience, and those must be felt, acknowledged, and transformed through your inner work. Letting go of attachment to being a part of this family is the next step so that your progress on your Soul path is not hindered by your personality 'requirement' to belong to your family of origin. Lastly, lifting your family of origin to the Upper Room using the mantra from Paul Selig, or other tools you may have of your own, to create the opportunity for a breakthrough.

I know who you are in truth and love
I know what you are in truth and love
I know how you serve in truth and love
You are here, you are here, you are here
You are free, you are free, you are free
You have come, you have come, you have come
You are in the Upper Room
Behold! I make all things new

If your family members are operating from a state of consciousness where they would deny the hurtful impact of their actions, the same actions they would condemn in another, then you know you will not make any progress through having Personality-to-Personality dialog. That is why the preferred approach is to simply work the energy, lift the consciousness, and converse Soul-to-Soul. Even from the Soul level, you may be surprised to hear how the person has blocked ability to see their own hurtful behaviors, which allows that person to stay in the victim position. The victim position keeps a person stuck, but also keeps them from having to admit uncomfortable truths about themselves; so often a Soul who is not ready to 'wake up' will prefer to be stuck than move forward into healing the circumstances.

As a person who has left the 'stuck' world behind, you may find it very uncomfortable to experience the stubborn denial of your family of origin to accept response-ability for their part in the dynamic. It might really challenge you to witness the lengths to which people will go to avoid seeing themselves with clarity. Since you have plunged into your shadows, you may feel utterly perplexed at the obstinate denial, since you know the freedom and Love that lies on the other side of facing the truth. A big trap here is to make your relatives wrong for choosing to cling to old perceptions and patterns. **The energy of making someone wrong, and making yourself right, serves to further entrench the denial and prevent realization.** It is not an excuse, but remember that a strong denial program is born from trauma, and used to wall off pain. You have to let it go, stop trying to change the dynamic, understand that there is a block preventing realization, and focus on your path.

Letting go of your family of origin does not mean that you shun them back, nor that you stop caring for them. It means that you realize that they're not ready to become personally accountable to their role in creating the family dynamic. **Rather than engage at the human level of drama, elevate your response to the Soul level and send them love and healing energies using your tools.** Heal the places within you that feel wounded by the shunning you've received, and strengthen your knowing of yourself that was challenged by your family's conviction that 'you are the problem'. If there is something you need to explore about yourself that was triggered by your family of origin, then dive into those shadows and heal yourself.

Trust that the Divine will unfold for them in perfect timing, and at the very least, they will realize what happened when they cross the veil and are restored to clear vision. They will not 'get away' with this deception, and you are not responsible for making them realize their mistakes. Do not take the actions and attitudes of your family of origin personally; their perceptions are not who you are, it's who they want you to be so that the old familiar paradigm stays in place. As the light on the planet increases, it will get more difficult to hold onto old paradigms and structures, and your family of origin may come to realize their mistakes in understanding and perception. In the meantime, give yourself nurturing and support in whatever ways you can create that for yourself.

Create a new family for yourself of people who see the person you are today, recognize the program of denial and actively disengage it, and share the same understanding of what it means to be in loving relationship.

For those members of your family of origin that can bridge to be part of your new family, dig into the uncomfortable conversations provoked by the negative perspectives about you held by your family of origin. Make clear boundaries that relationships are one-to-one, and dismantle the family-vs-one dynamic that your family of origin has been operating with. In other words, when you interact with the one member of your family of origin, make it clear that this interaction is between you and that person, and does not involve any other members of your family of origin. Do not speak about them, and do not involve their energies in this new bond you are forming one-to-one with this specific individual from your family of origin.

Also realize that this one person from your family of origin is still subject to the strong pull of family-vs-one dynamic that the others are operating from and use caution to keep the energies and conversations clear, neutral, and loving.

In the process of making a new family for yourself, you will likely feel a lot of pain of loss of your family of origin. Even if your family of origin treated you poorly in comparison to your new communities of spiritual support, a part of you will still long for their love and connection. You may even feel guilt at abandoning them to pursue more loving connections, even though the current reality is they have chosen to exclude you.

Be aware that you are moving from one understanding of Love to a higher understanding of Love, and in that process you get to work with your inner child to transform the definition of Love and to offer a new Source of that Love. The Divine Mother is working with us all in Earth School, so perhaps at some point members of your family of origin will come to realizations that lead them to reach back out to you with an olive branch. There are no guarantees.

So in the meantime, what you have to work with is yourself. **Respect yourself enough to be in relationship with people who treat you respectfully.** Love yourself enough to be in relationship with people who love you unconditionally and can allow you to grow and evolve, as you allow them to grow and evolve. Send love to your family of origin when they rise up to your awareness. Then let them go again and let it unfold. Be in your current now moment and appreciate those who are with you.

You cannot teach anything to your family of origin. Anything you try to teach will fall on deaf ears. It seems to be that sharing close ancestral DNA intensifies the experience of triggered shadow patterns. It's easier to work on these triggered shadow patterns with others who do not share such close ancestral DNA. Because of this, your family of origin's path to evolution will likely be based on seeds planted by others.

Trying to teach your family of origin will likely inspire them to be even more belligerent. If there are unloving patterns of behavior, lovingly and compassionately set a boundary through action; that action may be to gently step away and not to make yourself endure unloving behaviors due to a sense of martyrdom. Absence reveals important insights through the space, the void, of interaction. It is not a slammed door. **It is a gentle stepping away.** In the absence is the opportunity to reduce the clutter so we can see ourselves better.

Over time as you honor yourself, you may find yourself with an expanded emotional capacity and greater tolerance that allows you to be in relationship with your family of origin as they are—even if they are acting from patterns of suffering. You cannot rush yourself into the state of being that is capable of holding this kind of space for your family of origin. **You are grown into this capacity by your dedication to self-love and the practices that help you heal the Mother Wound.**

You can test the waters from time to time to see how you are able to handle being around your family of origin as they are, without trying to change them. And then if you need, gently step away to regroup and heal at a deeper level. When gently stepping away for personal reflection and healing time, it's a considerate idea to communicate something like "I value our connection and family, and right now need some time to process alone so that I can show up with even more love. I'll be in touch when I'm ready."

❤

Suggestions

Unblock the Rivers of Love Decide to unblock your heart from unforgiveness towards a certain person. Visit a river where you can sit and put your feet in the water. Open sacred space, and open your heart and mind to the Divine Mother. Speak your desire to unblock your heart and stop withholding your love. Close your eyes, breathe, and allow the river to wash away the blocks as you blow out your resentments, and breathe in a clear flow of love through your heart. Invite the Mother of the Waters to cleanse you of anger, grief, fear, and judgment: let it slide out your feet into the water with your out breath. With your in breath, pull up clear river water through your feet into your being and up to your heart. Annoint your third eye, throat, heart, will center, sacral center and root chakra with the river water. "I am allowing Love to flow." Stay with yourself through any discomfort with one hand over heart, the other over your belly. Feel the tensions with this other person melt away. You can keep the love clear and flowing while standing in your truth and boundaries.

Claim Your Medicine Remember the list of all the unloving ways you were treated by your mother? Reflect on the gifts of wisdom, skills and life experience you gained from your wounds that are now valuable assets in your life's work and relationships. Make a list and claim your gold. This process is alchemy: transforming your wounds into your wisdom. This process can help you shift from karma (your struggle) into your dharma (your purpose). Notice yourself standing taller with each discovery of your soul's curriculum. "Thank you Coyote teacher for this powerful medicine." Feel gratitude swell.

Quotes

"When you are your own best friend, you don't endlessly seek out relationships, friendships, and validation from the wrong sources because you realize that the only approval and validation you need is your own."
— Mandy Hale

"Inner peace doesn't come from getting what we want, but from remembering who we are."
— Marianne Williamson

"Stop wearing your wishbone where your backbone ought to be."
— Brené Brown

"When you hold resentment toward another, you are bound to that person or condition by an emotional link that is stronger than steel. Forgiveness is the only way to dissolve that link and get free."
— Katherine Ponder

"There is no love without forgiveness, and there is no forgiveness without love."
— Bryant H. McGill

"Sincere forgiveness isn't colored with expectations that the other person apologize or change. Don't worry whether or not they finally understand you. Love them and release them. Life feeds back truth to people in its own way and time-just like it does for you and me."
— Sara Paddison

"The weak can never forgive. Forgiveness is the attribute of the strong."
— Mahatma Gandhi

Changing Your Perspectives

As you shift into alignment with the Divine Mother, you will discover you also shift perspectives on long-held patterns and belief systems. The extreme focus on building material wealth transitions into a focus on cultivating a strong spiritual foundation. Up until now, you have allowed your energy to be pulled in a thousand directions—and now you strengthen your center, your inner Source, and learn to magnetize to yourself, rather than spraying arrows in every direction. Sacrificing yourself for others is exposed as martyrdom, and you realize the necessity of being Self-ish with inner exploration, time to wander, and self-care so that you can authentically give to others from overflow.

Cultural paradigms also shift as you and others realign to the Divine Mother. You realize the origins of violence as remnants of the reptilian brain inside your human mind, and activate the frontal cortex for higher consciousness with the art of diplomacy. The unquenchable thirst to consume, consume, consume that plagued you as you immersed in the conditioning of Western culture now loses its grip on you as your heart opens with genuine gratitude that inspires generous giving. Your eyes are opened to the pattern of entitlement in your life, your family, and your country—and your heart reminds you to be grateful even as the structures and institutions you relied on for security fall apart.

Opening yourself to the Divine Mother, you are able to challenge your cognitive understanding of 'God' as something external and distant to feel a deep knowing that you are immersed in the Great Spirit. You realize you are never alone because you are inextricably connected to All That Is.

Your increased sensitivity and perception helps you notice the harshness of judgement so you can soften and speak with love. And your self-respect allows you to relax expectations and judgments of people in your life so you can Let Others Voluntarily Evolve.

♥

Pulled In A Thousand Directions

Time and again, a mother has come to me in my practice on the verge of a spiritual awakening, economically strapped, overworked, and responsible for the care of multiple children with no support from the father, or with combativeness from the father that disempowers her maternal authority. I've met women and mothers who are entrepreneurs like me, who climb mountains every day to keep everything and everyone moving forward.

After a while, it feels like you're telling the little child within you "Just hold it until we get to the top of that mountain." Then you get 'there' and there's another mountain to climb, another distance to 'just hold it.' Can you relate?

These mothers desperately need support to move through their spiritual awakening, and yet they're pulled in a thousand directions without help. They'll often say "I can't do it right now...I'm needed here and here...and when XYZ happens, *then* I can focus on me."

Guess what? There will never be a time to focus on you. There will always be another mountain to climb. This is part of the Mother Wound passed down generationally to women and mothers of our time. Just a few generations ago, women were expected to raise the children and stay in the home; and then women's liberation opened the door to a woman having a career *and* children; and now the Great Awakening is calling us forth to a whole new paradigm. We are discovering our balance between motherhood and womanhood, family and career, matriarchy and patriarchy, personal and collective.

Just three generations ago in my family, my maternal great-grandmother birthed and raised 13 children as a migrant farmworker with scant means. All of the children had a job; even my grandmother from the age of 3 was taking care of her two younger sisters. When she was a young woman, my grandmother met my grandfather who got a job for the oil company out in Midwest Texas. She transitioned into being married to a man who had his own home, and being a full-time housewife, mother and volunteer for the town church. My mother left the small town of Kermit where she grew up, and moved to Dallas where she got a job and married my natural father. Then she unexpectedly got pregnant with me and her life took on a new meaning: find a suitable husband and father figure to raise me. Once she met husband number three, my Dad, she was able to start expanding her personal horizons and go to community college because she had a supportive husband to help raise me.

My mother stayed married to my Dad for 45 years, and had what many would call a successful marriage. She surpassed my grandmother in education by getting her Masters degree in child psychology from the University of Texas when she was midlife. But she never had a career, per se. She dedicated herself to taking care of my Dad who was the breadwinner of the family and had many health complications from the stress of his work.

I'm the first woman in my family lineage to have a 4-year college degree from a prestigious university. I'm the first woman in my family lineage to be an entrepreneur, mother, best-selling author, speaker, and influencer. I've generated enough sustainable revenue that having my own home and enough money for self-care (spa days, massage, pedicure) has been a given in my life. I should have been grateful and happy.

So why has my life been riddled with intense self-doubt, over-indulgence of wine and other comforts, and depression/frustration with the experience of being a mother and a wife?

I believe it is because the definitions of 'mother' and 'wife' are radically changing in my generation of women, and the ones following my generation. My generation has the ability to decide what it means to be a 'mother' and what that role looks like. We have unprecedented comfort that gives our kids a soft cushy Disney experience, at the same time that our children are under the most mental and emotional stress of previous generations because mothers are working jobs, paying household bills, driving kids to and from school and extracurricular activities, and doing all of this oftentimes without help from the father. With all the chaos of our lives, there's rarely a sense of the family pulling together to put a meal on the table, as there was in my great-grandmother's generation.

When my great-grandmother was birthing children, the goal was to keep them alive. Survival was very motivating for the children to learn to chip in through effort to help the family thrive. Although I was not alive at this time, I imagine that the life of the little Q'ero children I've seen walking 5 miles to and from school is very similar to the life my ancestors experienced only a few generations ago. Living close to the Earth, grounded, grateful for food and shelter, and brought together with comradery through the challenge of surviving.

Just a few generations later, my sons expect to have a room of their own, high-speed Wifi, a car to drive, and college paid in full. The fact that, as a spiritual mentor, I haven't had the resources to take them on exotic travel vacations like their father has given me some black marks in the 'Which Parent Buys Me More' book. Getting them to do chores around the house can be an exercise in frustration. Eat a family meal together? Why do that when you have your faraway virtual friends awaiting you on the computer in your room?

I imagine my great aunts and uncles around the family dinner table after a long day of being a migrant farmworker, and I imagine they had a lot more family bonding than happens around my dinner table.

How did my children get this way? Because of how I parented and how their father parented. From watching us while we were still together, and how we prioritized ourselves at every turn with vacations and dinners out. From receiving countless gifts at Christmas and birthday, and presents for doing what they're supposed to do. And because of the Mother Wound.

The Mother Wound within me made it so that I walked on eggshells with my husband and my children. I never wanted to exhibit anger toward my children because I had received too many tongue lashings as a daughter from my mother. I expected myself to be patient and kind and listen and be available to my children. I was a latchkey child, and I wanted my children to have a mother who was home. So I worked from home as an entrepreneur and hired a nanny to help until they were old enough for part-time daycare and then school. Constant interruptions to my work were the result of working at home as a mom, and as a writer who needs to immerse in flow to deliver the 'good stuff', that was hard. Sometimes I snapped and then judged myself for doing so.

Disciplining the children was a tangled mess between my husband's need to be right and my need to not create conflict. The children always needed something, and I was the first stop much of the time because of how 'reasonable' I was and because I was in the role of mother. I defended them to their father whose punishments often felt erratic and ungrounded in a system of teaching. I was caught in the middle between my husband and my children, frustrated about being in the middle, and helpless to do anything about it. When we moved to Texas to be around my parents for support, I ended up receiving what I perceived as harsh criticism from my mother whose parental style was disciplinarian. Now the Mother Wound deepened, and in reaction I got even more resistant to stepping into motherhood, not wanting to be like my mother, and instead retreated into distractions and entertainment.

When I started studying with my first spiritual teachers, I learned about codependency as an energetic that could bind you into behaviors that are disempowering. I increased awareness of these patterns and began extracting myself from them bit by bit which was only made possible because of the fact that I had left the children's father. I used powerful spiritual methods learned at school to reclaim my energy from others, to cut cords, and to create new boundaries that held each person accountable for themselves. I expanded my understanding of my role as a mother and realized that I could not protect my children from the lessons they needed to learn in this lifetime. Actually, trying to protect them from their lessons really gunked up the works for all of us. I changed from being constantly available to having boundaries that protected my purpose work, my relationship with my new husband, and my time with my children.

Becoming a thought leader added extra lessons about boundaries and investment of my time and energy for greatest potency.

What I see in the women and mothers who cross my path is often an inability to prioritize self-care of a spiritual nature. You may go for a massage, but you have many reasons why you are unable to invest in deeper inner reflection and rewiring of your inner matrix. "I can't do my inner work right now because my daughter just had a baby and I have to drop everything in my life and be there for her." "I can't do my inner work right now because the class is not at a convenient time when someone doesn't need me, and I can't set a boundary to claim space for myself."

What is the addiction to being needed by others that keeps you from focusing on the self-mastery work that will set you free from an unfulfilling, powerless life? When are you going to prioritize yourself?

Many women are unwilling to upset the apple cart and disappoint the people in their lives who have become reliant on them, and are pulling them in a thousand directions all at once. If this is you, you need to set boundaries, and dedicate to your own path and purpose. You need to let your children and significant others do much more of the heavy lifting in their own lives, and not rush in to save them by being the finder of all solutions.

I've heard just about every excuse for why a woman cannot commit time to herself for reclaiming personal power. As with any unhealthy behavior, the reason you don't change is because you get an underlying benefit from maintaining the status quo. **The addiction to be on call for loved ones stems from an underlying lack. You feel loved and needed by being on call for loved ones, and you avoid the harder task of cultivating true self-love through inner inquiry.**

The excuses to put off personal spiritual development stem from a root fear: If you change, your life will change, and you may realize you are responsible for loving yourself. You may realize that no one else has ever been responsible for loving you, and most of the constructs you've created in your life that disempower you are fully based on your need to be needed. You may discover an addiction to being a martyr, above reproach and yet helpless to change your life.

Many women would not recognize a boundary even if it came up with a sign that said "You need to put a boundary for self-care right here."

Once you realize you are responsible for taking care of yourself, loving yourself, and rewiring your inner matrix through self-mastery practices, you are on the path to reclaiming personal power. **That pathway to your power reveals every disempowering construct in your life, one by one, for you to witness, release, and replace with a conscious choice.**

It's true that when you turn your phone on mute, there are people in your life who will feel abandoned by you. Doing so gives a greater gift. It teaches you how to source love within, and it teaches the others how to find the answers that they're coming to you to get.

What are you teaching your sons and daughters by allowing yourself to be constantly pulled in a thousand directions, spreading your energy too thin to be fully present and engaged in any aspect of your life? What would you be teaching your children if you stopped to take care of yourself along the journey and created healthy boundaries, rather than waiting for a convenient destination where no one will 'need' you so you can claim time for yourself? How tense are the muscles around your root chakra from trying to hold it all together? Have you felt your hips and rear lately? Breathe into the clenching and encourage yourself to relax and receive.

What expectations have been placed on you that are extraneous to the role you actually play in your loved one's life? **Can you let go of being the one that always has the answers, and let them go through the uncomfortable journey to make their own realizations?** Can you take a break from being 'on call' and see what that feels like? What would happen if you were able to dedicate to yourself for one hour? One day? One week? One month? Your focus on yourself will activate the inner wellspring of love so that it spills forth in excess and can be easily gifted to others without draining you of all desire to act on the inspirations you've heard in your own heart.

If you're operating in the paradigm of being pulled in a thousand directions, you've likely also placed yourself in this role with your work, volunteerism, friendships, and so forth. Even small changes towards setting boundaries to stop scattering your energy, and focusing to create an inner sanctum for peace and self-reflection, will grow your resources. **Once you're truly full inside, and you have appropriate boundaries with others, you can begin giving from a resourced place of Divine inspiration.**

You are raising humans who must eventually take care of themselves. There is no time like the present to learn how to do that in age-appropriate ways, and to create space for yourself to listen to the inner child that is tired of 'holding it'. Watching you set boundaries, take response-ability for your 'stuff', heal within, and go after your passions are all wonderful ways to model conscious response-able living for your children.

❤

Sacrificing To Selfish

The world as you know it has been built on a paradigm of codependent structures that require you to do things for others, and others to do things for you, based on obligation. You have been conditioned with entire rulebooks that outline the protocols of human interaction, and you use these rules to assess whether another person has behaved appropriately; and if not, then you can have an excuse for judging the person, holding them accountable, and indulging in your feelings that you are choosing to feel such as being abandoned, victimized, let down, disempowered, and so forth.

In the collective rulebook up until now have been special rules for women, and special rules for men, added expectations of wives and added expectations of husbands. As women have stepped out into the workforce, the previous expectations around men providing economically for the family have fallen on the shoulders of the women and mothers in addition to all the expectations that already existed for women and mothers for keeping the house, nurturing through cooking, entertaining and inspiring the minds of family, and the list goes on. Of course there are exceptions to every rule, and certainly I have witnessed fathers who took on the bulk of the responsibility to raise the children; among them, my beloved Akeem.

The most extensive set of rules in the collective book of law have to do with how a mother should behave with her children, her husband, her own mother and father and siblings, and so forth. As the understanding of early childhood development has expanded, our collective desire to provide environments conducive to producing the most successful offspring have increased, and the expectations on mothers has multiplied. Additional performance pressures for mothers come from the unresolved childhood traumas that negatively impacted self-esteem; a mother who is aware that how her parents treated her was unloving often places high expectations on herself to be better as a parent than what she received.

The level of expectation placed on a mother is impossible to achieve without the mother sacrificing herself. If a mother is to excel at being a mother, her life becomes an act of service to everyone around her. As a mother fulfills the 'needs' of those around her, if she were to dedicate herself to doing so, at the end of the day she would have but a few minutes to take care of herself. **Very quickly, the well runs dry inside a mother who does not take adequate time for self-care and the personal work of self-mastery.** Her mind alone will deplete her resources with endless criticism for failing to be loving enough, or to find the solution to help her child with a problem.

Without time to dedicate for her personal inner growth and mastery, a mother will soon feel exhausted, inadequate, and depleted. In this beaten down space creeps self-doubt, self-judgment, and the harsh inner critic. Now add the very natural occurrence of a child having a challenge, and the mother takes responsibility for this, as if there's something wrong with the child that was caused through her inability to parent the way she 'should' have been able to. Is it any wonder that often we see mothers with that forced smile and high-pitched voice when responding "I'm fine! Everything is great" when you can clearly see the tension lines across her forehead, the deep dark circles under her eyes, and the vacancy in her spirit. She's still trying to meet all the impossible expectations out of an intense fear that she's really screwing up her kids.

Whew! Can you feel how tight, restrictive, and punitive this mother cage is? For single mothers, add to this the lack of financial and parenting support from the father, or dismissive comments from the father in front of the children that denigrates her wisdom. If this mother is also healing a Mother Wound with her mother, she can feel even more insecure and overwhelmed.

Sometimes as a mother in this culture, it feels as if the whole world is against you while simultaneously sucking you dry as the only source of sustenance.

This paradigm is not sustainable. I've seen too many single mothers struggling to be everything and do everything for their children without the necessary emotional and financial support from family. In fact, 'family' often hold the mother back from exactly the thing she needs the most through enforcing historical rules of conduct.

What does a mother in this situation need? Self-care. Space. Reflection. Rejuvenation. Pleasure. Resources for self-mastery. She needs to back up a few steps with every challenge so she can 'get' the lesson she's being taught while holding the most vital and responsible role a person can play for another person: being a mother. She needs less to do, not more, so she can relax and drop deep into her heart and come from Love. She needs financial support so she doesn't have to struggle and worry about providing. She needs emotional support so she can counter the inner resistance to the endless presence a child requires. She needs self-love so she can fully show up as a teacher with her children, and not be holding back from doing what she knows needs doing because she's afraid of losing the only love she has in her life. She needs to be self-referencing so she doesn't just hand down the same old dysfunctional patterns that her ancestors have been passing along for generations. She needs self-confidence to follow the wise woman within and trust what she feels in her heart, her womb, and her gut.

Imagine a medic tent during a war, and there are soldiers coming in one after the other with wounds that need immediate tending. Everyone is in pain and wants help, right now. In the medic tent is a person without medical training, getting on-the-job training as she firefights each new situation. It's an endless stream of problems, and each problem is one she has not seen yet. At some point, the mental and emotional stress of trying to figure out the best solution to an ever-revolving door of new problems is going to lead to a breakdown of the resource meant to be in service to others. Add to this an endless barrage of criticism for how this untrained service professional is helping, and you have an idea of what it is like to be a mother who is not in her power and her knowing.

What mothers need is the training that puts them in their power and their knowing. The greatest power is Love and a mother in touch with her Love will know exactly what to do in the moment, and will trust herself to do it.

The state of our world today is a direct reflection of generations of mothers out of their power and their knowing, disconnected from Love.

The pathway back to Love and being an empowered mother is currently called being 'selfish'. Ideally, a mother receives the training to discover her connection to Love before becoming pregnant. That is not the current situation, and so you work with what you've got. You start where you are by shifting gears and taking time out to learn some tools and practices that lead to an inner knowing of Love. **As a mother, when you find your inner well run dry and you feel burned out with giving, you must put the mask on yourself first just like the flight attendants tell you to do on planes.**

You must become 'Self-ish' to look within, care for yourself, and nurse yourself back to health. You cannot give to another what you do not have, so how can you give love to others if you don't first love yourself? We are in the middle of a transition between a world that feared a mother's power to world that reveres a mother's Love. It's big work for anyone in a body that birthed a baby. You've got to have tremendous self-awareness to liberate yourself and future generations from behavioral and mental conditioning based on the control and subjugation of women.

Becoming 'Self-ish' is the first step towards self-realization which is the liberated actualization of your consciousness, the freedom to live and express as you choose, and the power to chart the course of your life as inspired by your higher power. In my experience, a wise woman who has claimed her power by being brave enough to be 'Self-ish' is a far better teacher because she's leading through demonstration how her children can live with sovereignty.

You have a unique Soul curriculum to explore, and sometimes to others it might look 'Self-ish' if you act on the inspiration of your heart. But who decides what is a 'valid' reason to do something and what is not? The rulebook you inherited from ancestry and society may judge your choice to go to a self-discovery retreat as selfish, and encourage your sacrifice to be present for your daughter's soccer tournament. How can you hold space for every person in the family to be self-actualized, independent, and aligned to their Soul's curriculum while also feeling loved, held, and supported within the context of the family? **You must move from obligation as the motivation for doing something to genuine heart-felt inspiration. Your authentic 'Yes' is pure magic.**

In my own mind and heart, one thing is sure: the new 'family' paradigm will include a distribution of responsibility. Each person in a family must become responsible for their own self-love and self-care; the mother cannot be fully responsible for holding the family together. In my book, an ideal family is one where the children learn to contribute to the family experience by chipping in at family mealtime, supporting each other in celebration of individual goals, and becoming responsible to chart the course of their own life curriculum. I feel that pampering our kids and trying to lessen their struggles because we don't want them to fail has led to a generation that doesn't know how to find the solutions for themselves.

We need to teach our kids to be life entrepreneurs, and that takes learning how to listen within for the answers, take calculated risks, and cultivate the inner resiliency to roll with life's redirections.

The new paradigm definitely includes a healthy dose of being 'Self-ish' to make choices based on inner direction rather than outer approval. Ironically, as you become 'Self-ish' and tune into inner wisdom, you will be guided to the solutions that make things better for all concerned. Trust the process.

♥

From Violence To Diplomacy

In a violent world, children need to learn how to be independent and self-reliant and so part of growth is separation from the mother bond as a sort of violence that establishes this independence. And in the Western world it is normal to throw your parents away as disposable when you are on the path to true independence and self-power. This is because the Western world is about hierarchies of power where children who stay in the family system do not gain their power until the patriarch or matriarch dies because it is clear that within the family there is a permanent hierarchy with parents on top and children underneath. You can have your power in your own house.

In this paradigm, elders are tossed away in nursing homes as independent lives take priority to serve the needs of youth that pursue their desires as priority, disconnected from a larger context of family, tribe, or world. Independent agents in a violent world compete against each other for what is perceived as limited resources because they are not aware of a larger design that actually has a plan and place for each that serves the whole. The concept of whole is incongruent with the 'me/mine' mind.

In a loving world, children need to learn how to stay in the conversation of the family and tribe so the initiation to become an adult member of the tribe is not about separating from one's mother so much as deepening into relationship with the Divine Mother, Mother Earth. And in indigenous cultures this is done through a rite of passage called the vision quest that facilitates a youth forging a bond with Mother Earth to become horizontal with adult members of the tribe and have an equal voice. In this paradigm, one stays in the conversation with family and tribe and learns respect for ones elders. One learns how to tune into the Divine Mother for guidance about one's journey and role in the tribe, and there is harmony through allowing a larger force to lead.

The Westward expansion is at its combustion point. We are six degrees of separation from every person we throw under the bus to claim our power and independence. It's time to see through a new lens of love, surrender to the divine Mother Earth, and learn the harder lessons of staying in the conversation that our indigenous brothers and sisters have been learning for ages while we set out to conquer and be kings and queens of our own houses.

War is what ignorant children of violence do when they want what they want when they want it.

Diplomacy is the art of being an adult that knows we are One Human Tribe.

❤

Consuming To Giving

When you are afraid that life will not provide you a steady supply of what you need to survive, you stockpile much more than you need so you can feel secure. The toilet paper crisis during 2020 is an example of this way of thinking. Perhaps Divine Mother was asking whether we needed to consume so much toilet paper, or whether we could be more mindful about our usage to reduce the number of trees we kill so we have something to wipe our bums. Maybe Divine Mother was inviting you to see that you can take only what you need so that your neighbors also could have what they need.

The mentality of the European settlers who wrestled American lands from indigenous people is still present in our capitalistic culture. To defeat indigenous people, settlers to America killed the buffalo in vast numbers to take away the primary food source of these tribes. Today, corporations from America buy water rights from 3rd world countries and bottle up their water for sale; and if you read *"Confessions of an Economic Hit Man"* by John Perkins of the Pachamama Alliance, you may realize that coercion, intimidation and violence is involved in the sale of these precious resources.

The consumer culture keeps you running to earn the money to consume the next thing that television advertising tells you will satisfy your feelings of not-enoughness. Your standard of living increases alongside your salary, and your promise to share your wealth with those less blessed keeps getting pushed back because you still just don't feel like you have enough to be giving it away.

There's a reason that religions encourage you to give from your time, your talent and your treasure to others: sharing with your brothers and sisters rather than taking. **In Western culture, it is time to learn how to share privilege, power, resources, technology, innovations, and money as a global community.** Western societies have taken from their neighbors for centuries, and now it's time to share.

You must shift your consciousness from lack and scarcity, which causes you to take more than you need, into prosperity consciousness which leads to generosity and sharing. To make this shift, consider the analogy of flying in an airplane during a storm. On the ground in the plane, there are dark dense thunderclouds and lightening all around you. It feels as if the whole world must be saturated by thick humidity and threatening storms. This is the fear matrix of lack and scarcity that many Western people find themselves immersed in during times of 'crisis' where there might not be toilet paper on the shelves.

And then the plane takes off, steadily rising, Rising, RISING. As the plane moves through the clouds, all you can see is the storm. You think the storm is everywhere, and everyone is experiencing it just like you…this fear storm.

Until the plane rises above the clouds and you see blue sky. Eternal blue sky stretches into infinity.

The Western consciousness is now going through a fear storm of lack and scarcity and impending doom as systems crumble and structures break apart. When you're IN the storm, you feel saturated by it without the higher perspective. It influences your perceptions, even if you know fear is an illusion. The fear becomes so saturating it starts to seep into your consciousness and the egoic patterns of your mind expand to protect you. It becomes harder to relax and trust, and your mind spins thoughts about how to get control in uncertain times.

You have to move yourself through the clouds, knowing they are there, but not real. You have to guide yourself back to the eternal blue sky. From this eternal blue sky, it is safe to give, to share, and to only take what you need. Your Soul will lead you to live from the eternal blue sky. The eternal blue sky of the Divine reminds you that life is precious, and as more love fills your heart, you instinctively want to share your prosperity with others while you are still breathing. Pure giving from love and the overflow of your own heart is a beautiful experience and a way to respect and honor life. When you are inspired to give of your time, talent or treasure, that is the Divine tapping you on the shoulder and inviting you to share your Love so you can feel the high vibration of pure giving. **Giving keeps you honest about your consuming, Death keeps you honest about the blessings of your life, and by giving blessings and honoring Death and Life, you become a healthy cell in the body of Mother Earth.**

♥

Entitlement To Gratitude

When you enjoy certain blessings as a normal aspect of your culture and life, you expect to receive those amenities and even feel entitled to them. **What you may not realize from your wealthy reality is that not everyone enjoys the blessings you feel entitled to receive.**

I went to Smith College, an Ivy League all women's college, and was surrounded by people of privilege after attending junior high and high school in blue-collar neighborhood. It was a shock for me to hear the complaints and conversations that many of these women shared as this level of privilege was not previously part of my reality. I remember one day walking down the dorm hall I heard a woman on the phone with her father: "Daddy <whining>...do we have to go to Paris again?" I think my mouth dropped to the floor. I almost knocked on her door to say "I'll go in your place if you don't want to go." I had never flown outside the country before college. Going to such a prestigious college among daughters of the wealthiest families in the world totally changed my perspective about what was possible.

My next brush with entitlement came when I moved to Silicon Valley and began working in the high tech industry. Living in Silicon Valley from the birth of the Internet until I birthed my own sons, I witnessed a change in culture as the technology industry made millionaires overnight. Silicon Valley became a pressure zone where to prove your worth and compete for status you needed a Lexis or Mercedes or BMW, to live in an expensive neighborhood, and to send your children to the best private schools. Unless you lucked out with a successful startup or climbed your way into executive management, living in Silicon Valley with a sense of privilege required two high tech incomes with at least 70 hour work weeks. Living on a budget meant feeling deprived as everyone around you ate expensive meals and drank wine at swanky restaurants.

Before children, my then-partner and I had wined and dined at pricey gourmet restaurants on a regular basis throughout the years, feeling entitled to some pampering after a long work week; satiating our appetites with expensive meals was the way we learned to honor our relationship. I had become accustomed to waiters that wiped breadcrumbs from your table and described meals in such a succulent way that your mouth watered.

Although these outings were generally the highlight of my week, at some point I noticed that I was becoming angry if the waiter missed my 'sign' that I needed something, and that I was dissatisfied if the meal or service had any kind of imperfection...enough to complain and 'make a stink' about it. I started noticing my girlfriends being rude to wait staff if things were not done to 'impeccable standards.'

Realizing that I was unhappy, drowning in not-enoughness despite being surrounded by opulence, I decided it must be time for children. In retrospect, I see that it was actually time for a spiritual journey. However, I took the road most traveled and had children which did, in fact, change my priorities. My body began teaching me about more sacred matters like motherhood and deep psychological healing. The awakening of motherhood and onset of hormones spurred a craving for greater meaning in my life. To fill this thirst, I plunged myself into my art and set out to make a living selling beauty in a world more interested in status. For a while I tried to keep up with the Jones' while honoring my call for purpose, until the pressure was simply too much. $30K in debt from my lack of high-tech income, we chose to leave Silicon Valley and move to Texas. The home the father of my children and I bought and renovated together in the downtrodden College Park neighborhood of San Jose listed for a million dollars as we exited the mayhem to move to the country in Texas.

These glimpses into how entitlement had infected me and the culture around me were just the beginning of many deeper insights. As I look back across my life, I can see entitlement everywhere in my history as a Western person living in the wealthiest country in the world...starting with my own father. My Dad was a beautiful paternal provider who unwittingly, through his generosity, bred an atmosphere of entitlement in his children because we knew we could always depend on him to buy family dinners, splurge on birthday and holiday gifts, and help us out with cash when we needed it. After a lifetime of being invisibly entwined in the pattern of entitlement, I received a powerful insight about my entitlement during my first sacred journey to Peru. It was a profound moment for me, a realization of the role of gratitude in my life up until then; gratitude was something I felt when I got what I wanted when I wanted it. But because of the experience I am about to share, gratitude became something more fulfilling.

On this July day in 2014, I was hiking up to a sacred monument called Puma Marca in the Sacred Valley of Peru with other tourists from my retreat group. As we passed through a village on a dirt road, our teacher Alberto Villoldo stopped at a small building made of mud bricks and spoke to a woman who was standing in the doorway. They reached agreement and he turned to us and said, "She is offering to let you come and see her home." I felt my throat tighten as realization sunk in that this was where she lived with her whole family. I went to the doorway and peered into the one-room house that was 20ft by 10ft at most. It had a large mattress on a wooden board on one side where the family slept, a wood burning stove and 'kitchen' on the right side, and directly in the middle was a wooden table where the family gathered for meals. The woman threw a handful of corn on the ground under the table and a flurry of fur appeared as guinea pigs scrambled to eat the corn. The guinea pigs were not pets—they were animals the family loved and kept in their home until it was time to eat them.

Here I was standing in my REI gear that probably cost more than everything in this home, including the house itself, and feeling impoverished. What this Q'ero woman had that I did not at the time was worth far more than anything money could buy: she had gratitude. She could see the blessings of her life and feel grateful for her life's circumstances. She was generous and kind, not burdened by the feeling of 'not enough' and the curse of entitlement. She even cooked several of those guinea pigs for us and brought them to where we were camping later in the trip.

Being a mesa carrier in the tradition of the Q'ero has helped me to open my heart and feel grateful for the blessings of my life—even the things that do not feel like blessings. My mesa connects me to the wisdom of Mother Earth, and working with the Divine Mother has revealed to me, layer by layer, the ways I have been domesticated to be entitled by our Western culture. Many tough lessons I had to go through to liberate me from entitlement, including letting go of my inheritance from my Dad.

Being angry because you think you're owed something is a kind of sickness. What is much healthier is being humble and grateful for the gifts you are given by the Divine Mother.

It was work to lift myself into gratitude from entitlement. Entitlement really gets its hooks into you through comparing yourself to others and what they have, then feeling lack and anger that you do not also have what they have, then demanding that you should also have what you perceive they have because you deserve it. I mean, there's a million reasons why you deserve to have it more than they do, right? You can detect plenty of their flaws as justification why they do not deserve what they have that you want.

Comparison and entitlement work together to destroy your happiness by keeping you in a state of jealousy over what you perceive others have that you want, and striving for what you do not yet have so you can feel like you got what you're owed. Entitlement generates a great deal of suffering internally and projects negative energy onto others that you feel owe you something. **To lift yourself out of the tangled mess of entitlement you have to radically let go of everything you think you are owed, and practice daily gratitude for what is present in your life.** When I went through this rewiring, there were days that it was hard to bring myself to genuinely feel grateful; and the days I was able to reach gratitude, my heart expanded in such a gorgeous way that I kept dedicating myself to the process in hopes of reaching that ecstasy again.

Many people study the Law of Attraction because it appeals to their desire to manipulate forces to get what they want; to attract the prosperity they feel entitled to receive. And yet through studying the Law of Attraction, you're inevitably led to the realization that having more prosperity is a matter of adopting a state of gratitude that makes you aware of the prosperity that you already have. You also learn that the most fulfilling forms of prosperity are not typically based in material wants, but in receiving what deepens your sense of gratitude, love and awe.

I have had the privilege of engaging in a prayer practice with a spiritual community whereby we witness one another's gratitude and prayers around an altar during sacred ceremony. Listening to the genuinely grateful prayers of those more practiced with gratitude, and feeling the way my heart opens as the vibration of gratitude fills the space, is one of the reasons this is my favorite ceremony of the year. What I always notice is how the energy falls flat when any nuance of entitlement enters the space. Luckily, doubling down on gratitude clears it away so we can all feel grateful for what is here right now, and for the truth that our prayers will always be answered in Divine timing.

♥

External God To Immersion In Spirit

"You don't believe in God," the man said to me as he wept.

I was walking past this man, heading for what would be my most powerful channeling of Divine guidance from White Eagle to date, when I felt the pull of this stranger's sadness and stopped to help. My friends and I were on the way back to the conference where I would be delivering my speech, and we were in a hurry to get there, but I saw this man weeping and I felt a pull that made me stop my stride and ask him, "Are you ok? Is there anything I can do to help?"

His response as he wept, "You don't believe in God."

My husband who was there with me urged me to leave the man to face his inner challenges. The man was clearly encountering difficult things inside himself, and I could feel the energy turning toward aggression. We continued our journey as I silently sent blessings.

Still, his words tugged at me. What was it I felt? A tiny bit of fear? A little bit of doubt?

Back in the conference room I quieted myself and went internal, closing my eyes, tuning into my own heart, and listening. Everything happens for a reason. And many things happen to test our faith, our knowing. I knew this was such a test for me.

I was about to deliver a spiritual ceremony from an Earth-based heritage to a group of thought leaders whose personal beliefs ranged from Christianity to Agnosticism and everything in between. I knew there were potential landmines of fear in the group consciousness having to do with centuries-old lies about shamanism, paganism, and Earth worship.

In fact, my husband later told me that an African American attendee asked him during the ceremony what the greater meaning was, and that he was concerned to offend his Christian ancestors by participating in the ceremony which was intended to send our prayers for the collective healing and enlightenment of humanity to the Great Spirit.

Thank you for asking that question. I have another question. Does it offend your African ancestors that you practice the religion of the colonizers who stripped them of wealth and power, enslaved them, and even led them to believe that they are sub-human?

There is a story of 'God' that has been created by men to control a population into denying themselves sovereignty, subjugate themselves in order to be 'saved', and beg for forgiveness for being born sinners and unworthy of Love. This story of 'God' is used to punish people, and is a misuse of authority on the part of unenlightened people who wanted 'Power Over' others and clearly misunderstood Love. The cultural and spiritual beliefs and practices of entire continents of people were wiped out to create a system of control through Fear, and obedience to authority, that has stripped generations of people of the awareness of who they truly are.

If Fear is needed in order to enforce participation in a religion, how can that religion be about the principle of Love? If you do what we say, then you are loved and included. If you do not do what we say, then you are cast out into the pit of hell. If you are like us then you are chosen. If you are not like us, then you're going to hell. When I learned that there are families of devout Christians who collectively decide to cast a family member into 'hell' for their own good, I was heartbroken. How is this way of thinking in service to Love?

Love is All That Is.

All That Is.

Love is not about making things conform to your perspective or world view. **Love is about YOU opening yourself to understand how what you see before you is a part of Love, which is All That Is.**

I do not believe in a 'God' that would give all the instructions to being 'saved' to one group of people, make them the 'chosen ones' and then leave all the other people on the planet to go to hell and suffer because they don't have the special book.

I do not believe in a 'God' that would birth you on a planet and then tell you to be afraid of interacting with it. It's preposterous that a Loving God would tell you that the very materials you're made of are evil, and you should stay away from them.

These thoughts do not come from 'God'. They come from people who had to differentiate themselves from those they were conquering and slaughtering mercilessly so they could maintain a belief in being 'good'. Thus the concept of 'savage' was created and the disdain for everything in nature was set into motion as a way of differentiation by conquering Westerners who also wanted to be 'good' Christians.

This is a huge part of the Mother Wound of our planet.

Fear of Earth-based spirituality is a false construct born of 'Power Over' religion that keeps people from experiencing the deepest Love available in the material realm, the Love of the Divine Mother Earth.

At this point in history, we have had centuries of lies about 'God' told by billions of people from a 'Power Over' matrix of control. It's a hot mess. It's tangled up in our brains as domestication from our parents, our ancestors, our churches, our schools, our communities, our governments, and so forth. We've only had a sprinkling of enlightened people on the planet over the last few centuries, so we can assume that every single one of us is still reaching for that top part of Maslow's pyramid of needs: self-actualization.

If we want to clean up the mess made by religious clashes, we need to stop debating it for a while and get quiet. Let the noise and the fear of doing it wrong subside. Stop looking to other people to give you a connection to Source, or to interpret 'God' for you. Go within to the Divine Source that lives there. Find your own presence and peace. Inspired knowing always comes from presence because that's where the Divine lives: In Spirit. The chattering mind is the ego trying to do it 'right' and be powerful. The chattering mind fills up all the space if you let it, and the space is where Spirit enters your awareness.

What we share in common is that we were all birthed onto the Earth. In this way, the Earth is our common Mother. Earth-based spirituality is a birthright of every human being. Lying belly to belly with the Earth, and inviting yourself to be tuned to the heartbeat of the Mother, is the quickest way to restore yourself to a temporary state of sanity. As soon as you commune with a group of people again, you're back in some level of insanity. The more time you spend on the Earth getting quiet, the more you'll become aware of the patterns of insanity in your own human consciousness, which will help you become aware of it in others.

People whose traditions involve Earth worship demonstrate that quiet reflection with nature results in feeling peaceful and grateful. How peaceful and grateful do you feel? How long do your feelings of peace and gratitude last? If you want to liberate your mind from the conditioning that has robbed you of a visceral knowing of Love, and of yourself as a part of All That Is, you have to be willing to challenge your fears and the fears of your ancestors. **You have to be willing to open to the possibility that there is a vast intelligence within all things that you can learn from once you get quiet and listen.**

The practice I shared at the conference that day was despacho from the Q'ero people in Peru. We collectively breathed or softly spoke our intentions into little flowers, and the biological material of the flower captured our intentions for ourselves in service to humanity and the planet. I created a boat made from banana leaf and filled it with kintus, or prayer bundles, to ask for support from the Four Directions and the Mother Earth herself. And we put all the little flowers inside the boat, then walked together to the river and placed the boat on the water. Mama Cocha, the Mother of the Waters, took the prayer boat in a little circle in front of us, and then carried the prayer boat upstream against the current. Upstream against the current.

If you are reading this book you are part of the reawakening of the awareness of the Divine Mother to Western consciousness. You and I are flowing upstream against the current of the historical paradigm that has enslaved humanity. **We are flowing upstream to Love.**

♥

Soften and Speak with Love

The world has gotten very loud with the voices of humans arguing over their perspectives. Feeling passionate about the injustices of the world and how to resolve them, we raise our voices rather than our hearts. We want to raise the consciousness of the planet, but find ourselves shouting rather than listening. One day, I heard what I sound like when I'm doing this.

I was listening back to a recorded conversation and I heard my voice adopt that edge that happens when I'm feeling pain and being strong, passionate and convicted to get through it. I heard that abrasion underneath the conviction of the point I was making. I heard the defensiveness protecting the vulnerability covering up the pain.

I learned how to bring the edge to my voice during my upbringing. Listening to my mother become very passionate about world events, I learned that the correct response to perceived injustice was to bring outrage and censure; to convey judgement with abrasive accusation in your voice. I learned how to make someone wrong by overpowering with rage or bitterness while holding hard inflexible walls in my voice.

Through my training as a healer, and learning to sing medicine songs from the jungle called *icaros*, I learned that my voice is powerful because it's connected to my heart. When I speak, my voice resonates with the energy I'm feeling and it goes directly into your heart. Singing icaros from my heart while I am focusing intention on love is healing and beautiful medicine to receive. When learning to sing these songs, I learned how to melt the restrictions within my heart and voice, and soften into a space of trust and love. **We all have this capability to sing from our hearts and share healing vibrations.**

However, this day listening back to my voice of passion in that recording, I felt how it feels to receive me when I'm all 'fired up'. It made me pull back from myself, recoil, and want to hide. I realized it made me feel how I felt as a child listening to the adult anger being expressed in the house.

I realized in this moment that it was hard to listen to me when my voice was screaming of the pain I was feeling. I always had a hard time hearing that voice as a child, and even as a woman.

And I also understand why that abrasion in my voice was there. Pain. I wanted someone to listen and validate that pain: "What you've been through is so painful, Kerri."

Now when I hear that abrasion in my voice, or in someone else's, I can have the consciousness to know it's a cry for help. Hear my pain please. The answer is to melt the abrasion with validation and comfort from the heart.

Through the validation of the pain is a softening. This happens with the realization that everything you went through, that you endured, that you survived: made you strong. And now it's time to become wise, compassionate and loving because of it all.

You're wise enough to melt the abrasion within you, with Love and compassion.

You're wise enough to forgive all that came before and let it be the history that made you who you are today.

You're wise enough to recognize learned patterns and reprogram yourself with Love.

You're wise enough to soften the abrasiveness of your voice and to know that Love in flow—not anger in force—is the most powerful vibration to carry your messages.

The whole journey of life seems to be a softening back to a whisper, like a gentle breeze on a warm day. The art is to notice the nuances, the leftover remnants of defensiveness, and bring love and grace to it. In softening the energy around the voice and heart, new words to speak may also present themselves that offer even more grace. Notice the words you use to tell the familiar stories of your life, and be aware of the tensions in your body and throat as you speak them. What happens if you breathe love and compassion into the tensions and then soften the tone of voice you use to speak as well as the words and framing of the story?

Before might be something like this: "The painful drama of my marriage to a narcissist forced me to stand up for myself, walk away from being bullied, and stop abandoning myself."

After might be something like this: "My marriage was a catalyst for me to see what needed healing inside of me so that I could hear myself, honor myself, and love myself."

Do you feel the difference? In the first statement, the focus is on the other person as the source of the wounding, and there is self-judgment when describing the actions taken to support the self. In the second statement, the focus is on the inner transformation and ways that the relationship opened up healing for the self.

Become aware of the stories you tell unconsciously about your life and relationships, and start examining them. Play around with how to revise them so that the focus is on the healing you received, and the higher vibrational feelings you were able to claim for yourself as a result. Notice how it feels to speak this new story; does it soften your heart and throat? Does this new story feel lighter?

The words you use to tell your story, and the vibration of feeling with which you speak it, says a great deal about the depth to which you currently love yourself. Just minor tweaks in language can open up beautiful gifts of release, forgiveness, and compassion.

♥

Let Others Voluntarily Evolve

I heard this acronym for love and it resonated strongly with me: Let Others Voluntarily Evolve. Enthusiasm for the spiritual path can make you want to share your discoveries with friends and family who have known you long before you 'woke up'. Your desire to share, while likely to be well intentioned, may not have the positive effect you imagined. Your sharing might result in resistance, obstinate behavior, and even hostility.

We are certainly in a critical juncture on Earth where we must evolve to save our species and the planet. And, Earth is still a planet of free will where trying to 'wake up' a person before they are ready can further delay the progress of that individual. When your sharing provokes debate, evokes a sense of superiority over another, or makes you feel like you need to prove yourself, it is time to back off and breathe to release your need to convince the other person that what you have experienced is 'the way' they should also walk.

I learned a powerful lesson about Letting Others Voluntarily Evolve years ago when my Dad found out he had an incurable form of leukemia, and yet it was in stasis which the doctors could not explain. Interestingly enough, this form of leukemia was exactly the same as the leukemia that took my grandmothers life just months before my Dad discovered he had it. At the time, I was in training with the Four Winds Light Body School where we were told that the spirits of departed loved ones could be attracted to your energy body and attach there, causing disease. We were practicing how to set the Soul free to cross beyond the veil so they could come back as a spirit guide without having a negative impact on those they loved.

I suggested to my Dad that his leukemia could be caused by an attachment from my grandmother, and urged him to have this energy healing done to remove her (and the leukemia) and help her cross over. Rather than being enthused and interested, my Dad was closed to the potential. He had chosen to go with Western medicine and was planning a doctor visit to find out about chemotherapy and other treatments available. I was crushed that my Dad would not listen to me and kept pressing in, which caused him to keep pulling back. We reached an impasse and stopped communicating for a while.

Then a spiritual retreat with a mentor at the time helped me to realize that although I felt my parents were judging my spiritual path and rejecting me, it was actually me who was judging my Dad's choice of medical treatment and rejecting him because he would not listen to me. That night I went to visit my parents and just listened. After about 30 minutes, my Dad stopped and said to me "I notice that you've been just listening and I really appreciate that. You're a strong leader. But in my life, I need you to follow." This was a message I will never forget.

In other people's lives, we are followers. There are some things you can control and subjugate people into in this material dimension we are experiencing; but waking up is not one of those things. Waking up is a Soul choice. Any attempt to force a person to wake up will result in a backlash that actually delays the process. Gentle open-handed invitations, loving and kind demonstrations, and patient witnessing are the best tools for encouraging those around you to open the door to the spiritual journey.

There is a big part of the population on Earth that do not understand spirituality because they have not yet crossed that bridge of realization about themselves. They are immersed in historical structures that are crumbling before their eyes as the energies on the planet support people in transitioning from material perception to spiritual knowing. During this time of chaos that is the catalyst for the awakening, people are going through pain as the world they understood falls apart. Have compassion, and practice self-mastery when confronted by your own frustration with stuck points of view or lower vibration behaviors and patterns. As the light increases, people may be even more provoked into acting from their shadows.

Wounded people do wounded things. Then wounded people breed more wounded people that do more wounded things, often in the name of love, simply because they thought love was supposed to hurt. Because for them, it always has hurt, up until now.

It seems nearly impossible for wounded people to accept response-ability for their mistakes, humble themselves, and express regret to the people they've wounded. It seems that the hearts of wounded people are calloused by life, and from this unfeeling space they mock sincere attempts by those they've wounded to come to reconciliation and peace.

I remember what it felt like to be wounded. I remember the dark depression and worthlessness of being a wounded person. I projected my pain out on to others, blamed them for my feelings, and resisted being accountable because it hurt too much to be responsible for the torrential suffering inside of me. I consciously and unconsciously lashed out at people close to me. I hit rock bottom and wanted to die.

And then I turned a corner because **I chose** to open to receive help from something bigger. I humbled myself before the Great Spirit and surrendered to a greater will. I was fed up with the way I had been living and I was ready to heal.

Only from this place of personal choice to face myself and heal was I able to own my part of the mess. It was hard work of self-mastery to review my life choices and own them, to admit the impact I had on others and myself, to express heartfelt regret for the wounds I inflicted on others, and to forgive and ask for forgiveness.

For 20 years I thought I wanted to heal as I showed up weekly in psychotherapy sessions. But really, I was deluding myself. I wanted someone to tell my story to; I was not ready to change that story. Until it was painful enough that I was willing to let the Truth restore me, until that moment of despair, I was not ready to evolve my consciousness.

All those years, I now witness that the therapists who sat with me in weekly sessions were planting little seeds. The friends who had already realized some things I had not, gently planted some more. My bosses and mentors patiently planted some more. But there was no way those seeds could grow until I chose to let the LIGHT in.

Once you're in the LIGHT, you can bring yourself there when the people around you are being un-loving, refusing to claim response-ability, judging and shaming and blaming. Being around the LIGHT wears down the shroud of darkness people wear to keep out Truth and Love. **Once you know better you have to do better, and sometimes people aren't ready to do better, so they hide from the LIGHT.**

Let Others Voluntarily Evolve.

If that means that people disappear from your life, then allow yourself to grieve what has fallen away. Holding onto hope that certain people will join you in conscious awareness can hold you back from your own path of ascension, and even physically hurt your body because it's like you're holding onto the past while your body is trying to move into the future.

During a deep trance in ceremony one night, I had a powerful experience of reprogramming my energy body using the sacred songs that healers were singing. My Soul guided my hands to clear away the shadows from the light of my aura, and as my auric field cleared, the shadow condensed until it was a hard dark nugget which I then felt in my stomach.

I pleaded with the dark obstinate nugget to accept the light and receive the Love. It refused. So I purged it into a bucket because it was not compatible with the new me. And then I wept over the puke.

Sometimes we have to purge people from our lives who are not yet ready to evolve because staying in connection with them keeps us from our own ascension path. Other times, our ascension path is directly to hold space for these people with loving compassion. And sometimes, both are true at different times.

Let go of the desire to fix it, and stop chasing after those that do not wish to be a part of your life. Sometimes relationships that have gone out of alignment will come back into alignment, and sometimes these relationships do not recover. They die. They set like the sun so that a new day can begin. Honor what was and is no more. Let yourself feel the grief at the same time as you welcome the sunrise of a new potential with anticipation. Rather than be crippled by the loss, embrace what is to come. A new adventure awaits your willingness to receive it.

You cannot force another to evolve. We are all conscious Divine beings with choice. We get to choose our lessons. If a person evolves, it is because she chooses it.

Be in the world as a witness without feeding the fear and lower vibrational patterns. Witness without believing. The art of the shaman is to hold the higher truth amidst chaos. Find the peace and love within and radiate. Allow realization to do the work by being a demonstration of higher principles in your life. As you are demonstrating higher principles, whoever is ready will realize a truth, and in this realization this person will no longer be resonant with the lie that was obscuring the truth.

The truth is always present. Our ability to witness the truth depends on the structure of lies within our consciousness. Realizing a truth instantly exposes the lie that was covering up or distorting it. Lies are illusion. Truth is everlasting. And this is a way to be in service as a demonstration of truth that, when a person is ready to wake up, can be in service to that waking up.

♥

Suggestions

Schedule YOU Into Your Calendar Have you ever noticed that what gets into your calendar typically happens? That is because the act of putting something in your calendar is commitment. Commit to yourself, your soul's curriculum, and the self-care needed to flourish. Invest time and resources into your spiritual path, and reap the dividends on your investment.

Authentic Yes! Are you ready to run an experiment that will drive your inner Pleaser nuts? For a whole week, say 'no' every time you are asked to do something by another person. Do not explain yourself, nor apologize. Just be with a firm kind 'no' and notice what the voices in your head say, and how your body reacts. Hold yourself with compassion as you dismantle this deep domestication. This experiment will help you have the confidence to pause before answering so you can give an authentic answer. Until you can say 'no', your 'yes' will lack the realness that inspires deeper connection.

Practice Gratitude When you find yourself complaining, take three deep belly breaths and say "I am willing to be grateful." With your eyes closed, feel your heart. Breathe into your heart several times. Notice any energy shifts, and listen for whispers of reasons to feel grateful.

Soften with Love The more you listen to your inner matrix, the more awareness you'll have of self-judgments and criticisms. Soften these with love and compassion. This mantra is helpful: "Om mane padme om"

Quotes

"The strongest action for a woman is to love herself, be herself, and shine amongst those who never believed she could."
— Unknown

"You will never gain anyone's approval by begging for it. When you stand confident in your own worth, respect follows."
— Mandy Hale

"Think like a queen. A queen is not afraid to fail. Failure is another steppingstone to greatness."
— Oprah Winfrey

"The mere mention of the word "selfish" can ignite a host of sundry emotions from the politely offended to the overtly judgmental."
— Sarah Marshank

"When you arise in the morning give thanks for the food and for the joy of living. If you see no reason for giving thanks, the fault lies only in yourself."
— Tecumseh

"Gratitude turns what we have into enough, and more. It turns denial into acceptance, chaos into order, confusion into clarity...it makes sense of our past, brings peace for today, and creates a vision for tomorrow."
— Melody Beattie

"Wear gratitude like a cloak, and it will feed every corner of your life."
— Rumi

Restoring Matriarchal Balance

As humanity shifts into the Age of Aquarius, the opportunity is granted to you to restore matriarchal balance in your microcosm of the macrocosm. When anything is out of balance in your life, you must turn and face the opposite and lean into your discomfort to give energy and momentum towards that which has been neglected. If you have been indulging in too many rich foods and living a sedentary lifestyle, to restore balance you must lean into the discomfort of eating more vegetables and fruits and getting daily exercise. Thus to restore the Divine Mother energy within you, you must lean into the discomfort of loving and honoring the representation of Mother in your life, even if you have not felt loved and honored by your biological mother. To heal the relationship with Mother, you must claim all the ways you are a good daughter (or son), and reframe what that means from historical social-familial book of law to Soul understanding. And if you are a mother, you must forgive yourself for everything you think you did wrong.

Just as Love is a river flowing through your heart, Divine Mother energy is also a river of vibration that can flow through you to heal your heart and bring comfort, resiliency, wisdom, compassion, and guidance to your life and the lives of those you meet. When you act on the suggestions in this chapter, your actions signal to the Divine Mother that you are ready to heal your Mother Wound. As you heal your Mother Wound, you allow the Divine Mother to flow through you with wisdom that heals the masculine energies in and around you, and liberates your children from the old paradigm.

❤

A Place Of Honor

Depending on your experience of your mother, this teaching might be very challenging to receive. And I know it to be true: to heal the

Mother Wound, you must give your mother a place of honor in your consciousness. **Honoring your mother restores the ancestral lineage to a flow of love and wisdom, and it opens the door for you to authentically honor yourself (especially if you are a mother).**

The gifts of your ancestral DNA are inherited from your mother and father. If you do not honor your mother, then how can you receive and honor the gifts of your maternal ancestry? When you refuse your mother a place of honor, or shut her out of your heart, you also interrupt the flow of ancestral gifts into your Divine feminine consciousness; you cut yourself off from your inheritance.

You may not want her inheritance, especially if you have cultivated a negative view of her based on your life's interactions with her. But if you refuse her inheritance, you also refuse your maternal grandmothers, great-grandmothers, great-great-grandmothers, and so forth. There is wealth in your maternal ancestral line that you do want to claim, and it is worth the price of forgiveness to honor your mother. Once you forgive your mother by honoring her, warts and all, you are able to restore the flow of Love all the way back up your ancestral line. By honoring your mother, you also open yourself to receive the gift of being honored by your children; the potential opens for your children to honor you by feeling the resonance of honoring the mother figure you established in your family tree.

Create a personal ceremony to enact the honoring of your mother. You can create a ceremony from your heart, and make it as simple or lavish as you wish. If you have an ancestral altar, you can add something to it to signify your mother's place of honor as an ancestor (whether she is living or departed). An ancestral altar is a space you create with pictures of your ancestors and other offerings like candles or flowers; you visit this space periodically to honor your ancestors and to pray for and with them. In this way, the ancestors know where to converse with you, and they stay out of other areas of your life if you set that boundary.

If you are working on healing the Mother Wound, you can create an altar to support your work and to introduce an element of honoring your mother (see "Returning to Ritual and Ceremonies"). Maybe you add a little throne for your mother to your altar along with one for yourself. Stones and crystals are very supportive for altar work, and you can allow yourself to be guided to ones that will support your healing and unfolding. Rose Quartz, Spirit Quartz, Amethyst, Moonstone, and Red Silver Leaf Jasper are some of the stones that were used on my altar while writing this book.

Open sacred space before creating an altar or initiating a ceremony. When you visit the altar to talk with your mother, open sacred space again to invite the Divine into the communication for healing and transformation. If you place flowers on the altar, be sure to refresh them when they begin to wilt to show respect for your intentions.

The simple act of creating an altar or performing a ceremony may seem trivial; yet the healing that can ripple out from that act of Love is immense and powerful.

If you are a mother, it is important that you claim your own throne as a matriarch and honor yourself. You can create a ceremony or ritual, or make a symbolic representation of it in your home, to honor yourself in this way. You do not need to announce it; it will announce itself in the energetics.

Once you are in this place of honoring yourself and your mother, you can recognize your partner and children with their own places of honor. Seeing your sons and daughters as worthy of inheriting the immense Love of their ancestry, just by virtue of being born, will help create the vibration of unconditional Love that helps everyone feel accepted through the ups and downs of learning in Earth School.

It's especially important when merging families after divorce that each person in the blended family be given a 'throne' or place of honor energetically by the mother and the father. It clears up the energy lines and helps to reassure each child that they are loved and important in the new context.

The place of honor is unconditional for each member of the family, which allows you to have boundaries for the temporary circumstances of life when lessons about respect need to be enforced.

Young adults going through wild rebellious phases that disrupt the family's harmony learn that they always have a place of honor in the family even if their engagement with the family shifts into a new phase of living apart.

As you create and hold a space of honor for your mother, yourself, your partner, and your children, you'll notice how the vibration of gratitude heals the Mother Wound within you and helps you to shift your inner perceptions. These inner shifts change how you feel about yourself, your mother, your family, and the Earth. **Focusing on what you're grateful for about your mother will activate that energy of gratitude in return at the higher levels, and help to heal the wounded stories.**

Visiting your Mother Wound altar, you can light some candles and speak from your heart the things for which you feel grateful. Keep speaking your gratitude until you feel it open your heart. Say some Ho'Oponopono to access the vibration of forgiveness: *I am sorry, Please forgive me, I love you, thank you.* You can use this mantra to receive compassion: *Om Mane Padme Om.*

Perhaps you'll feel emotions rising to the surface or tears welling up in your eyes. No one is one-dimensional; we are each complex beings with many aspects, some of which we can feel very grateful about. Allowing yourself to witness the things you love and appreciate in your mother, and honoring her as the mother you chose for this incarnation, will help to heal the Mother Wound.

Run the experiment and see what happens. Be mindful of any secret expectations you have that your biological mother will change through your practice of devotion. **This practice is about healing the Mother Wound within YOU...not her.** She may receive the healing vibrations and be inspired into new behaviors, or she may not.

Either way, the truest test of this teaching is how it makes you feel inside.

❤

I Am A Good Daughter

Strained or non-existent relations with your biological mother can lead you to feel like you are a 'bad daughter', unworthy of love, not good enough, selfish, and a thousand other judgments. Sometimes, keeping you feeling bad about yourself as a daughter is a control tool used by a mother who has an unhealed Mother Wound. A mother who has not yet learned key Earth School lessons like forgiveness, empathy and compassion, is not in a developmental place to acknowledge the ways you have been a good daughter.

To heal this aspect of the Mother Wound, you must help yourself to realize what a good daughter you actually are, even if your biological mother has not recognized you as such. For this, you must invite the love and support of the Divine Mother who does not operate in the realm of the human egoic personality, and is thereby aware of a larger context of how you are a good daughter...and even what being a 'good daughter' means.

I have felt the sting of judgment from people in my family of origin and my mother's friends as I have charted my own course to heal the Mother Wound within me. As we have covered in other sections in this book, perspective is a matter of the information you receive and the source you receive it from. **The work in this section is about helping you to know, for yourself, that you are a good daughter, regardless of what other people believe about you.**

With the exercise, the invitation is to make a list of the ways you are a good daughter, from your perspective, that soothe the inner naysayers and allow your inner child to feel 'good enough'. I have shared my list with you below for inspiration. Feel free to copy aspects of it that resonate for you. After you make your list, speak it out loud in sacred space and then burn it if you wish to release it.

∞

I AM A GOOD DAUGHTER

I was birthed into being by the Divine Mother. I am automatically a 'good daughter' since the Divine Mother does not make me earn her love. The Divine Mother loves me unconditionally.

I agreed to incarnate on Earth into my biological mother's web, inheriting her Mother Wound, and accepted a life of service to my mother and her ancestry to heal the patterns of suffering and unforgiveness. The Divine Mother sees me doing 'the work' every single day, and knows I am a good daughter for doing my best.

I gave from my heart unconditionally to my biological mother throughout my childhood, despite psychological, emotional, and physical abuse.

I dedicated myself to personal growth in thousands of hours of weekly psychotherapy session for over two decades to heal the Mother Wound I inherited from my biological mother.

I dedicated myself to spiritual practice for nearly a decade, spending every cent of my retirement fund on the programs, healings, and trainings I needed to support me to heal the Mother Wound I inherited from my biological mother.

I resisted all urges to yell or express anger at my biological mother, even when anger was yelled directly at me. I used my tools to process my difficult feelings, and leveraged the support of spiritual groups and programs and healings that I purchased with my own money.

I stayed alive through the pain that sent suicidal ideations through my brain, making me want to escape this incarnation.

I listened to the Divine Mother and my Soul and acted to fulfill the Soul's curriculum I came here to embody and perform in service, even when that meant losing the love and support of my biological mother and family.

I used my voice as a Messenger of the Divine as respectfully as I could, every step of the way, to honor my healing process and my biological mother's life. Every time I realized I could do better using my voice more consciously, I adapted the use of my voice and message to be more conscious.

I slept at the home of my biological mother after my Dad passed, even though I did not feel safe there. I stayed for several days and nights to support her in the loss of her partner, until she asked me to leave.

I called my biological mother every day for weeks after my Dad passed, checking on her and offering help, until she asked me to stop calling.

I kept silent on social media, podcasts, books and other forums about many of the things I felt hurt by that occurred within my family, and with my biological mother, out of respect for their privacy. I used my spiritual tools to heal myself and come to terms with these things, and I used spiritual practices to send forgiveness, compassion and love to those involved.

I did my best to teach my sons higher practices for relating with family while being mindful of teaching these lessons without harming their relationship with their grandmother.

I worked daily to forgive my biological mother and to find ways to come to peace with our relationship, and then shared the wisdom and practices in this book for the benefit of others to heal their Mother Wounds.

I consistently worked to see and heal the patterns that were affecting the relationship with my biological mother, and to see her as a sovereign Divine being of choice, worthy of the unconditional love of the Divine.

I owned my own healing of the Mother Wound 100%, and released my biological mother from all response-ability for my own state of consciousness.

I AM A GOOD DAUGHTER OF THE DIVINE

♥

Forgiving Yourself As A Mother

When you look back at how you raised your children, you may find yourself in some judgment from your current vantage point of wisdom and experience. You may wish things had turned out differently, or that you had made better choices or been wise enough to know what you know now. **The more you know about the impact that your mother had on your consciousness, the more you may cringe when exploring the choices you made as a mother before you had the level of awareness you have now. Be gentle with yourself.**

As described in my first book, *Awakening To Me: One Woman's Journey to Self Love*, I essentially starting taking a wrecking ball to my life when my youngest was just out of preschool. Then I burned it all down and left my marriage when my youngest was in 3rd grade, my eldest entering 6th grade. The state of mind I was in during their young lives can be best described as "light is on, no one is home" with moments of presence sprinkled here and there. Often my mind was somewhere 'adult' when I was spending time playing with them. I remember talking about this in therapy and doing my best to stay present and not in my head. I just wasn't very good at it; I had a lot of mental chatter, confusion and emotional energy which I funneled into artwork production to stay sane.

Then after I left my children's father, the next several years was a steep spiritual climb to build a new foundation for my life with weekend and week-long spiritual healing retreats, absorption in the healing process, and finding my own voice as I tried to pay attention to theirs. Gradually I was increasingly able to stay present with my boys just as they neared the ages that they didn't want to connect with their mom, and preferred to do their own thing. Now I was totally ready to be a fantastic mom: and my boys were off with friends or interested in computer games.

I was blessed with a couple of years of deep connection with my eldest son, and a budding honest dialog with my younger son, by the time of this book being published.

At several points in my healing process with the Mother Wound, I felt severe self-judgment for being the kind of mother I was, especially during those honest dialogs with my sons. It was heart-wrenching to hear their perspectives on growing up as my children. I wished I hadn't been so immersed in healing my own trauma, although that's exactly what I had to do to stay alive and not let suicidal ideation take me out.

I had to heal on the inside to be the mother they needed, and I couldn't be the mother they needed when they needed me because I was trying to raise them and heal myself at the same time.

Finally awake as my eldest son turned 20, I grieved the loss of the childhood I would have witnessed him having had I been healed when he was born. The wishing well became a deep yearning for what never was and would never be. All I had was moments of tenderness I could replay in my mind when I felt connected to him as he grew. He was no longer that boy, and I was not ready to let that boy go. I wanted an encore, but had to let go and embrace his next act…which he would invite me to if he chose, when he chose.

I realized during this time that I could really beat myself up good for all the mistakes I made, and all the potential wonderful experiences I missed out on while I was otherwise occupied. I could blame myself for every perceived flaw in my son, and visit the wishing well even more often, hoping for a different reality than the one I was reviewing in my mind and heart.

Yet the messages kept coming to me during healings and channelings that my children chose to be born into my mother's web. And my mother's web was what I was here to experience in this lifetime, and to heal from the inside out. **Could I forgive myself for doing the best job I could do, every step of the way, from the consciousness at which I was able to meet the moments?**

I had to surrender to the divine plan and trust that my flaws produced the opportunities for wisdom and growth that my sons came into this incarnation to experience.

In one meditation on this subject, White Eagle asked me "How do you make an omelet?" I thought this was quite obvious… you crack some eggs and put them into the pan. Then I realized that cracking the egg is how the potential gets out, and once it's cracked open you can do something beautiful with it. My egg certainly got very cracked by my early life's traumas; and having that crack is what allowed me to move through the adversity by releasing some innate gifts locked up inside me.

Sometimes the very thing you think was awful that you did as a mother is exactly what your child needed to 'crack the egg' for personal evolution.

Still, it helps to show that you've learned your lessons and you acknowledge your mistakes to feel like a better person as you contemplate the mother you've been. What if you could share everything you've learned with the young mother you were at the time of your first child's birth? What would you say to yourself to prepare you for what was to come? When I wrote a letter to myself, it helped me to bring some closure to the tangled up mom mess inside me. Here's what I wrote:

Dear momma,

Welcome to the longest marathon of your life. You'll feel depleted. You'll want to give up. You'll doubt yourself. You'll feel frustrated, guilty, not good enough, and even resentful. You'll want to hide or run away.

Hang in there. The good stuff is around every corner.

He will laugh and your heart will melt. He will finally 'get it' and you'll rejoice inside. He will seek your counsel and you'll feel honored. He will tell you how he really feels and you will grow because of it.

This little being, so helpless at first, is your opportunity to master love. How you love him reveals how you love yourself.

I know a few secrets you do not know as you're birthing this baby over twenty years ago.

...you don't love yourself yet.

...you have no clue how to love him.

...you think you're teaching him, but he is here to teach you.

If you can hear me all the way back there in time, here is some advice.

Listen, listen, listen way more than you talk.

Make it safe inside you so you can be his safe harbor.

Be kind and gentle to yourself so you can be kind and gentle to him.

Get quiet inside so you can hear your heart and womb guidance.

Do what you know is right no matter how anyone else tries to invalidate your mothers wisdom.

Be more interested to discover who he is than to make him into what you want him to be.

And most importantly, forgive yourself for how much you are about to fuck up. He knew you would. He loves you so much he chose you to be his momma anyway.

Love,
Me

Consider writing a letter to yourself as a new mother from the experienced wise mother you are today. I hope it brings you peace.

I also offer you this prayer: *The Fierce Love of a Mother is present through the ups and downs of growth and perspective. I am learning to be the Love inside the storm.*

♥

Initiating Your Children

The indigenous cultures had a very smart cultural tradition of rites of initiation into the overall tribe. When sons reached that age where they were feeling that rebelliousness and push for upheaval which is a built-in natural process for evolution, the tribe knew it was time to send that son out into Mother Earth for lessons. So the son ventured out on a vision quest for days alone with no food or water or support of any kind except for the Divine Mother. This initiation took the explosive energies of a boy becoming a man and gave them to the larger consciousness that knows what to do with it, how to transmute it into power and beauty.

Today our sons are trapped in a culture that cannot handle the explosive nature of the transition from boy to man and is suffocating our men under a system of punitive control and conformity. Our polite society that cannot tolerate rebellious expression is suffocating our boys and turning that aggression inwards, leading away from self-empowerment that builds a real man in the world. So we create selfish men out of a desire to suppress nature's process for evolution.

And where could our girls and boys go to be wild today? We are cutting down the forests and blanketing the planet with human consciousness through 5D... You know, you actually need to get away from humanity in order to evolve humanity. You need to commune with Mother Earth directly without the noise of human thought. You need to be vulnerable and without comfort to create that crack in your egoic consciousness that lets her love pour into your heart. **You need to get lost in the wild and untamed expanses of nature to help you become more civilized.**

The modern day vision quest can be found under many highways in homeless camps. People who no longer have the heart to keep lying that this material life is fulfilling have let go completely of all possessions and allow themselves to live at the mercy of the Divine Mother. In doing so, they reclaim their self-respect because they're no longer living a lie, and then they become teachers for the people who cannot look them in the eye at traffic stops. It used to be that just a few people chose the homeless path. Now the 'problem' is becoming so large it's hard to ignore, isn't it?

What do you think the 'problem' is? Do you think that large swatches of people just went insane and threw away their lives because of mental illness? When will we, as a society, realize that it's our mentally ill society that is making people sick enough that it's better to live under a highway than it is to live 'normal'?

When we don't need the money of the elite anymore, they will cease to have power over us. The structures that held their control in place will crumble, and we can return to the Divine Mother. Our children will finally be free.

♥

Healing the Masculine

As a mother, your relationship with the father of your children, or with men in general, has a profound effect on your son's relationship with masculine energy. This is particularly impactful for sons who are learning to express their own masculine energy.

Sons of mothers who have been abused often do not want to be like their father and so they reject the masculine energy altogether. This causes the sons to become more feminine in nature, more in touch with their emotions, and more capable of communication which is all positive. However, in pushing away their masculine energy, the sons never fully step into their power as men. In judging the father figure, sons not only push away their masculine energy, they embrace the feminine energy to try to not 'be like' their father, and then they go against their true nature which ends up causing resentment toward their mother.

It is important to realize that there is a positive pole of masculine energy and a negative pole of masculine energy. At the negative pole are control, domination, subjugation, disrespect, and diminishing of a woman's wisdom and value. In other words, all the behaviors and energies that promote a world view where women cannot think for themselves, or take care of themselves; this world view is disempowering and judgmental of feminine energies. At the positive pole are support, container, providing, and lifting the woman to her highest expression (which does not mean rescuing). The positive pole of the masculine can tune into the subtler energies of emotion and sensation and nuances of communication, and is heart-open and able to communicate feelings and empathically connect with women.

When the father figure is operating from the negative pole of masculine energy, the son experiences a rejection of his own masculine energy out of empathy for the abuse he witnesses his mother enduring.

Also in the household of a single mother, sons do not typically get initiated into manhood by masculine energy. So many sons of single mothers stall out on their hopes and dreams, lacking the confidence to take initiative towards manifesting their desires into the world. Other sons of single mothers cross boundaries to become the father figure of the house, claiming responsibility to 'take care' of the family when the mother/father are not able to. This is assuming more responsibility than should be placed on a son in optimal conditions, and leads to a lifetime pattern of personal needs being usurped by others who seem to be helpless or martyred.

A son's need to protect his mother can be so strong that he holds back from telling his truth, not wanting to be one more way the masculine 'hurts' his mother. He diminishes himself and retracts his power so as to avoid being threatening to his mother who is healing from her childhood abuse from the masculine, or from her life relationships where the negative pole of masculine (aggression, domination, subjugation, disrespect) was in effect.

It's almost as if the son's subconscious cries out "How can I be myself without hurting you mother? Because I love you and don't want to hurt you. I witness you have been hurt enough."

A son needs to express his power and step outside of the umbrella of his mother. Yet a mother's love is often tangled up with her desire to protect her son and make sure nothing 'bad' happens to him; to make sure he doesn't hurt himself on his way to his manhood. Her desire for him to not repeat abusive patterns from the negative pole of the masculine adds pressure that he may translate into self-judgment as his needs clash with his mother's.

To be a blessing, mother's love must be uncaged from fear. If the son encounters hardship, the mother can be a supportive witness and a constant source of encouragement to move through the difficult challenge and harness the wisdom of the experience. In this way, the mother demonstrates her faith in her son's ability to go through challenges and get to the other side with wisdom. Do you see how this is a profoundly more empowering message than the up-until-now message of fear that the son will hurt himself and must be protected from doing so, or cautioned at every turn about the potential dangers and pitfalls he faces?

By facing the challenges head-on, the son gains inner confidence that he can do it. In the positive pole of masculine, this is the role a father can play with his son. Creating challenges for the son that seem out of reach, and then pushing the son toward it with great encouragement. Tackle it son! You can do it!

This positive pole of fatherhood has been lacking in great measure on the planet at this time, and mothers have been rearing their sons without the benefit of the masculine initiation into manhood. Even if the father is present in the family, he may hold back or immerse himself in work outside the home to avoid messing up the way he perceives his own father or grandfather did. He may shy away from engagement rather than dig in and make the way for his lineage to embrace positive male mentorship. Without a direct example of what this positive masculine looks and acts like, many men up until now have avoided the situation altogether, preferring to serve the role of provider which is far less entangled.

On the way to the new paradigm, there are many bumps and mistakes over which the father may judge himself harshly, and which may trigger deep wounds with a mother who experienced an overly aggressive or controlling father figure.

For sons to witness their mothers wounded and disempowered by their fathers makes it difficult to find their rightful place in manhood. "How can I be a man without hurting my mother? What kind of man can I be that is a blessing to my mother and to the women I meet, while still honoring my personal power? How do I claim my personal power without the benefit of a positive father figure who initiates me with love into my manhood?" These are all questions deep in the subconscious of masculine humans on the planet at this time who are awakening and desiring right relationship with the feminine humans that surround them.

A mother's love can feel oppressive and stifling to her son when it does not give the son freedom to express himself and take the risks that will build the confidence he needs to transition into manhood.

The first step is for mothers to be brave enough to create the space for their sons to tell the truth. "Please do not lie to me son and pretend you have not been wounded by my lack of self-respect and dignity, and by my lack of courage to stand up for myself. Tell me the truth so we can move beyond it into a new truth of our co-creation."

As a mother, it's your job to be strong and resilient and to claim your power. It's your job to stop blaming the masculine and wallowing in victimhood; you must do the inner work to become self-sufficient. **You honor and love yourself so that you can love your son and hold space for his growth and healing, whatever that entails.** You cultivate good boundaries to not take it personally when your son tells you a truth that pierces your heart; his words only touch a wound that was already there…and often, the truth hurts on the way to healing.

If you desire your son to claim freedom in the expression of his masculine sovereignty, you must heal the Mother Wound within you so that you can communicate freely and you can hear your son's truth without making him responsible if that truth crushes you. Are you not strong enough to witness your son's anger without flinching? Can you keep your heart open through the pain, knowing that the pathway is 'feel it to heal it'?

The alternative is to tiptoe across the issues, skate at the surface of relationship with small talk, and hold your son to traditions like Mother's Day out of obligation. Meanwhile you will watch your son walk on eggshells within himself to avoid triggering the women in his life, and stuff all his feelings of anger and resentment at having no true space to express himself truthfully.

I had a client who was a 30-something adult male, over 6 feet tall, who had been repressing his own manhood due to the Mother Wound and an overly oppressive father figure. During the healing session, the guidance was to hold space for him to roar like a lion. He could not do it at first. "I can't yell at a woman" he said. He tried for a few minutes and could not get a squeak out. Then I broke the ice and roared like a lion in front of him. He felt the raw power of the energy and was amazed at my strength. I encouraged him to try again. After a few attempts he finally got the roar going, and once it was going he could not stop for 10 minutes or more, releasing decades of pent-up anger. Then he began to weep, and I simply held space for him. He held himself back his whole life because he thought he had no right to feel these things. He thought that if he confessed to feeling these ways, he would be 'bad' and 'scary'.

I was able to hold space for this stranger to roar in my presence, but then found myself scared when my son vented anger to me one day several years later. His anger being expressed triggered a deep fear from my childhood and a primal fear in my body, and I stood still like a deer in the headlights. I stayed present and grounded through the experience, but had absolutely no idea what to do. My son had never expressed these feelings to me before. I was shocked. Very importantly, we bridged back to connection and understanding in the days following this outburst; it's important for our sons to know the love is still there after the anger.

It seems to me that trying to stop anger from being expressed is the very thing that makes anger lead to violence in the masculine. In facing feelings of anger myself, I have noticed that meeting anger with grounded presence dissolves the anger after a bit. And then underneath the anger is something very real that needs to be expressed and understood. As women and mothers, can we be willing to invite the expression of anger in 'safe' ways before the anger accumulates within to cause an explosion? Or until the well of anger is so deep it leads to a bottomless depression?

Mothers and sons have a unique opportunity to bridge to a new balance between the masculine and feminine that honors the wisdom and power of both. The work I see for myself as a mother is to remember to be present and curious with my sons as they grow, encouraging honest expression of their truth to me and staying alert to navigate boundaries of personal responsibility.

❤

Liberating Our Children

As a mother, I have always wanted to give my children a good life filled with love, prosperity, purpose, joy, support and connection. The question is, how? How can we guide our children to be sovereign co-creators and receive the freedom and prosperity that is their birthright? Especially when we see the state of the world today, how is the dream of a New Earth going to be birthed in the middle of this mess?

The mess is part of the magic. And you can do your part as a parent to lighten the load on your children for creating a sustainable Earth. Since you cannot give what you have not yet received, to give your children these gifts of sovereign co-creation you must first claim these gifts for yourself. In doing so, you become the demonstration of a pathway to freedom, as well as an embodiment of healing that is received by your ancestors seven generations back and forward...which includes your children as beneficiaries.

An aspect of claiming sovereignty is releasing history—liberating yourself from history as well as setting your children free from history. **Your personal history of who you think you have been dictates a trajectory of who you think you can be.** You must release this personal history and identity so that you can open to a far greater potential along a trajectory that only your Soul can imagine, since it is beyond the limitations of your mind and personality.

You must release the familial history of who your family says you are based on their mental projections of you from their frozen-in-time moments of remembrance of you that became the family story of you. **Your family's story of you likely bears little resemblance of who you are now that you have been in the process of transformation and Soul alignment.** To continue that evolution, you must release that familial history. This is also a gift you actively give your children to set them free for their own liberation.

You must release your ancestral history which you carry as ancestral DNA in your body. While your ancestral DNA offers you access to wisdom, skills and talents held by your ancestors, it also carries with it anything unforgiven when your ancestors died. What has not been forgiven during your ancestor's lifetime is brought forth as an ancestral pattern and revisited upon future generations. In this way, you continue the work of your ancestors in your own life.

In one medicine journey, I received the Spirit guidance to welcome my ancestors to use my physical vessel to 'forgive it' — whatever they could not bring themselves to forgive during their lifetimes. I felt whoosh after whoosh as ancestors released stuck traumas and un-forgiveness from the ancestral DNA in my body. I became very cold, my teeth chattered, and my body shook as the healing process continued. After what felt like an hour, the whooshing ended, and I warmed back up feeling much more liberated within my body. This clearing of the old opened me up to all new potentials; so although it was an act of service to my ancestors, I was a direct beneficiary.

You must release the collective history which dictates who you must be because of your ancestry, country, religion, cultural heritage, color of skin and so forth. While I do not advocate spiritual bypassing the impacts that this collective history still has today on your experience of life, I do advocate that you extricate yourself from its grip so that a whole new potential can reveal itself at a higher octave of expression in your life. This is a dance between acknowledging what has been, and healing it in the quantum field to release that cultural memory and open to a new potential. If you cling to the old wounds, you will continue to experience the old wounds in your life and in the collective. **You must heal and let go so you can transform beyond your wildest dreams into a new human experience.**

When you truly remember who you are, you release fully the history of you, the Book of Fate, and you grieve the loss. Those you leave behind will continue the familiar storyline for as long as it serves them. And you are free to chart the new course for yourself, your lineage, and humanity overall.

Do not drag yourself back to the old stories out of longing for what was. If you do, you will miss the opportunity to write the Book of Destiny with your Soul, and to witness the beauty that your children create for themselves as they choose their own identities.

This is not a spiritual bypass. This is not discrediting what others are experiencing as collective reality based in historical context. This is not walking around in collective reality disassociated from it. This is liberating yourself from identification with the current narratives of your family and community so you can fully experience it, witness it, move around in it, view it from all angles, and alchemize it using your gifts. We are not shifting thousands of years of history by throwing it in the toilet and flushing it down. We are alchemizing it with higher frequency and compassion.

You are the adventurer at the edge of human consciousness. It is no different than the loss of family of origin that settlers felt in traveling thousands of miles from family in pursuit of a better life, never to see those loved ones again. The information age has offered the illusion of always staying connected. Yet a leap in consciousness creates just as steep a gap between yourself and others as a continent: it is a gap in vibration.

Do not diminish or lower yourself trying to be where others are by suffering to belong with them, but hold a high vibration and abundant flow of Love and lift others to it through energy and demonstration.

♥

Suggestions

Honor Your Mother Create a sacred ceremony or ritual to honor your mother and the ancestral lineage of matriarchal wisdom she passes down through her to you. You may choose to create an altar as described in "Living As Sacred Ceremony" or you may make up your own ceremony from the heart. Your genuine desire to restore honor to the matriarchal energy of your ancestry is the most potent aspect of this ceremony.

Honor Yourself The little girl, teenager, young woman and mother within you all deserve your love, respect, and honor. Let your heart guide you in a special ritual to uplift your inner females. What burdens do these aspects of you carry that can now be laid to rest? Lie belly to belly with the Divine Mother and release it all into her for transmutation. Invite the 'elder you' to time travel to the 'now you' and offer sage advice for how to heal, comfort, love, and support your inner selves. Open to receive the instructions for a personal healing ceremony, and then take the steps to make it so.

Forgive Yourself As mothers, we cannot help but make mistakes. It is part of the innate design of being a mother, and of being human. Through our imperfections we and our children stumble into the light. There is one perfect mother and that is the Divine Mother. The rest of us are learning. Commit yourself to the forgiveness exercise in this chapter and let that shit go! If you want a good relationship with your children, start here.

Quotes

"One of the oldest and most generous tricks that the universe plays on human beings is to bury strange jewels within us all, and then stand back to see if we can ever find them."
— Elizabeth Gilbert

"We need to reshape our own perception of how we view ourselves. We have to step up as women and take the lead."
— Beyoncé

"A woman armed with ancestral wisdom is a powerful force. You'll find her powers come from within, she is in tune with her spirit, and the magic of the universe. She trusts, values and follows her intuition."
— Lori Bregman

"In a child's eyes, a mother is a goddess. She can be glorious or terrible, benevolent or filled with wrath, but she commands love either way."
— N.K. Jemisin

"A mother is not a person to lean on, but a person to make leaning unnecessary."
— Dorothy Canfield Fisher

"When our minds move in harmony with love--through forgiveness or prayer or the simplest tender thought-- then mountains move and the universe shifts."
— Marianne Williamson

Becoming Earth Keepers

Sitting in a circle at 14,500 feet on Ausangatay, the Holy Mountain for the Q'ero people in Peru, I heard Alberto Villoldo explain that the shamans were about to give us an initiation: the Keepers of the Time to Come. He wove a mythic story that we were souls who had all sat around the fire together for thousands of years, and that we had agreed in this lifetime to be on Earth as wisdom keepers and medicine people. And as the shamans prepared the Anye Despacho for this initiation, I felt a deep sacred remembrance that what Alberto shared was true. It was the first real remembrance that I was a steward of the Earth come for the Great Awakening to help lift humanity into the Age of Aquarius. Up until this moment, I had glimpses into my Book of Destiny, but was so mired in my Book of Fate that I could not imagine myself reaching very far beyond the drama of my own life and family. My five-year journey up until this moment had been a scramble up the mountain to heal what I perceived was a broken self, and liberate myself from the suffering.

On the bus ride to Ausangatay, Alberto offered a chance to receive mentoring. I vied for my chance, and when it was my turn I shared with him the frustrations of not being able to get beyond my Book of Fate and into the Destiny that I was beginning to sense lay up ahead. He recommended that I do a meditation in which I put everything I thought I knew about myself, all my memories and stories about myself and my life, into a treasure box and close the lid for the duration of the trip to the Holy Mountain. He said "Let Ausangatay tell you who you really are." It was a metaphor for putting aside my personality, and opening to the potential of my Soul.

Back to the circle with the shamans, I felt the energy of Destiny calling me. I turned to Ausangatay and asked "Who am I? What am I here for?"

The shamans came to us one by one and gave us the rights of initiation as Keepers of the Time to Come, adding a special kuya (medicine stone) to our mesas (medicine bundle). As the initiation activated my energy body, I felt the seed of Destiny being planted in my heart.

That night sharing dinner in the dining tent, I sat next to Alberto. As he began to share about the next day's journey to the Rainbow Lagoon which was a sacred site at 16,500 feet, I felt my excitement grow as I sensed a piece of my destiny was coming into alignment. Then Alberto began cautioning that whoever chose to make the trek had to be sure they were committed to it because if anyone could not make it, everyone had to turn back. He surprised me when he turned to me, put his hand on my knee, and said "Kerri, you might consider not going since you've had some trouble breathing in the altitude. You wouldn't want to be the reason others had to turn back." I felt crushed and confused. I knew I felt called to the Rainbow Lagoon, and I had only had a brief issue with the altitude days ago. Why was he picking on me?

All night long I tossed and turned with the weight of the decision. And when the first rays of the sun crested the sky, I made my choice: I was going to put my faith in Ausangatay to get me to the Rainbow Lagoon.

It was a long challenging hike to the Rainbow Lagoon, and I was grateful for the coca leaves in my cheeks that helped give me the breath and energy to keep lifting my legs which felt so heavy in the altitude. I was at the back of the herd, doing my best, when I saw this pile of snow off to the right. It seemed so strange to see just one pile of snow in the middle of an immense landscape that stretched in all directions. Curiosity got the better of me and I walked over to investigate. As it turns out, it was a fallen white bird with beautiful wings. The moment a saw the bird, a voice spoke to me "Forgive yourself." I began to cry because I knew it was a message for me as well as my Cherokee medicine man within. Stepping out into the marsh, I wrestled some feathers from the end of the bird's wing, and placed them in my backpack as a reminder, and to accept this gift of forgiveness.

With the help of my fellow journeyers, I made it to the Rainbow Lagoon and witnessed for myself the crystal clear beautiful turquoise waters surrounded by mountain peaks. My heart was so moved by the experience that I sang a song to the Rainbow Keeper, the Spirit who guards the Rainbow Lagoon. I felt my love and gratitude returned to me as tears ran down my cheeks.

Back at the hotel later that night, I showed the feathers to Alberto and asked him what type of bird he thought it might be. He looked past me the way he always did when reading energy, and said "I believe it is a White Eagle." A chord struck deep inside me and I went online to investigate White Eagle Chief. I discovered a picture that looked just like the vision that had come to me so many times of a Cherokee Chief with a headdress, and I read how the role of a White Eagle Chief was to bring peace. Another realization stirred the buried grief from my chest as I remembered the guilt I felt on the Trail of Tears having advocated for peace. The voice came again: "Forgive yourself". I held the feathers to my heart and cried. I am only a messenger from Spirit. I cannot take the pain away, I can only walk with others and hold their hands as they face it.

Three years later in a medicine journey, White Eagle appeared before me clear as day and connected all the dots of my journey to remembrance so that I could publish his book, *The Second Wave*, with clarity and confidence.

If you are reading this book, you are a Keeper of the Time to Come. You agreed to be here at the turn of the ages to guide humanity back to Love. All the work in this book has been to help you heal the Mother Wound so you can close the Book of Fate, and open the Book of Destiny so we can create the New Earth together, a world we are all standing at the brink of together.

We are Earth Keepers, stewards of all of life on the planet, guides for our brothers and sisters. You've felt the call to purpose in your heart and you've committed to the path. I know who you are because you otherwise would never have picked up this book.

Your path to fully remembering your Soul purpose is unique and unfolding in Divine timing. **As you remember, your presence plants a seed of remembrance in everyone you meet.** Make an act of power to claim your Destiny with a personal meditation ceremony in which you surrender everything you think you know about yourself and your life into a treasure box, and then invite the Divine Mother to reveal insights that place you further on the path to your Destiny.

Commit to your spiritual path and connecting with Mother Earth every day to stay in the high vibration that supports insights and revelations from your Soul.

Now more than ever you are called to use your mastery tools to shift your mindset into beneficial directions. You can feel disempowered and disillusioned by what is happening, or you can feel inspired and curious about what is on the other side of the dismantling.

Stephen Covey shared a bit of wisdom years ago that there are spheres of influence each of us possess. The biggest influence a person can have is over their own thoughts, behaviors, and choices. The next biggest influence a person can have is with their own family. Then their friends, community and work environment. Some people branch further to influence their towns, governments, and industries. A rare few influence the world.

There are no more heroes.

There are everyday people like you and me that make daily choices to influence ourselves and others to create a better world.

We are Earth Keepers.

It starts with you. How do you want to feel? What kind of life do you want to live? What small actions can you start taking today to make an exponential change over time? What radical shifts must you make to claim the Destiny you feel in your heart?

Everyday people dedicating themselves to adopting sustainable living practices and opening up to Soul-guided living will be the way we collectively step into New Earth. There is no Easy button.

The path to New Earth is forged with moment-by-moment choices to become more conscious about how you live on this planet. You must overcome the inner resistance and stubbornness of your personality so you can unlock the sacred wisdom in your own heart. As you heal the Mother Wound, you grow your faith and the confidence to follow the nudges from your Soul.

Peeling back the layers of conditioning and fear makes you more sensitive and receptive to hearing messages from the Divine Mother. **Following the nudges aligns you to the greater consciousness of the planet so you can be guided to act in service to all of life on Earth.**

♥

Aligning To Earth Consciousness

To allow your instrument to be played in harmony with all of life on our Mother Earth, you must align your consciousness with Earth consciousness and become the hollow bone through which the Divine can flow.

I have had many beautiful experiences of collective harmony that happens when the egoic mind is out of the way. At the end of plant medicine ceremony, for example, is a time of community sharing of songs and poems and music; when it is your moment to share, the silence in the room is profound as the space expands before you to fill it. **You do not so much think about the song you will sing as you do feel that there is a song to be sung through you, and you allow it to be.** When the sharing happens in this way, it is Divine and sacred and beautiful. When the ego 'thinks' it is time to share, there's generally some awkwardness and fumbling.

The presence and awareness of the collective consciousness that plant medicine affords helps you to become aware of just how much your personality is running the show in your daily life. As you dedicate yourself to Soul-guided living, you will experience more occasions of harmony with the collective consciousness until that is your complete way of life.

As part of this shift, you'll begin feeling less fulfilled by television and more rewarded by meditation or time in nature. The pace of your life relaxes as your mind chatter diminishes and the quiet of your Soul expands. Your definition of 'fun' changes from getting inebriated to engaging in sacred ceremony. Your home fills up with rocks, stones and crystals. Rather than shopping for more clothes you buy a crystal singing bowl. You start noticing disconnection in relationships as your desire for heart-centered connection increases. You prefer spiritual community to friends that want to go out to bars. Sex with your partner evolves into Soul communion.

Actions to take to align yourself to Earth consciousness include:

-   Spending more time in nature on walks or hikes, allowing quiet contemplation as you move your body or sit and meditate in a beautiful spot.

-   Standing barefoot on the ground or lying belly-to-belly with the Earth every day for at least 15 minutes.

-   Opening sacred space every day as shared in the "Prayer To Welcome Earth Support".

-   Creating a personal altar to anchor your spiritual practice and placing on it sacred items such as candles (to add the element of fire), crystals and stones (to welcome their wisdom and gifts), feathers, figurines of animal allies, and so forth.

-   Listening to shamanic drum journey meditations or taking yourself on journey with your own drum or rattle.

-   Performing rituals to honor the new moon and full moon, and using these cycles to re-invest yourself in your intentions or release what no longer serves.

-   Tuning into your body (rather than the clock) to determine the optimal times to rest, eat, move, work and play.

-   Praying over your food with gratitude as you prepare and eat your meals.

- Working with plant allies to clear your energy field, heal your body, and illuminate your consciousness.

- Welcoming animal allies as spirit guides for a day, a challenge, or a lifetime.

- Meditating with crystals and stones in your hands or over your chakras.

- Singing sacred songs to open your heart and bring healing or express gratitude.

- Conducting personal ceremonies to welcome support from the Divine Mother, Great Spirit, ancestors, Four Directions, guides and so forth.

- Playing crystal bowls for healing and rebalancing of your chakras.

- Playing flutes, rattles, or drums as sacred offerings to Spirit.

- Creating power objects for your spiritual practice such as rattles, drums, mandalas.

- Making every day a walking prayer on the Mother Earth to learn from this ancient wise teacher.

♥

Living As Sacred Ceremony

Life offers painful moments and experiences, and yet you can transform that pain into beauty through ceremony. When I began studying Earth-based spirituality, I was introduced to the art of ceremony for processing the pain of my life and welcoming gratitude, love and awe. People in the shamanic path do not just sit down, close eyes, and meditate. We open sacred space, burn sage or tobacco, set up an altar, speak words of intention, honor the ancestors and spirits, and then pick up the drum and take a journey.

Ceremony is about the rituals that release your mind and open your heart, bringing you into an altered state of consciousness where your

Soul takes the helm and steers you towards exactly the beauty you need to witness in the moment to process your pain.

Every day of your life can begin as a ceremony when you open sacred space, welcoming the support of the ancestors and guides, the Four Directions, the Earth, the celestial bodies, and the Great Spirit. Watch the day unfold with more grace and awareness when you start it as a ceremony.

Every day can conclude with presence when you welcome the Divine to create spaciousness inside of you to be a witness of moments that need more of your attention to come to closure and reclaim your energy.

Altars are a key element of any ceremony as they become a portal to other dimensions of reality, such as the Upper Room that Paul Selig speaks of in his channeled texts. You can invite allies to bring their unique medicine and gifts to your altar, such as crystals or herbs. For the work of healing the Mother Wound, it is helpful to have several altars for anchoring different intentions: a personal altar for your daily spiritual practice, a distinct altar for Healing the Mother Wound, and an ancestral altar to honor your mother and relations. Each of these altars will have different elements to aid with the fulfillment of the intentions with which you establish the altar. When you create an altar with a focused intention, it serves to hold space for you as you move through your emotional and psychological processes.

The next sections offer recommendations for creating your altars as well as a mandala on the Mother Earth for initiating the healing processes in this book. There are also recommendations for ceremonies you can conduct at the new moon and full moon, as well as personal ceremonies for your transformation process.

There are so many aspects of life touched by the Mother Wound, and you deserve your dedication to creating beauty from your pain with ceremony.

Personal Altar

Set up a small table surface with a cloth that demarcates the area of the altar. On this cloth place a candle at each of the Four Directions that you light whenever you come to the altar for prayer and open sacred space. Add crystals, rocks and stones to the altar to support you in personal goals with their unique wisdom and gifts. You can find these at a crystal shop and select them by allowing yourself to be naturally drawn to them, or allow Spirit to present them to you as you wander in nature. Discover what animal allies are here to support you and obtain little figurines of these to add to the altar. Draw a tarot or oracle card and add that to the altar for as long as it feels relevant. Add pictures of guides and ascended masters like Guadalupe or Quan Yin. If Spirit leaves feathers in your path, pick these up and add them to your altar.

Mother Wound Altar

Set up a small table surface with a cloth that demarcates the area of the altar. On this cloth place a candle at each of the Four Directions that you light whenever you come to the altar for prayer and open sacred space. Add supportive stones and crystals for the healing work including: Rose Quartz (compassion), Spirit Quartz (harmony, alignment and spiritual growth), Amethyst (spiritual awareness, healing, and psychic abilities), Moonstone (new beginnings), and Red Silver Leaf Jasper (Mother Earth connection for nurturing serenity and tranquility). Place a little bowl or shell on the altar and fill it with tobacco to absorb any heavy or negative energies. Place images of goddesses or ascended masters on the altar such as White Buffalo Calf Woman, Guadalupe, Quan Yin, Mother Mary, and so forth. Place a picture of you as a young child on the altar to represent your inner children being healed. If you wish, you can place a throne on this altar for yourself to step into sovereignty as your healed self.

Maternal Ancestral Altar

Set up a small table surface with a cloth that demarcates the area of the altar. On this cloth place a candle at each of the Four Directions that you light whenever you come to the altar for prayer and open sacred space. Add a picture of your mother, grandmother, and great-grandmother to represent your maternal lineage. If there was a maternal figure in your life who was very helpful to you, add a picture of this woman to the altar. If you wish, add a throne to this altar for your mother to honor her as your connection to your ancestral lineage. You can place a stone in the throne to support clearing any negative energies and bringing more love and compassion; for example, rose quartz. As you pray at this altar, you can add little notes to your mother of things you wish to communicate with her. When ready, you can burn that note to release it to Spirit; first blow into the note how it makes you feel, and then light it on fire.

Mother Wound Earth Mandala

When you begin the healing process for the Mother Wound, create a mandala on the Earth to hold the container for your healing and support you with loving energies from Mother Earth. The procedure was described in "Aligning to the Divine Mother", and is repeated here for your ease and grace.

Find a private safe space outside on the Earth to create this mandala where it will be protected as you perform the work of healing over weeks and months. When I created mine, I acquired a rose quartz crystal in the shape of a heart; this was to represent my own heart. I gathered together white beans (lima preferred), pinenuts, tobacco, and tiny flowers to my liking. Collect what your heart calls forth for your mandala. Open sacred space over the ground where your mandala will be created. Then use the white beans to create a circle on the ground by intentionally placing each bean as you contemplate healing your Mother Wound with Divine Mother love. Once the circle is complete, begin in the south point of the circle and place pinenuts with intention as a line leading to the center of the circle to call the energy and healing power of the South to your mandala. Then create a line of pinenuts from the west point of the circle to the center of the circle to call the energy and healing power of the West to your mandala. Repeat to call the energy and healing powers of the North and East into the center of the mandala. Create an inner circle out of pinenuts to designate the Center of the Wheel of Life. Now place the rose quartz crystal heart in the center of the mandala where the pinenut lines intersect, inside the Center. Sprinkle tobacco all around the mandala, welcoming healing energies and protection from Spirit of Tobacco. Lastly, decorate from your heart and gratitude the mandala with the tiny flowers in a way that feels beautiful to you. Now that the mandala is complete, say a little prayer to the Divine Mother: "Thank you Divine Mother for healing the Mother Wound within me, and helping me to love myself unconditionally." Every day, visit your mandala and say prayers, remove 'full' tobacco and replace with fresh, add new tiny flowers and any other items you're called to add. You may sprinkle flower water over your crystal heart, for example. Notice the healing that happens in your life.

Moon Ceremonies

On the new moon and full moon you can perform a sacred fire ceremony to release what no longer serves you and bring more light into yourself. An easy ceremony is open sacred space and then make a list of everything you are ready to release from your history with your mother so that you can reclaim the energy that has been locked up in unforgiveness. When you are finished with your list, blow into the paper how all of those things make you feel, one-by-one, until you feel you have released it into the paper. And then burn the paper to let it go. Watch it burn and feel it release from your body. Now imagine as you stare into the flames that you are filling up with pure golden light and the clean energy of new potentials. Chant '*Om mane padme om*' or other chants to boost your feelings of compassion, gratitude, and love. You can also join me in sacred ceremony for the new moon and full moon as I perform despacho which is a tradition of prayer from the Q'ero in Peru.

Personal Ceremonies

Personal healing ceremonies come from the heart guided by your Soul, and bring tremendous transformation into your life when practiced regularly. You can create ceremonies to honor and release childhood trauma, relationships, loved ones who departed, and phases of your life. During the course of writing this book, I engaged in daily personal ceremonies to invite spiritual guidance from White Buffalo Calf Woman, weekly personal ceremonies for shifting my perspectives and healing myself and my ancestry, new moon and full moon ceremonies for setting intentions and releasing stuck energies, and periodic ceremonies where I welcomed support from other healers to go deeper into myself for healing.

♥

Embodying The Mountain

What changes have ancient mountains seen transpire before them as they patiently hold space for the dance of life? Billions of suns have risen over their peaks. Civilizations have risen and fallen, and yet they remain strong and present throughout the turmoil of life on Earth. The mountain spirits hold wisdom, and this is why the indigenous people pray to them for guidance.

Inside you is an eternal presence that has lived longer than any mountain on Earth. The ancient one within has seen worlds birth and die in cycles of evolution across the galaxy.

The knowing presence within you is the Source of peace and wisdom. When you relax and surrender to this presence, it can awaken each cell of your body from the frantic dream of the powerless human. You no longer need to worry and anticipate your next steps. This presence literally moves you to play your instrument when the orchestra is ready for your melody. Your body responds to the instructions of the presence, and you simply find yourself being as you are doing inspired actions. When it is time to stop, you stop. When it is time to play, you play.

Remembering to embody the mountain grounds you so you can relax into the state of being for the presence to dance through you. When presence enters the room, tongues silence and humans sit up and pay attention. To be the one who presence is flowing through is a powerful gift to receive: a gift that you will never own.

LOVE IS FIERCE: HEALING THE MOTHER WOUND

In the wake of presence moving through you is the intoxication of peace, love and joy. In the wake of presence moving through you is curiosity of when it will happen again, and who is it flowing through right now? You eagerly scan the room in rapt attention with delight.

You cannot control the presence, nor force it to move through you as you surrender to embody the mountain. You simply surrender. Even when you are not feeling the presence it is there, silently observing.

The presence is beyond names. It moves through all of life on Earth and throughout the galaxies. This is why people who have felt the presence do not harm another... When you discover something magical, you want it to happen again. You delight when you witness it happening for another person, and when you can share the presence moving between you and another person, time and space drops away instantly. All that matters is savoring, relishing, and immersing in the experience of the presence.

You can call the presence whatever you wish. Just notice how giving it a name puts it into a box in your mind. The presence is beyond all boxes. It truly defies all attempts to label it.

Remembering to embody the mountain helps you get anchored in your body which offers the conduit through which the experience of the presence can be unleashed to flow through you. The more the presence flows through you, the more the resonance of this infinite wisdom magnetizes your auric field. Your auric field then radiates out packets of light that are received by the auric fields of other humans in your midst, sharing the remembrance of the presence.

There is a dreamy flowy state to the presence which is in stark contrast with the flat, coarse, dense auras of people who have not yet discovered the presence within themselves. You can be in the flow of the presence with everyone, regardless of whether they have found it. It is you who must choose to stay in the presence when met by the rigid boundaries of human crust.

When the presence is flowing through you, the experience feels like peace, joy, love and acceptance. You radiate this experience everywhere you go and it can be felt. When you speak from presence, the words are infused with the vibration of peace, love, joy and acceptance. When you allow presence to flow through you during conflict, the conflict is transformed with love and compassion, and the outcome is elevated to a higher potential.

By embodying the mountain, you can bring the presence through uncomfortable things to transform them.

Think of the mountain as an ancient, wise mother. Allow her to embody you and pour wisdom out of your mouth as she floods love through your heart.

By embodying the mountain and allowing the presence to flow through you, you heal the Mother Wound and become a whole again. Your steady agape love blesses all of us.

White Buffalo Women Rise

Daring leaders who live into their values are never silent about hard things.
— Brené Brown

If there's one thing I know it's the power of a woman who has had enough. She loses all the pretenses and the pleasing and the pleading and she hits her backstop and then she snaps. *Enough!* she declares. And everyone listens because when a woman knows her truth it's indisputable.

When a mother speaks from her heart and grounded wisdom, the message is magnified in impact. A message delivered from agape love lands in the hearts of those who hear it and calls them forth to greater action.

Imagine a message delivered from women who have healed the Mother Wound, embodied the mountain, and are allowing the wisdom and power of the presence to flow through them into the world. Strong wise women from this consciousness—White Buffalo Women—can mend the Sacred Hoop and build the foundation of a New Earth.

YOU have the ability to heal the Mother Wound, become a White Buffalo Woman, and influence the world. You can influence what companies are supported through your family's resources. You can educate yourself through the prevalence of the internet and higher education. You can choose to speak your mind and vote through the ballot and your wallet.

What the world needs now is for you to get the courage to declare yourself a White Buffalo Woman and firmly say *Enough!*

Enough polluting our waters. Enough violence in our schools threatening our children. Enough killing endangered species and pillaging natural resources. Enough starving and homeless people. Enough sex trafficking and child molestation. Enough corporate greed and financial enslavement of the majority. Enough calling us crazy because we can feel how heartbreaking the state of our world is today. Enough calling us hysterical because we grieve for our children's future.

It's time to listen up humanity because we White Buffalo Women have a few important things to say.

Stop.

Stop ignoring the issues and arguing over 'facts'. We all know what's happening here.

Stop acting like it's business as usual.

Stop feeding us pills and shaming us to shut us up.

And.

And we care, that's why we are reasoning with you.

And we know your technology and gadgets and construction are fantastic assets for humanity.

And it's clear you were trying to create wonderful things for us to enjoy.

Listen.

Listen to the bigger picture. We need all of life on Earth to sustain humanity. One species gone is a domino effect. Who is going to pollenate the flowers that you give us on Mother's Day if all the bees and butterflies are dead?

Listen to the cries for help of our children who are committing suicide in record numbers. They're so disconnected they can't stand to keep living. What happened to family dinners and card games by candle light in a tent under the stars?

Listen to your own heart if you can find it under all that numbness. Are you willing to feel angry, afraid, depressed, and overwhelmed with all that's going wrong? Will you join me over here in the ugly truth? Will you hold my hand and promise to help me fix our home for our beautiful kids?

We do not have disposable children and this is not a disposable planet.

We are made of Earth and we belong on Earth.

Wake up.

White Buffalo Woman: when you've had enough, the whole world will listen up. When you get the courage to speak up, you'll give women around the world the courage to overcome tremendous odds.

Change your priorities today to make Earth possible tomorrow. Your grandkids are depending on you to stand and speak.

Rise White Buffalo Women.

Rise.

About Kerri Hummingbird Sami

Kerri Hummingbird Sami is a Soul guide, shamanic energy healer, award-winning best-selling author and inspirational speaker. Kerri has over 20 years of experience in leading by inspiration, and a special passion for empowering women to be the artists of their lives. She mentors women to rewrite the story of their lives through inner transformation, connection to essence, remembrance of purpose, and realignment to authenticity and truth.

She is certified in energy medicine by the Four Winds Light Body school, certified as a spiritual coach by the Artist of the Spirit Coach Training Program and HeatherAsh Amara, certified in empowerment and firewalk training by Sundoor, and certified as a Warrior Goddess Facilitator. She is the past President of the Austin Chapter of the International Association of Women (IAW).

In 2014, The Indie Spiritual Book Awards conferred the honor of "Best in Category" to *Awakening To Me: One Woman's Journey To Self Love*, and in 2015 it won Pinnacle Best in Category for Self-Help and National Indie Excellence Awards Winner in Category for Spirituality. Her 2015 best-selling book *From We To Me: Emerging Self After Divorce*, is a best-seller. Kerri lives with the love of her life, his two children, and her two teenage sons in the Austin area. She works with clients around the world.

Prior to her career as a Soul Guide, Ms. Hummingbird had a 20-year career as a technical and marketing communications consultant in both Silicon Valley and Austin high-tech communities. She has served in leadership since she began working, most notably serving on the Board of the Silicon Valley chapter of the Society for Technical Communication. She also inspired and led over 150 artists to open their studios to the public as the Executive Director of the non-profit Silicon Valley Open Studios in the Bay Area, California for several years in the early 2000s.

Award-winning, best-selling books:

The Second Wave: Transcending the Human Drama, 2019

Awakening To Me: One Woman's Journey To Self Love, 2014

From We To Me: Emerging Self After Divorce, 2016

Other titles:

Reinvent Yourself: Indulge Your Deepest Desires By Becoming Who You Are Starving To Be, Available at www.kerrihummingbird.com/gift

Printed in Great Britain
by Amazon